British Art Destinations

Written by
Emmy Watts

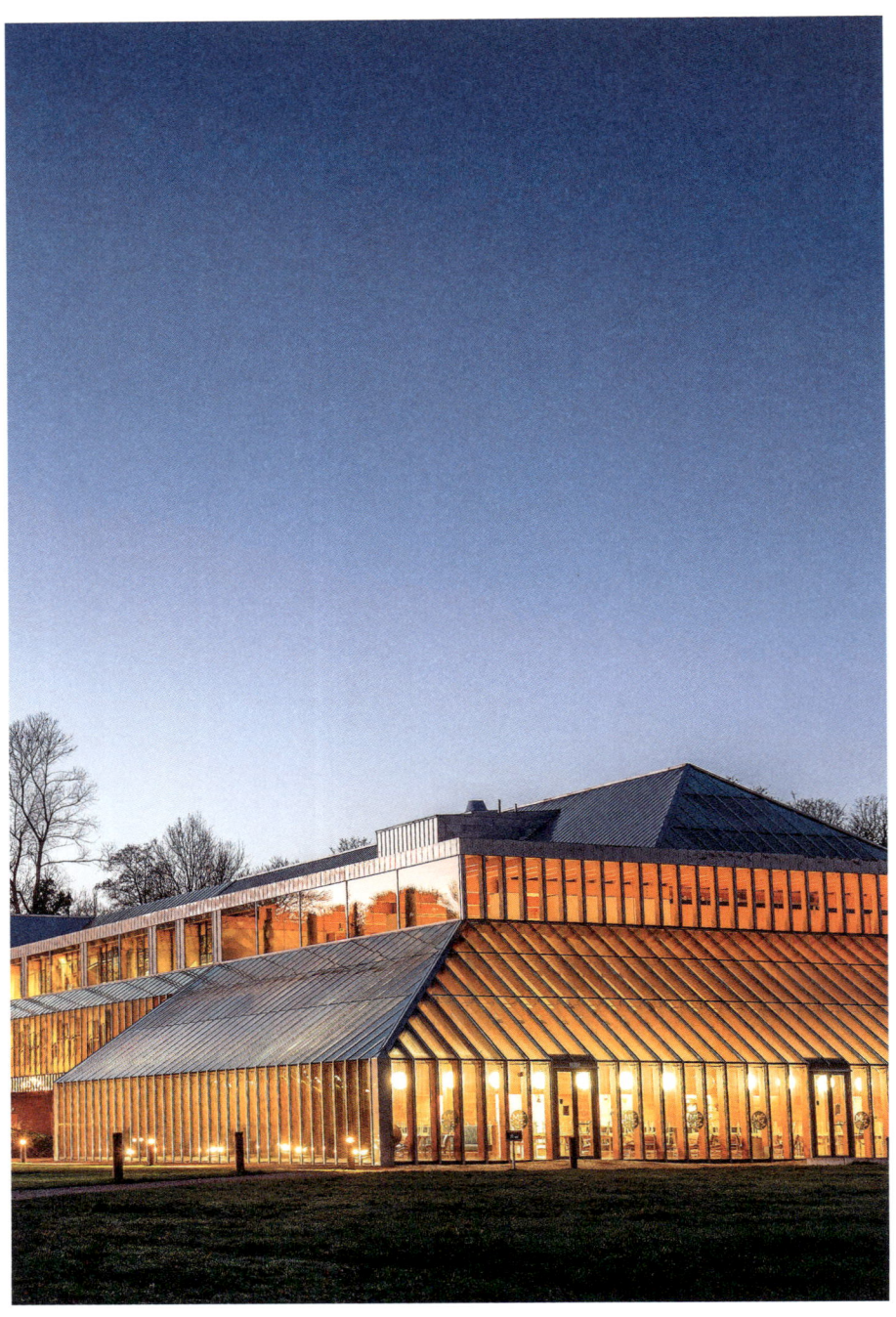

Above: The Burrell Collection, p.192
Opposite: *Angel of the North*, Antony Gormley, p.156

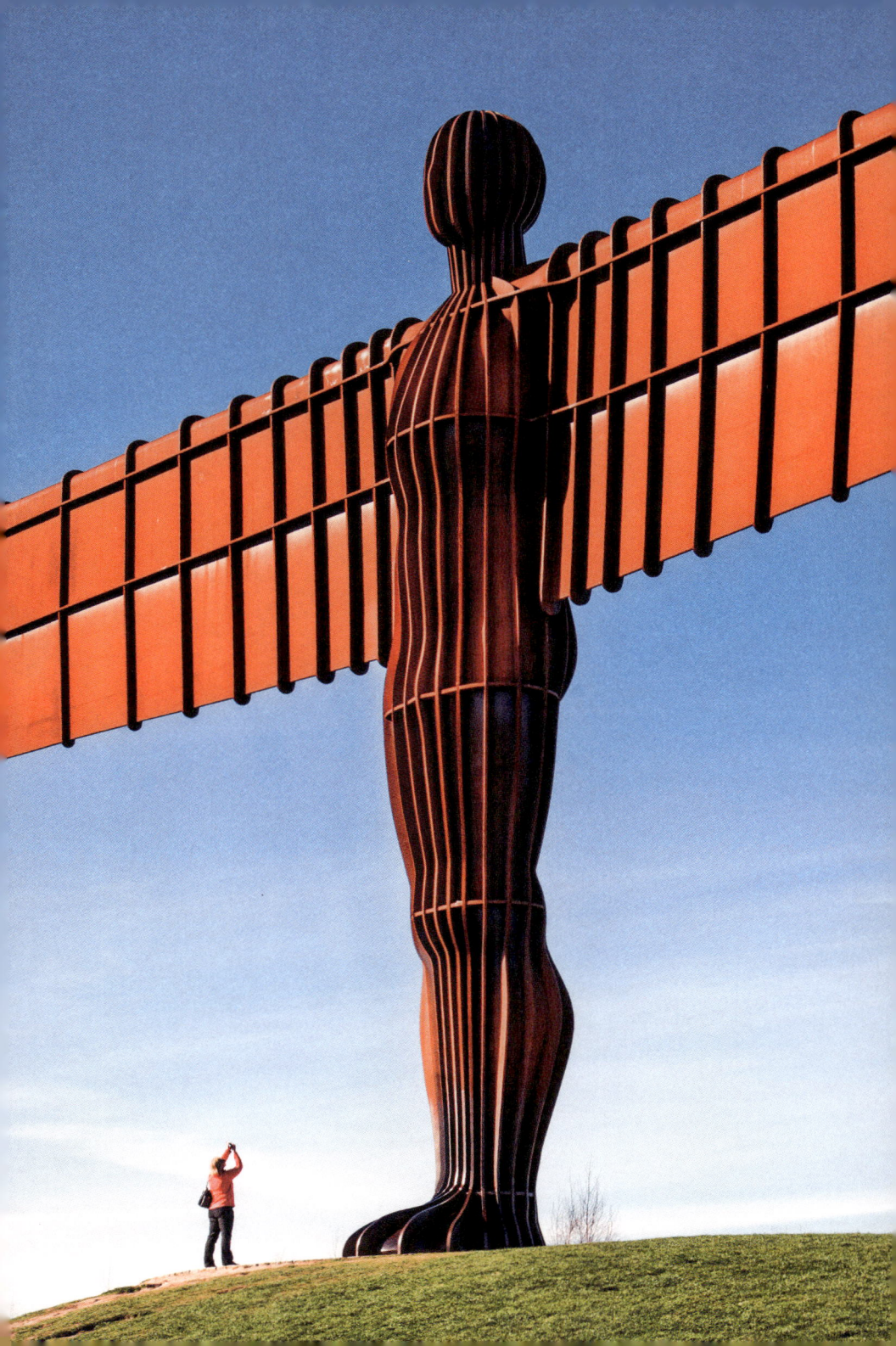

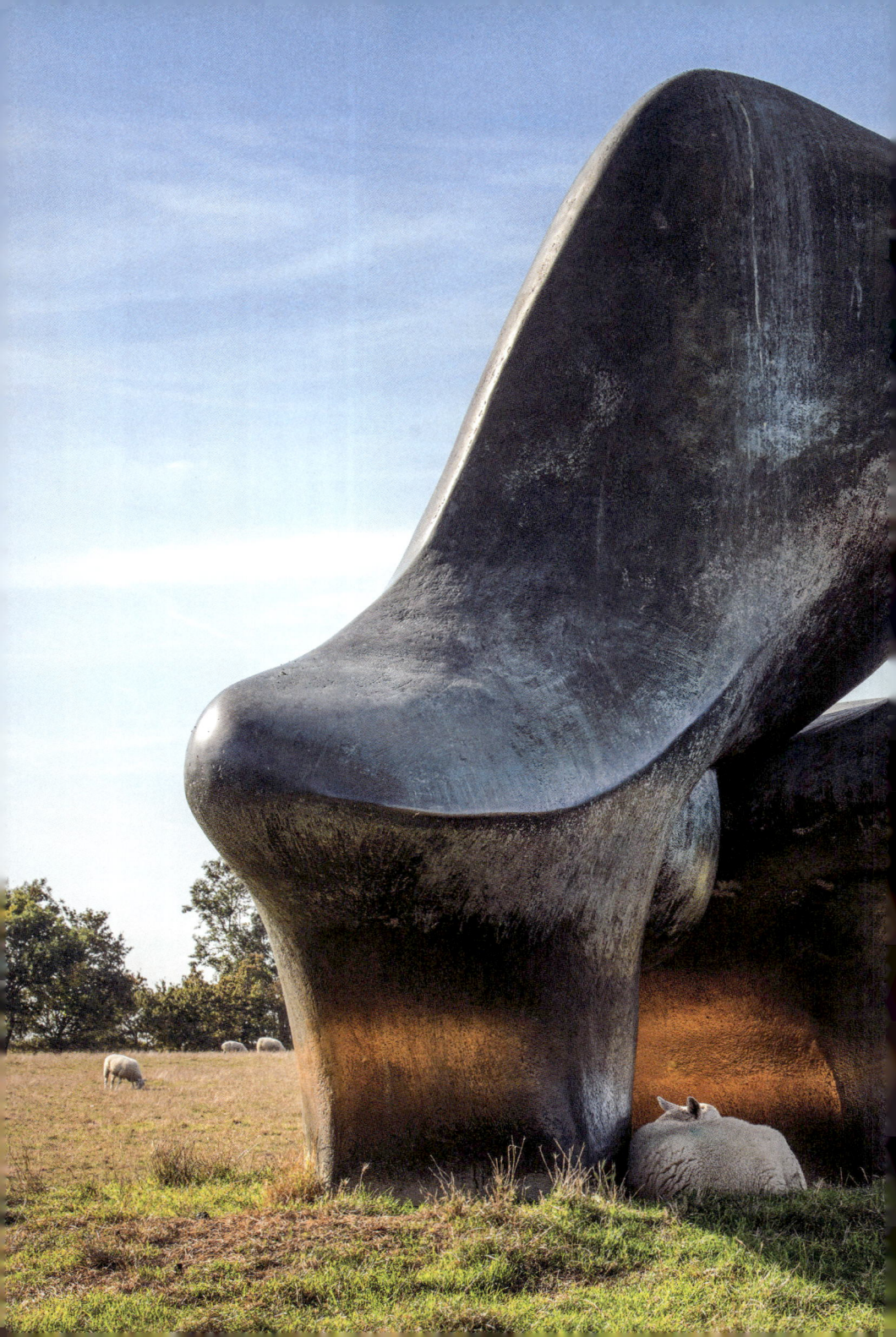

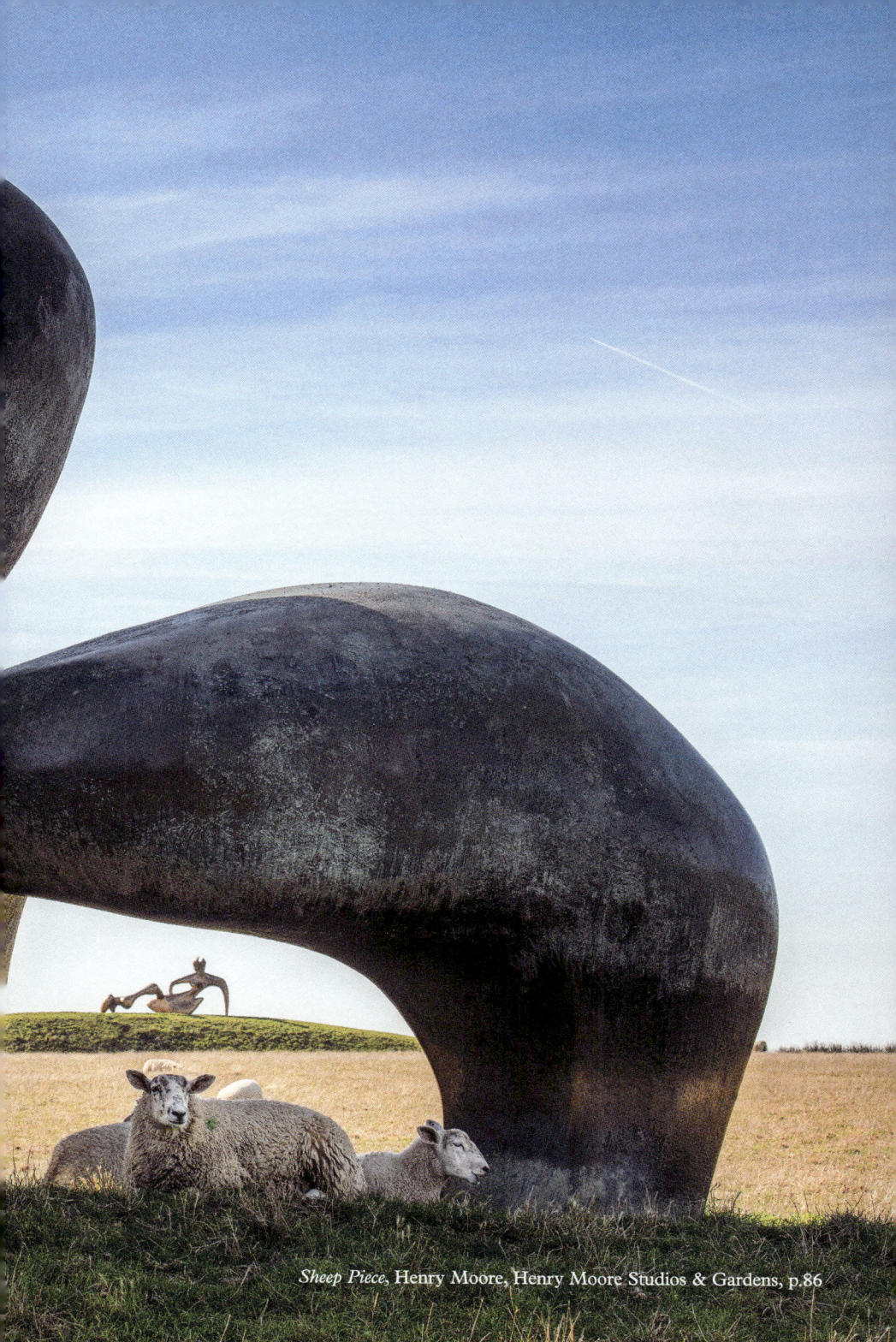

Sheep Piece, Henry Moore, Henry Moore Studios & Gardens, p.86

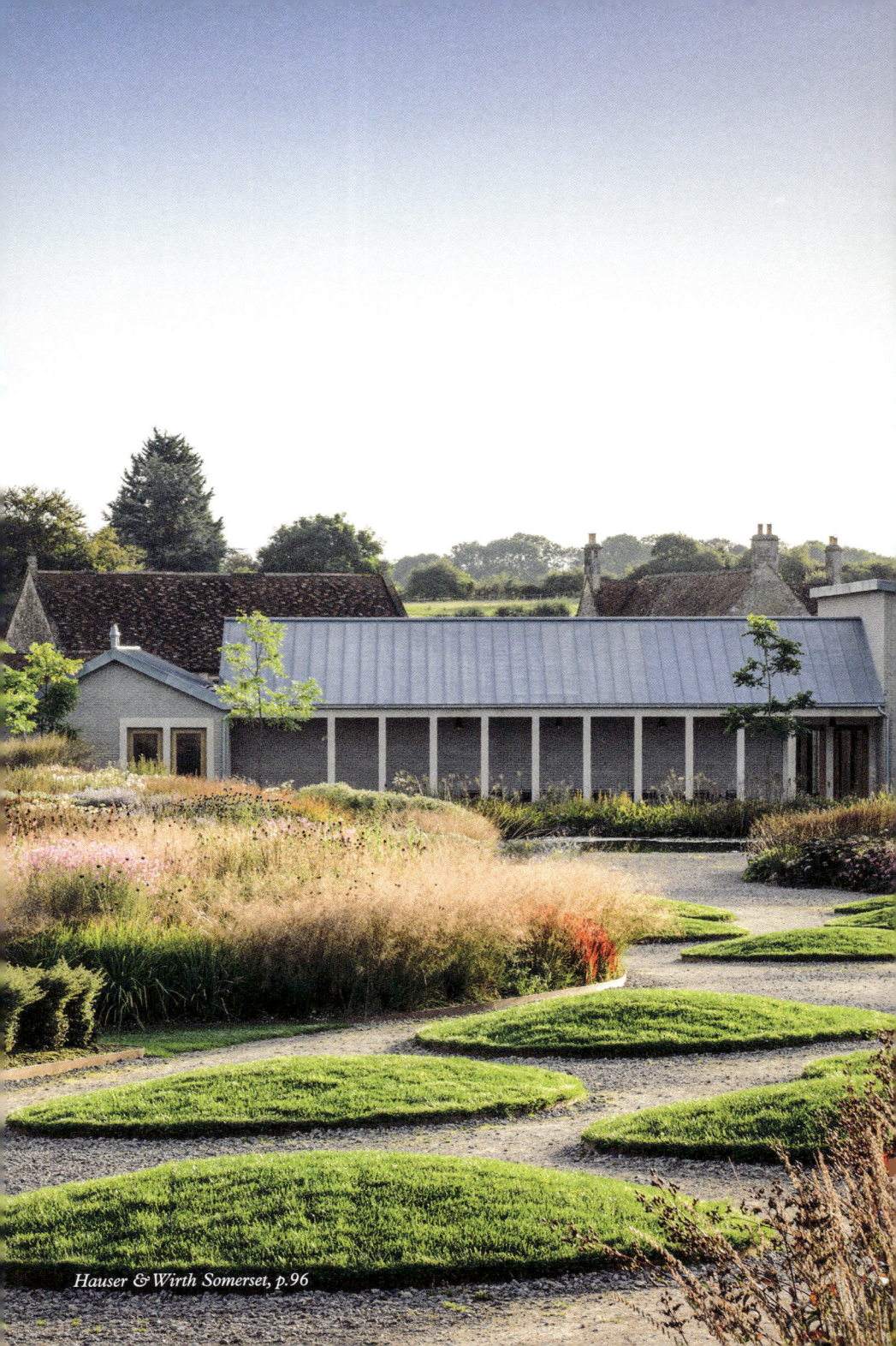

Hauser & Wirth Somerset, p.96

CONTENTS

THE BEST FOR...

INTIMATE INSIGHTS While their inhabitants are long departed, the houses where Barbara Hepworth (p.112) made the bulk of her work, Lee Miller and Roland Penrose (p.60) entertained their illustrious artist friends, and Vanessa Bell and Duncan Grant (p.68) lived out their bohemian dream still sparkle with their spirit, offering unique insight into their lives and labour.

RURAL ART AMBLES Prefer to get your cultural fix *en plein air*? Strap on your walking boots and set your GPS for one of Britain's breathtaking cross-forest sculpture trails. Choose from site-specific works in the Forest of Dean (p.104), nature-worn forms at Grizedale (p.158), or large-scale structures at tranquil Kielder (p.152).

CITY EXPLORERS Street-art tours and urban sculpture trails transform art appreciation into a cultural treasure hunt. Scout out works by Gary Hume and Anish Kapoor on London's The Line (p.14), or head to Bristol in search of Banksy's (p.118) formative works, which hide in plain sight across the artist's hometown.

SUN, SEA AND CULTURE Britain's seaside scenery has been inspiring artists for centuries. The arresting Turner Contemporary (p.70) is the jewel in arty Margate's cultural crown, while Tate St Ives (p.128) pays tribute to the town's artistic alumni. Meanwhile, the ambitious Creative Folkestone Artworks (p.74) scheme has transformed the town into the UK's largest urban outdoor art exhibition.

ALFRESCO ART The heady blend of culture and country air at sculpture parks is enduringly hard to resist. Jupiter Artland (p.198) offers a suitably otherworldly encounter just outside Edinburgh, while Wiltshire's Roche Court (p.108) is a 60-acre artistic Eden hosting work by Anthony Caro and Michael Craig-Martin.

| NATIONAL TREASURES | Longing for some Lowry? Sate your appetite in Salford (p.172). Hankering after Hockney? Set your satnav for Salts Mill (p.168). Or make a beeline for the big guns: London's Tates (p.26, p.46), National Gallery (p.36) and National Portrait Gallery (p.20), or Edinburgh's trio of National Galleries (p.202). |

| ECCENTRIC ESCAPADES | Arty escapades don't come much more eccentric than a trip to Prospect Cottage (p.76), artist Derek Jarman's former home in seemingly post-apocalyptic Dungeness. Then there's Tout Quarry Sculpture Park (p.116), an offbeat attraction that's evolved from the quarry that gave Buckingham Palace its stone. |

| SOMETHING NEW | The YBAs aren't so young these days, but thankfully there's no shortage of British galleries showcasing up-and-coming talent. London's Saatchi (p.18) is renowned for giving a platform to emerging artists, while Gateshead's Baltic (p.164) and Modern Art Oxford (p.50) are famed for their fresh and fearless shows. |

| A BITE TO EAT | Elevate your art adventure with a visit to one of the UK's picture-perfect gallery cafes. Yorkshire Sculpture Park's (p.176) Weston Restaurant dishes up seasonal, local fare alongside epic scenery, while South London Gallery's (p.40) South London Louie specialises in strong coffee and light lunches, and Messums West's (p.114) The Mess is unmissable in its own right. |

| A GRAND DAY OUT | When art meets stately splendour, you know you're in for an epic visual adventure. Chatsworth House (p.182), Houghton Hall (p.88) and Compton Verney (p.136) all offer a potent cocktail of culture, mixing impressive permanent collections with ambitious programmes – all in majestic surroundings. |

| ARTY ALL-NIGHTERS | Cotswold Sculpture Park's (p.100) on-site Airbnbs offer cosy abodes for culture vultures, while Jupiter Artland's (p.198) Artist's House cottage sleeps up to six. Meanwhile, Grayson Perry's House for Essex (p.58) promises an immersive experience. |

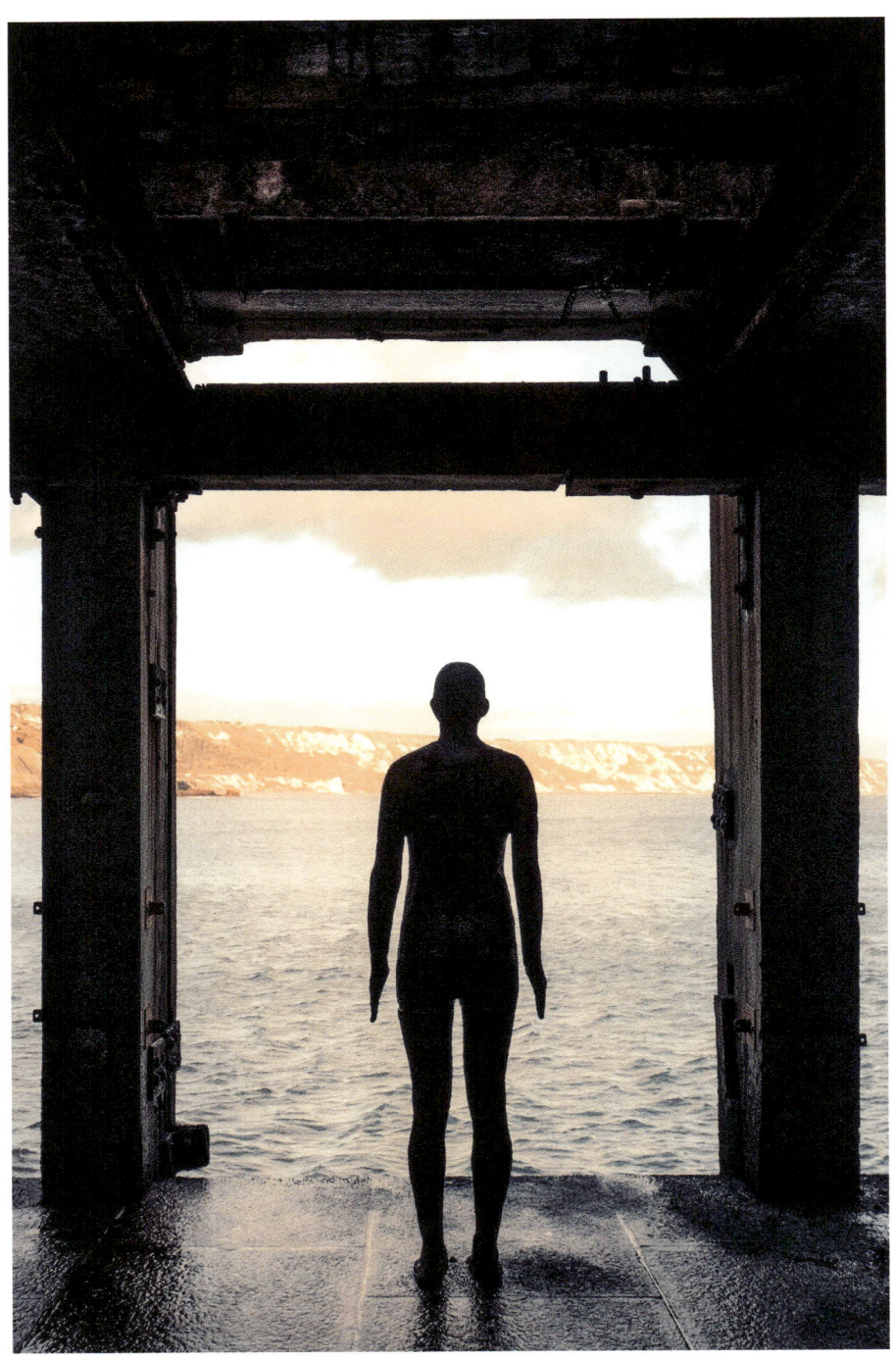

Another Time, Antony Gormley, Creative Folkestone Artworks, p.74

DESTINATION: ART

Art wields the power to move us. It can spark joy, elicit tears and transport us to infinite new worlds. It also quite literally has the power to move us, compelling us to trek across town and country on the off-chance we might witness something extraordinary. As it happens, we Brits have witnessed a lot of extraordinary things in the last few years, from Brexit to a new sovereign via a global pandemic. The upshot? UK gallery attendance is flourishing. Visitor numbers have largely returned to pre-pandemic levels, and more of us are consuming culture than ever before – no doubt prompted by a mutual desire for escapism in an increasingly unpredictable world, the diminishing affordability of foreign travel and probably a fair amount of TikTok-induced FOMO.

In 2024, *Van Gogh: Poets and Lovers* drew crowds of 335,000 to London's National Gallery (p.36) – many flooding in from outside the capital to catch a glimpse of the Dutch painter's legendary landscapes and still lifes, culminating in a 24-hour opening on its final weekend. Pre-COVID, Grayson Perry's *The Most Popular Art Exhibition Ever!* became an (almost) self-fulfilling prophecy when 180,000 people from across the UK and beyond descended on Bristol's Arnolfini (p.122) to ogle Brexit pots and Hogarth-inspired tapestries – in turn reversing the troubled gallery's fortunes.

But while a zeitgeist-capturing show can put you on the map, what tips a gallery (or sculpture park, or art trail) itself into 'destination' territory? A bougie, chef-helmed cafe? A hip, design-led gift shop? How about an inclusive events programme? Or an aesthetically pleasing play area? In reality, of course, the merit of a particular attraction is in the eye of the beholder. Art is subjective and visitors' needs are diverse, while the term 'destination' has become so diluted in recent years there's a sense that almost anything can be deemed one, be it a city-sized museum or a pint-sized novelty pop-up.

The locations in this book vary wildly in footprint, subject matter, and supplementary offerings. They stretch from Glasgow to Guildford and Dungeness to Derbyshire, and span galleries, trails, sculpture parks, stately homes, artists' homes, short-term rentals and 66-foot-tall sculptures on the side of the A1. Some will take little more than an hour or two to cover. Others demand multiple visits and even overnight stays to fully assimilate their contents. All of them, however, have one key thing in common: each one is tried, tested and 100 per cent worth travelling to – at least, in our humble opinion.

Beyond providing fodder for your Instagram grid, these carefully curated locations will feed your curiosity and nourish your creative soul, opening your eyes to long-bypassed local gems while luring you to corners of the country you'd never otherwise have ventured. Feeling inquisitive? Follow your nose to Sussex for a permissible poke around not one, but *two* charismatic artists' houses (p.60, p.68). Craving some salty air? Hotfoot it to Margate, where sea, sand and Tracey Emin-approved restaurants await visitors to the very gallery (p.70) that prompted the town's dazzling regeneration. Or make like Heron and Hepworth and chase that enigmatic light down to St Ives, home to the latter's atmospheric home studio (p.112) and Tate's unmissable fourth instalment (p.128).

The word 'destination' might be synonymous with 'journey's end', but many of these locations are just the starting point for a much grander adventure. The aforementioned 66-foot-tall motorway sculpture (p.156) is a sight to behold, but it won't take you long to do so. Luckily, it's only a 15-minute drive from Gateshead's glittering Baltic (p.164) with its award-winning rooftop restaurant, inimitable gift shop and proximity to Newcastle's buzzing city centre. Likewise, the petite but punchy Modern Art Oxford (p.50) is just moments from the diametrically opposed Ashmolean (p.48), among Oxford's many other delights.

Buying this book marks the beginning of your own very personal journey across the UK's artistic landscape. Reading it won't make you an instant expert on British art, but it will equip you with all the intel you need to plan boundless getaways within one of the world's cultural hotspots from city gallery hops to creative rural retreats and enriching seaside sojourns. If you're eager to squeeze more sculpture from your staycation, pack more paintings into your minibreak or simply shoehorn more art into your everyday, this book is an excellent starting point. All that remains is to fine-tune your itinerary, choreograph your transportation and get ready to be *seriously* moved.

Emmy Watts
London, 2025

THE LINE

Unique urban sculpture trail

A sliced-up sand dredger, a stack of supermarket trolleys and a pile of giant shop-mannequin arms might sound like a junkyard inventory, but this 22-sculpture art trail is anything but rubbish. Snaking nearly five miles from Stratford's Queen Elizabeth Olympic Park to North Greenwich's The O2, the ever-evolving Line proposes a more accessible alternative to the traditional sculpture court and simultaneously submerges visitors in the natural environment. Works by lesser-known and big-name artists feature, though Anish Kapoor's *ArcelorMittal Orbit* is perhaps the most famous, being both the UK's tallest sculpture and home to the world's longest slide (designed by scientist-turned-artist Carsten Höller). Ignore the number order and work your way backwards, beginning at the southernmost post and crossing the river via cable car, ending with an adrenaline-charged plummet down *that* slide.

North Greenwich Station, London, SE10 0PH

the-line.org

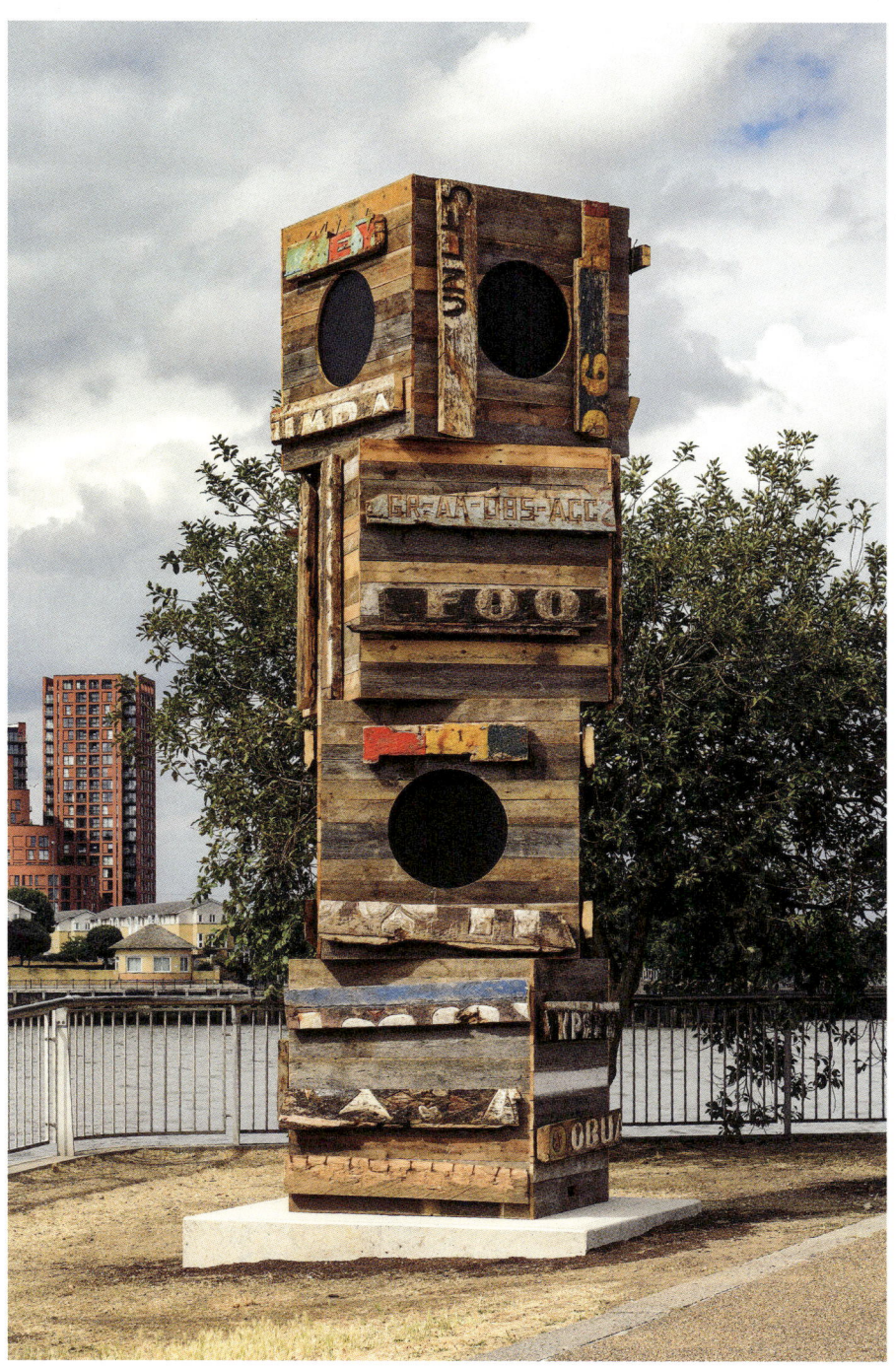

Tribe and Tribulation, Serge Attukwei Clottey

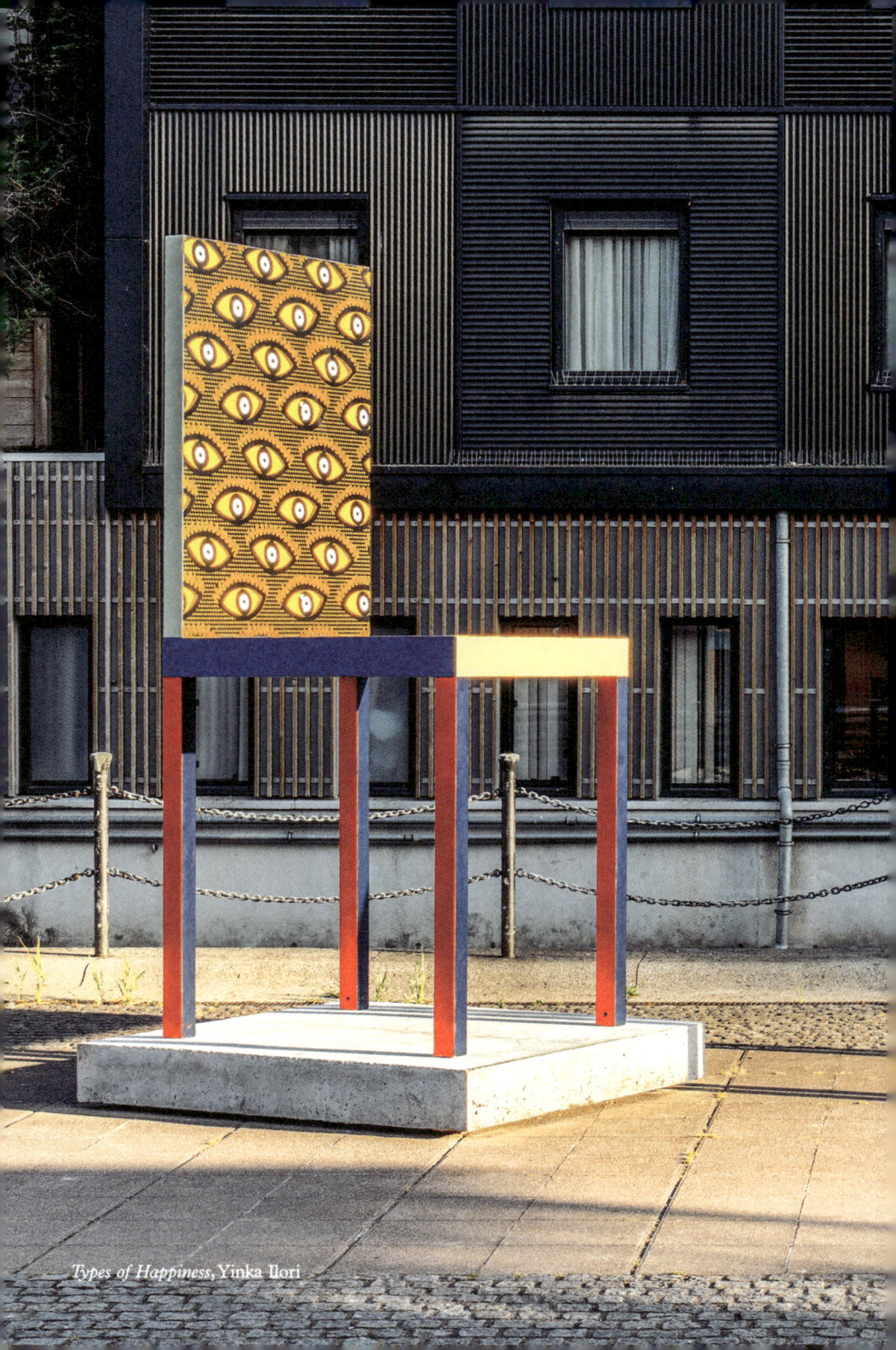

Types of Happiness, Yinka Ilori

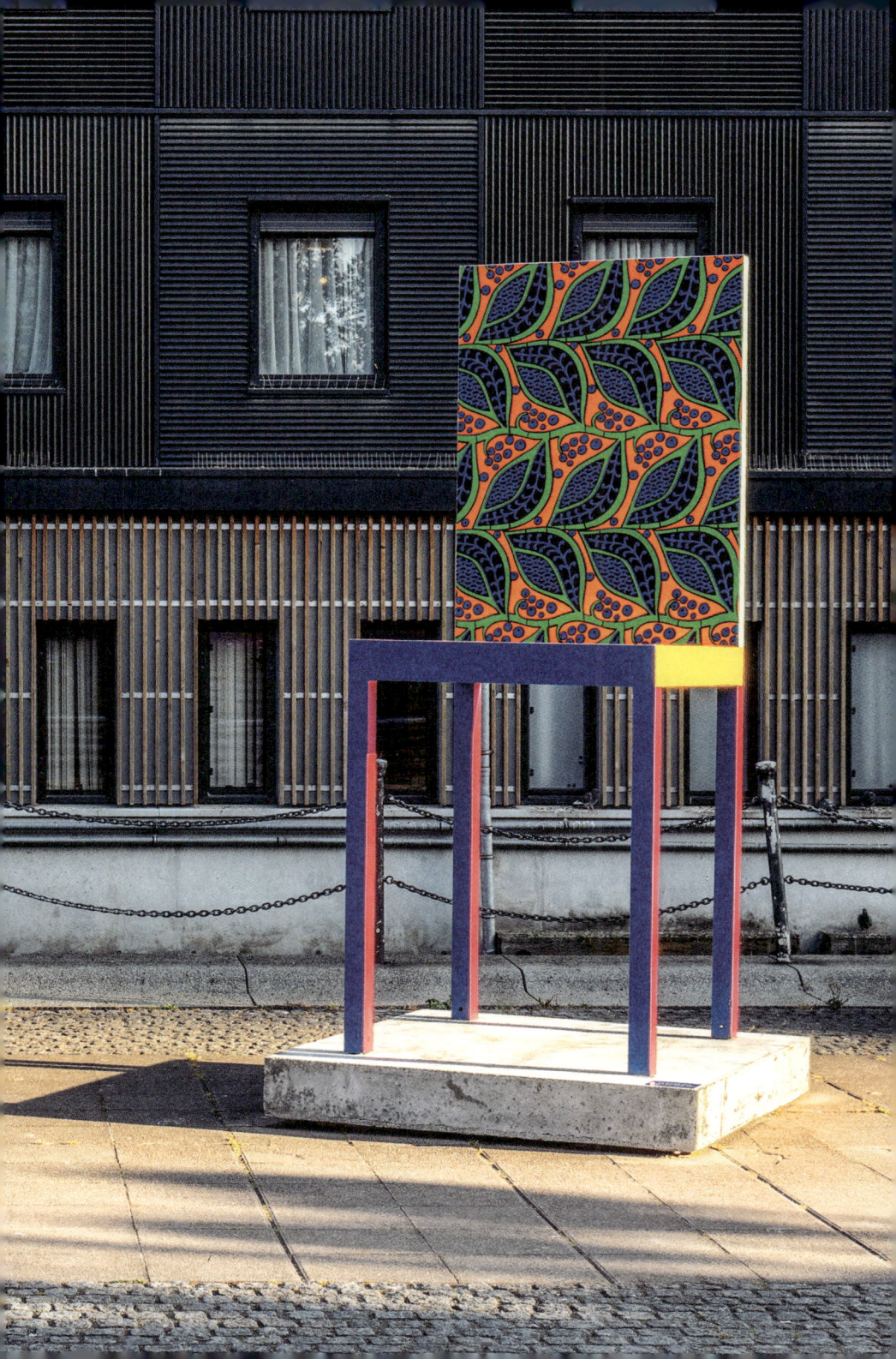

SAATCHI GALLERY

Breezy space platforming emerging artists

If it's cutting-edge art you're after, this cathedral of innovation is a great place to start. Guided by its overarching emphasis on freshness over repute, the Saatchi provides an unusually grand platform for emerging artists across its vast, stripped-back interior. Though no longer linked with controversial advertising mogul Charles Saatchi, the gallery's founding principles – namely making art more accessible to the mainstream and elevating work that would otherwise not be seen in London institutions – remain. Sun Yuan and Peng Yu's life-size *Old Persons' Home* diorama, the largest-ever solo museum show of French street artist JR, Richard Wilson's 2,000-gallon engine oil installation and street art exhibition *Beyond the Streets* are memorable highlights of the gallery's 15-year tenure in the Chelsea space, but its fast turnover means there is truly always something new to see. Do the 15 galleries in order to avoid missing out – and *always* exit via the excellent gift shop.

Duke of York's HQ, King's Road, London, SW3 4RY
saatchigallery.com

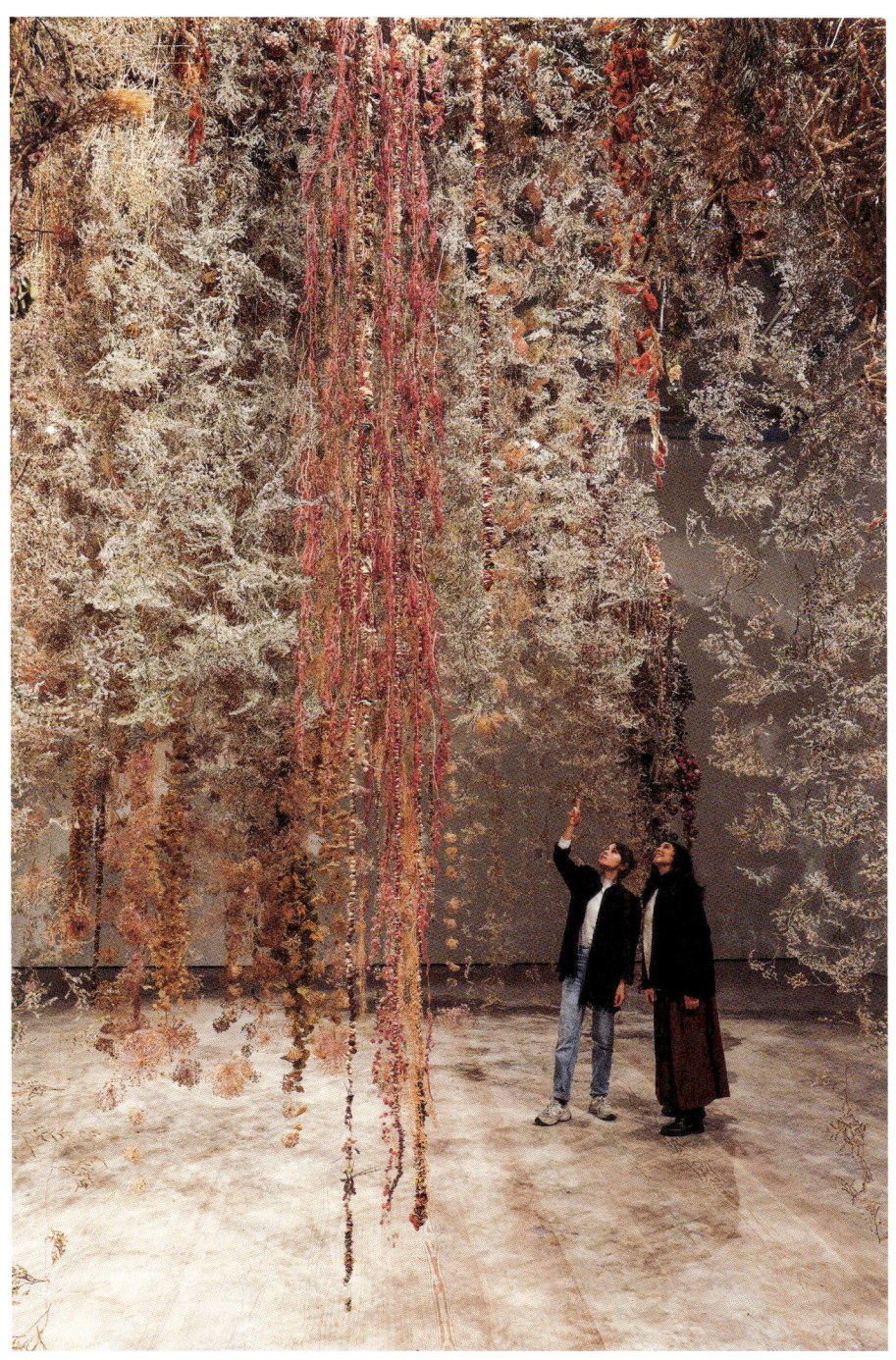

La Fleur Morte, Rebecca Louise Law

NATIONAL PORTRAIT GALLERY

Recently refreshed home of famous faces

Emerging fresh-faced after a three-year revamp in 2023, the NPG is now significantly more accessible, culturally diverse and representative of the UK today. This revitalised institution now boasts an entire gallery dedicated to female sitters, a Tracey Emin-adorned entrance and convivial public spaces. Once somewhat limited in terms of its sitter demographics, its rejuvenated walls are now host to social rights activists, feminist icons, silver-screen legends and Tudor monarchs, together forming the most comprehensive portrait collection on the planet. Head straight for the *History Makers Now* display – a powerful who's who of contemporary changemakers from Jeanette Winterson to Doreen Lawrence – before embarking on a free tour of the gallery's most illustrious occupants, from Anne Boleyn to the Brontës. Finish with a perusal of the gift shop and a fluffy coconut lamington from the elegant Audrey Green cafe – or a cheeky cocktail from 'secret' basement bar, Larry's.

St. Martin's Place, London, WC2H 0HE
npg.org.uk

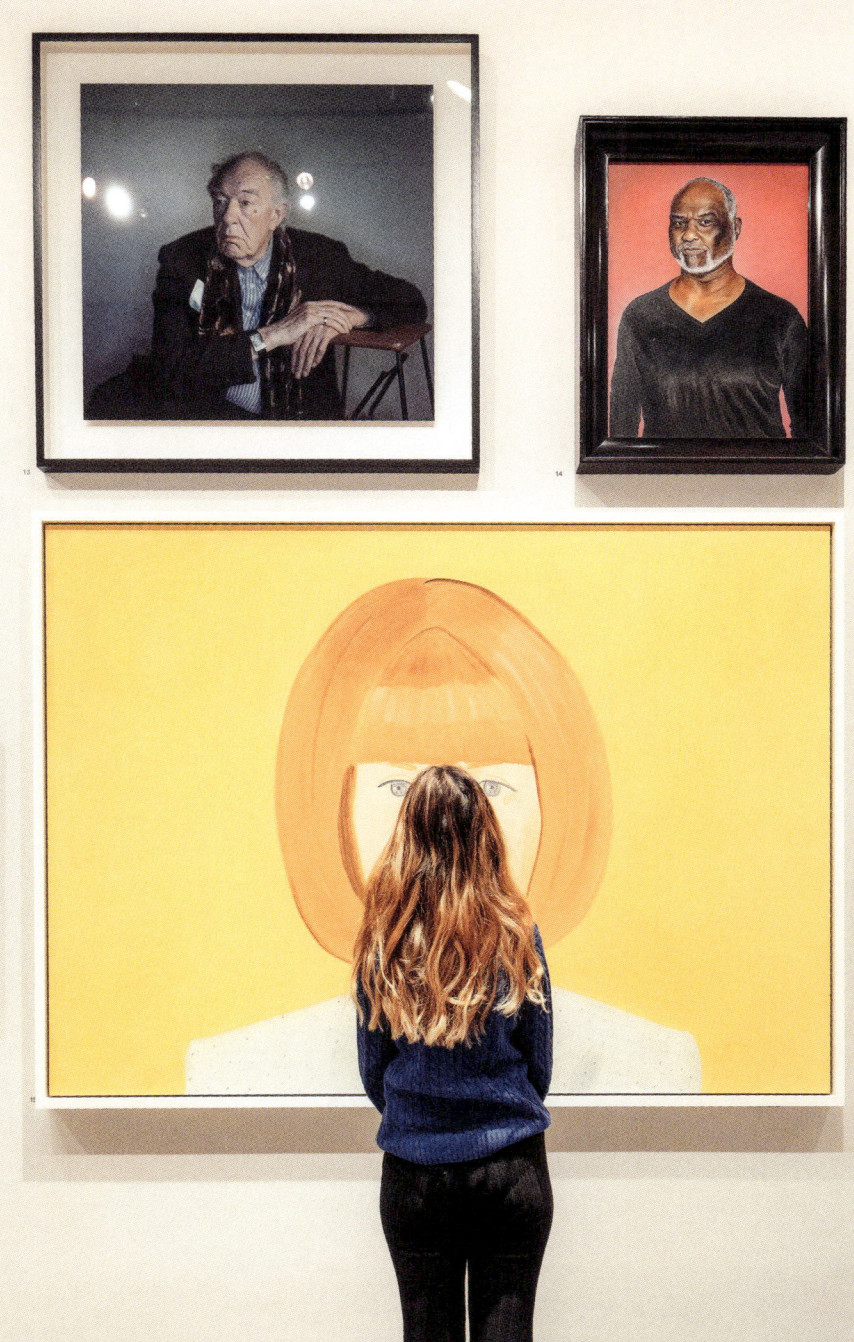

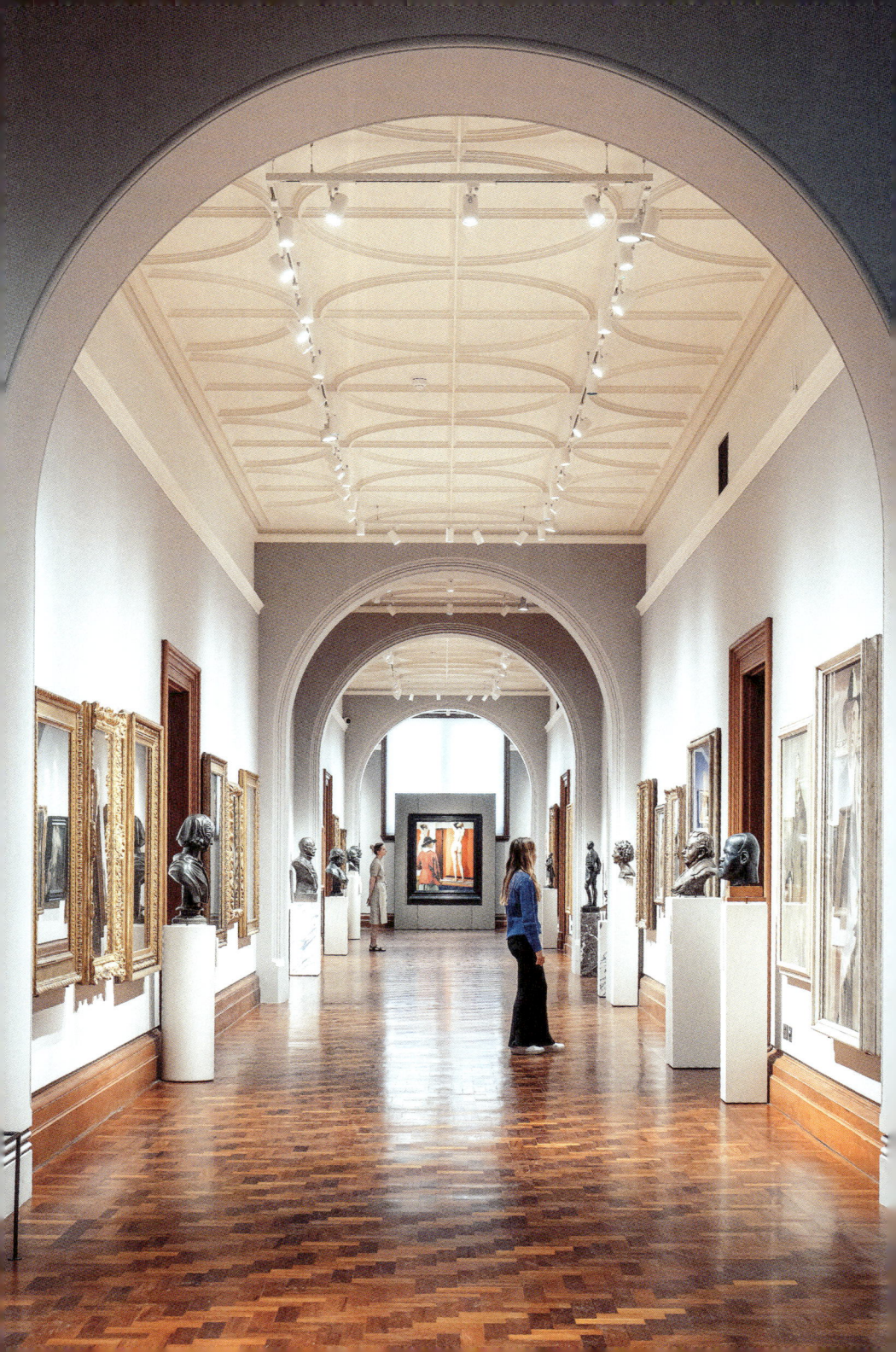

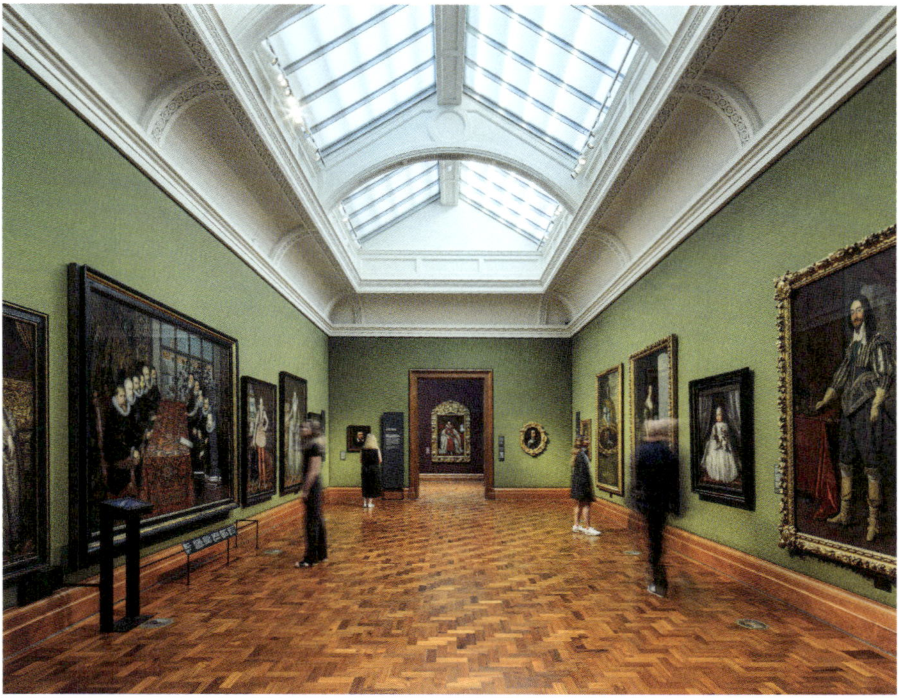

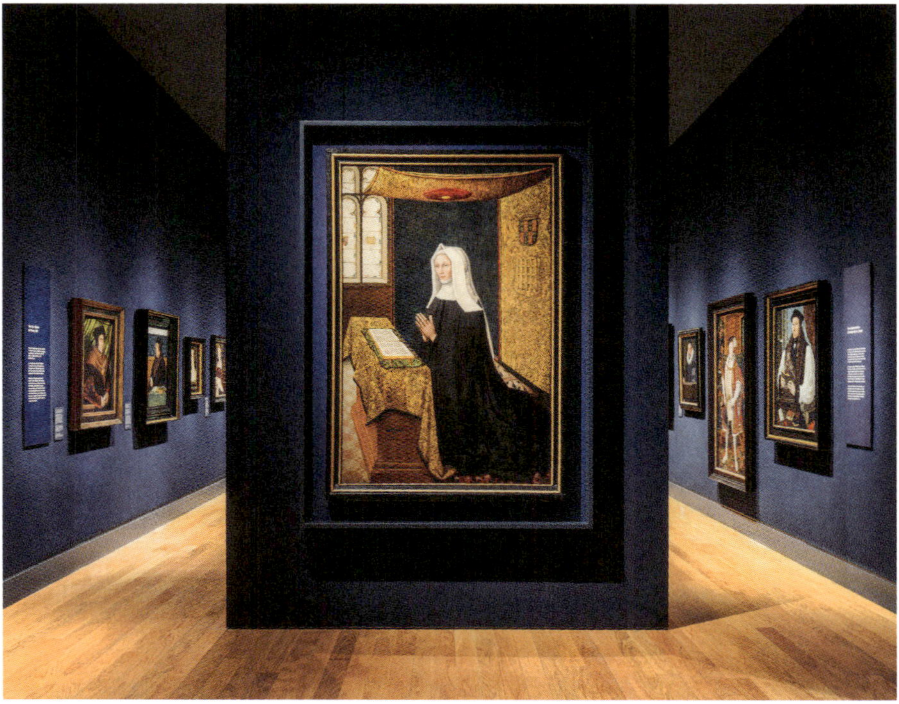

HAYWARD GALLERY

Concrete colossus known for big-name shows

Approach this Brutalist beauty from Waterloo Bridge and you'd be forgiven for thinking some art-loving alien race had landed beside the Thames, ready to impart cultural wisdom from their vast, protuberant vessel. Inside, the spirit of innovation is just as potent, with a new cutting-edge exhibition transforming the Hayward's chameleon-like concrete halls every three to four months. Carsten Höller's disorientating metal tunnels, Ernesto Neto's sensory textile 'playrooms' and Do Ho Suh's gossamer houses are just a few of the interactive structures in which the gallery's adventurous audience has immersed itself in recent years, while retrospectives of pioneers such as Bridget Riley and Louise Bourgeois have proved just as popular. Entry is paid, but there's always free art to be enjoyed, be it in the gallery's project space or its criminally underused but architecturally noteworthy outdoor sculpture courts.

Southbank Centre, Belvedere Road, London, SE1 8XX
southbankcentre.co.uk/venues/hayward-gallery

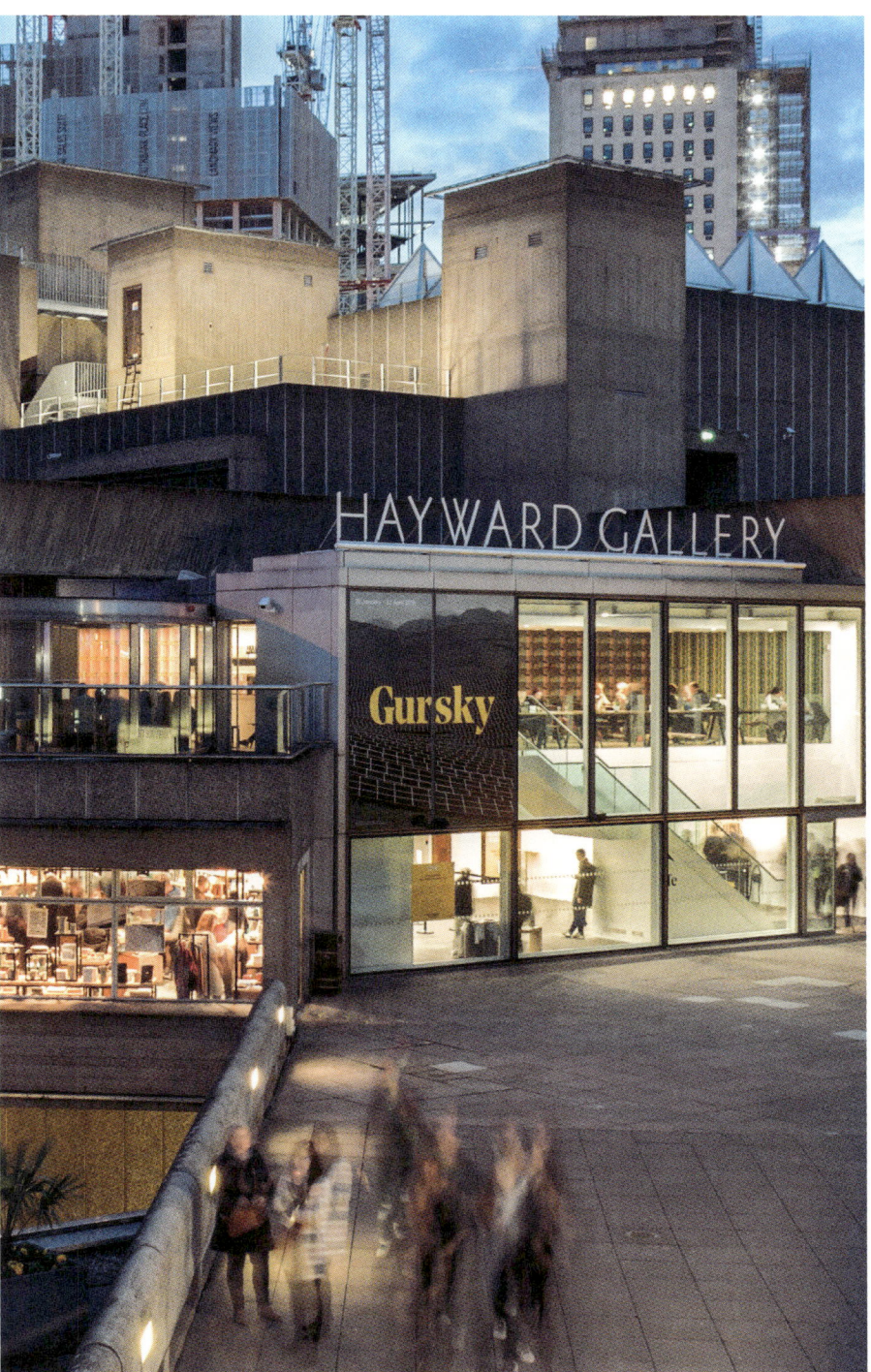

TATE MODERN

Electrifying art in ex-power station

No arty excursion to the capital is complete without a mosey through the Tate's sacred halls – home to modern masterpieces including Matisse's contemplative *The Snail* and Marcel Duchamp's infamous *Fountain*. Occupying nearly 8.5 acres on the Thames' vibrant South Bank, the imposing former power station is London's premier house of contemporary art; a Brutalist bulwark whose epic paid exhibitions make membership a no-brainer – though its free-to-view permanent collection is just as stimulating. At its centre, the awe-inspiring Turbine Hall hosts dramatic, large-scale commissions by some of the biggest names in art, with Olafur Eliasson's sublime artificial sun and Louise Bourgeois' mighty steel arachnid among the more memorable moments in the project's 25-year duration. Check out the Tate Lates programme of grown-up events after dark, and don't miss the Uniqlo: Tate Play series of free family workshops and interactive Turbine Hall installations, whose greatest hits have included opportunities to plaster a Yayoi Kusama-designed 'apartment' in stickers and construct a full-sized wooden playground with Woodland Tribe.

Bankside, London, SE1 9TG
tate.org.uk/visit/tate-modern

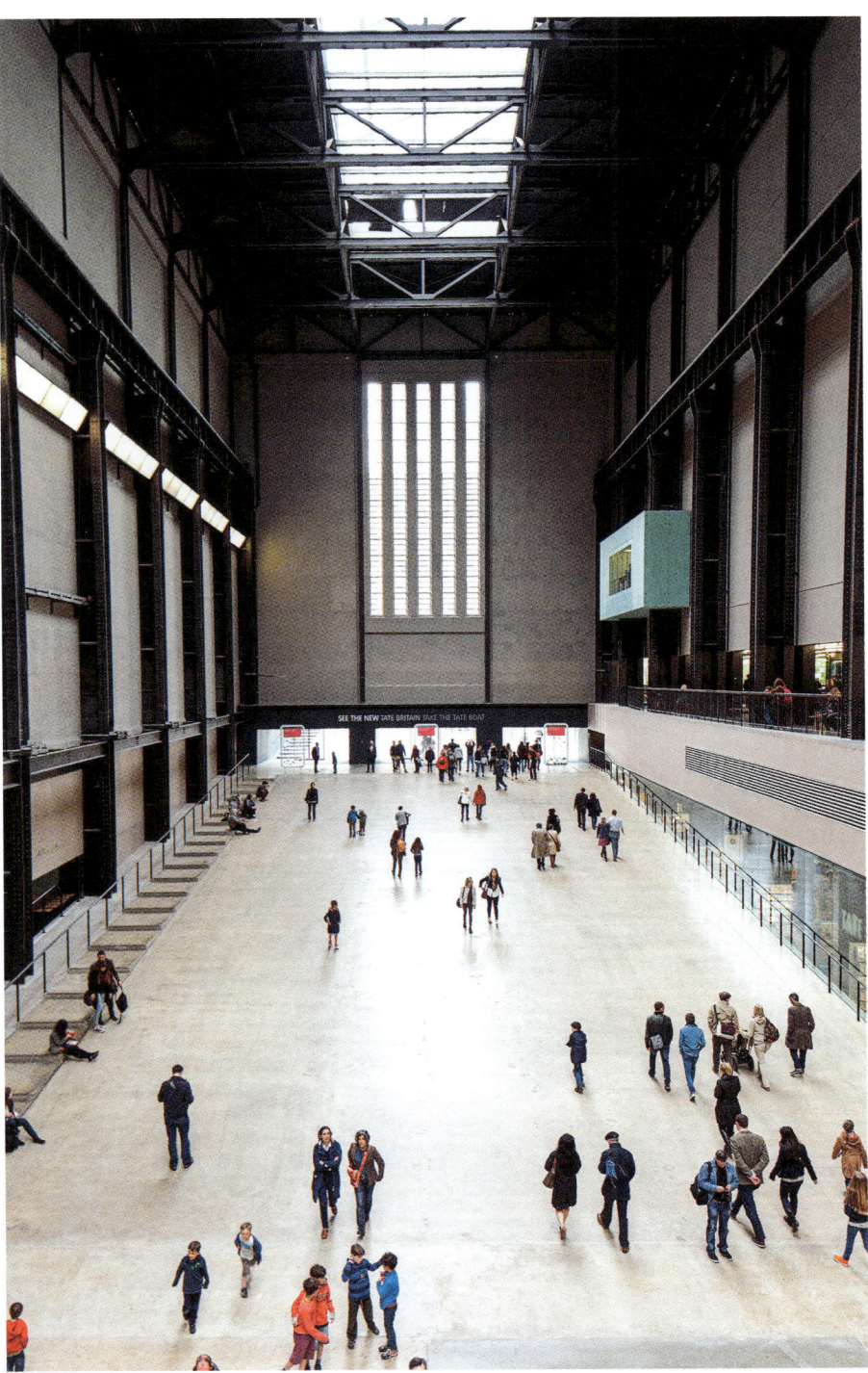

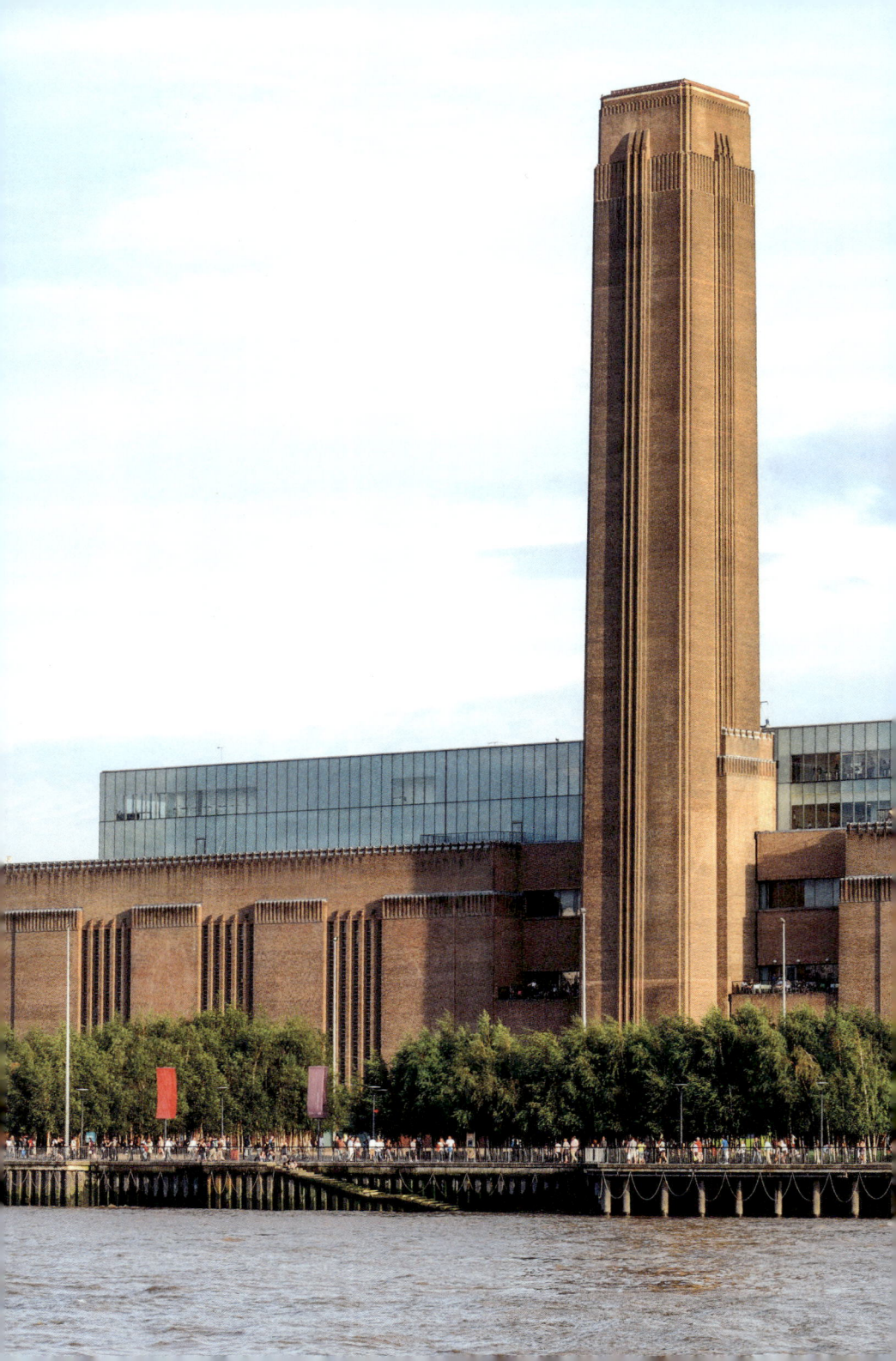

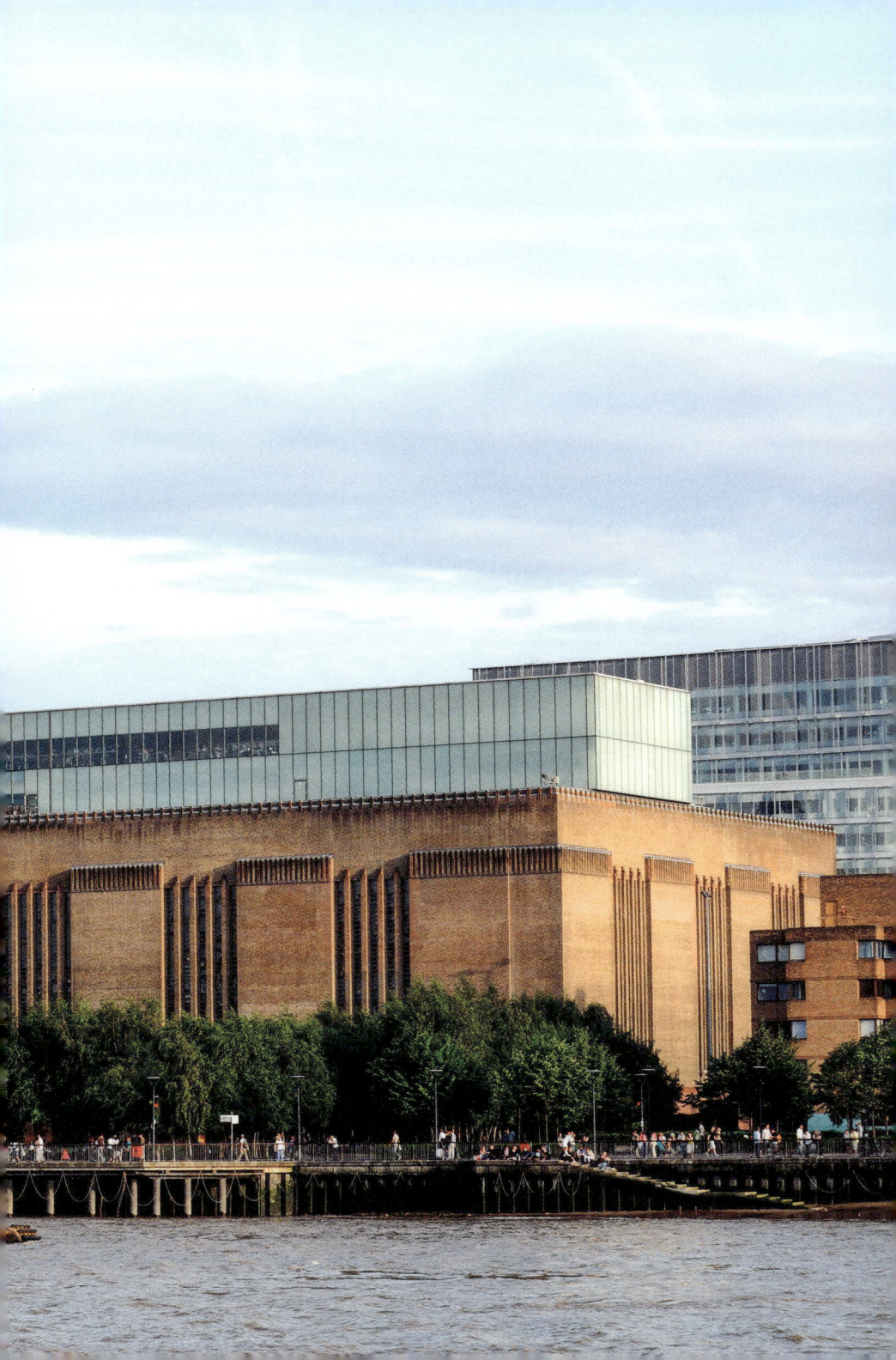

WHITECHAPEL GALLERY

Experimental exhibitions in stylish space

Nestled among the betting shops and fast-food joints of Whitechapel Road, this striking gallery is an unexpected treat, occupying an Art Nouveau building and its next-door neighbour, the majestic former Passmore Edwards library. Founded in 1901 to improve the lives of the masses in the poverty-stricken East End, the Whitechapel played a pivotal role in British post-war art history. Significant exhibitions, including 1956's *This is Tomorrow* and 1964's *The New Generation,* helped to catapult the careers of artists such as Richard Hamilton, Eduardo Paolozzi, David Hockney and Bridget Riley. You can always expect the unexpected within its walls, be it a soft-sculpture installation where touching is very much encouraged (see Sarah Marsh and Stephanie Jefferies' *Sculpting Conversations*) or a full-sized swimming pool courtesy of Elmgreen & Dragset, whose 2018 exhibition sought to highlight the downfall of civic space. Don't miss the Walther Koenig art bookshop – one of London's best – and the sunlit, parquet-floored cafe, whose playful residencies such as women-run Italian pop-up Alba make a post-gallery lunch stop inevitable.

77–82 Whitechapel High Street, London, E1 7QX
whitechapelgallery.org

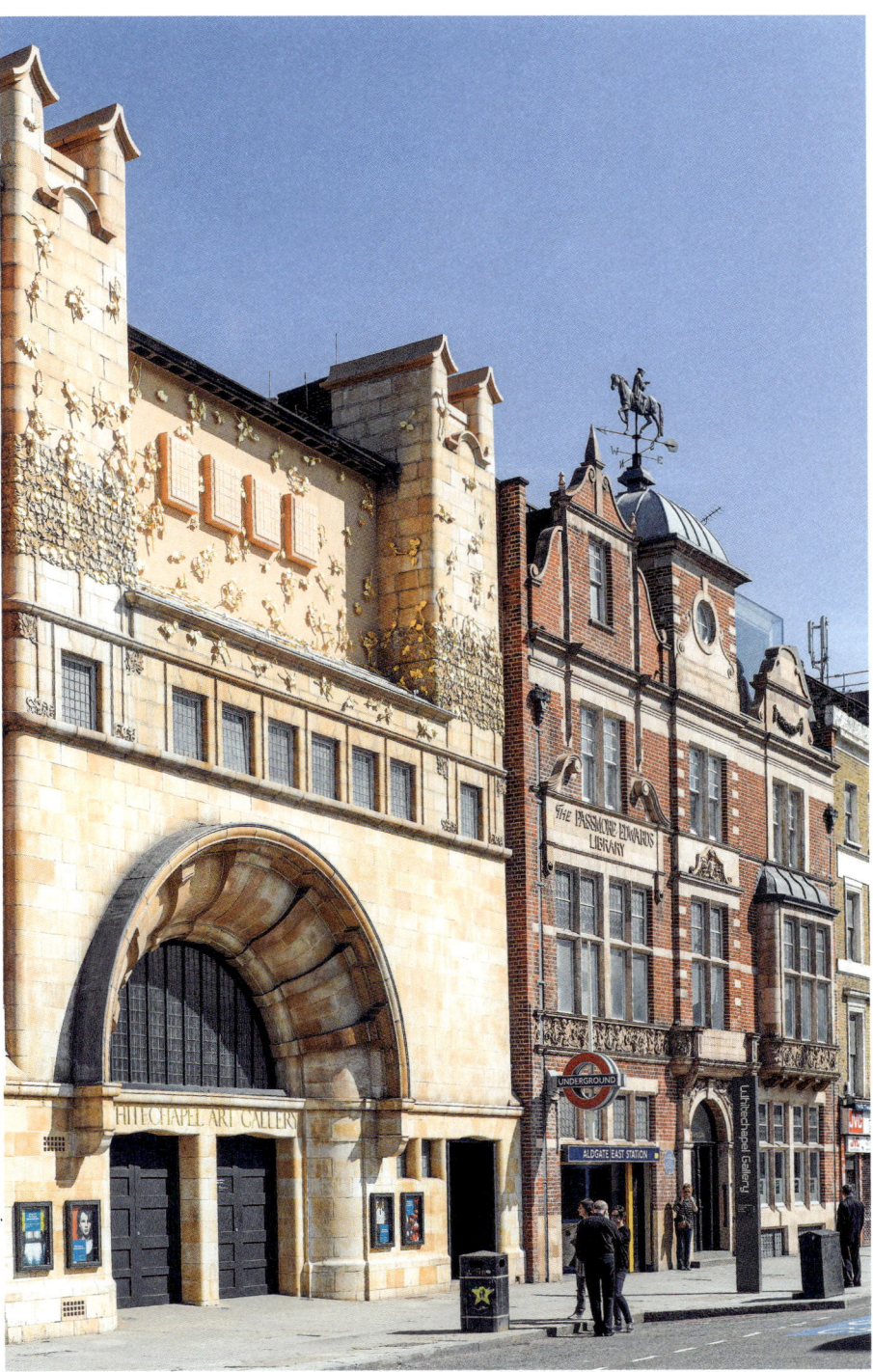

ROYAL ACADEMY OF ARTS

Eminent art establishment known for blockbuster shows

Famously snubbed as 'a big, fat, stuffy, old, pompous institution' by Damien Hirst in 1997, Britain's oldest fine arts organisation has worked hard to shirk its fusty image over the past three decades. Redeveloped in 2018 by architect David Chipperfield in time for its 250th birthday, today's RA is a joyful mashup of old and new, with meaty exhibitions presenting work by everyone from Michelangelo to Michael Craig-Martin, Constable to Cornelia Parker. It's perhaps best known as home to the world's largest and longest-running open-submission exhibition of contemporary art – an annual favourite comprising over 1,000 works spanning painting, sculpture, film, architecture and more, and preceded by the much smaller but equally unmissable Young Artists' Summer Show. True to its commitment to art for all, the RA's family workshops are outstanding (its monthly artist-led SEND activities reliably sell out within hours), while the buzzy Poster Bar provides a stylish spot to conclude grown-up visits.

Burlington House, London, W1J OBD
royalacademy.org.uk

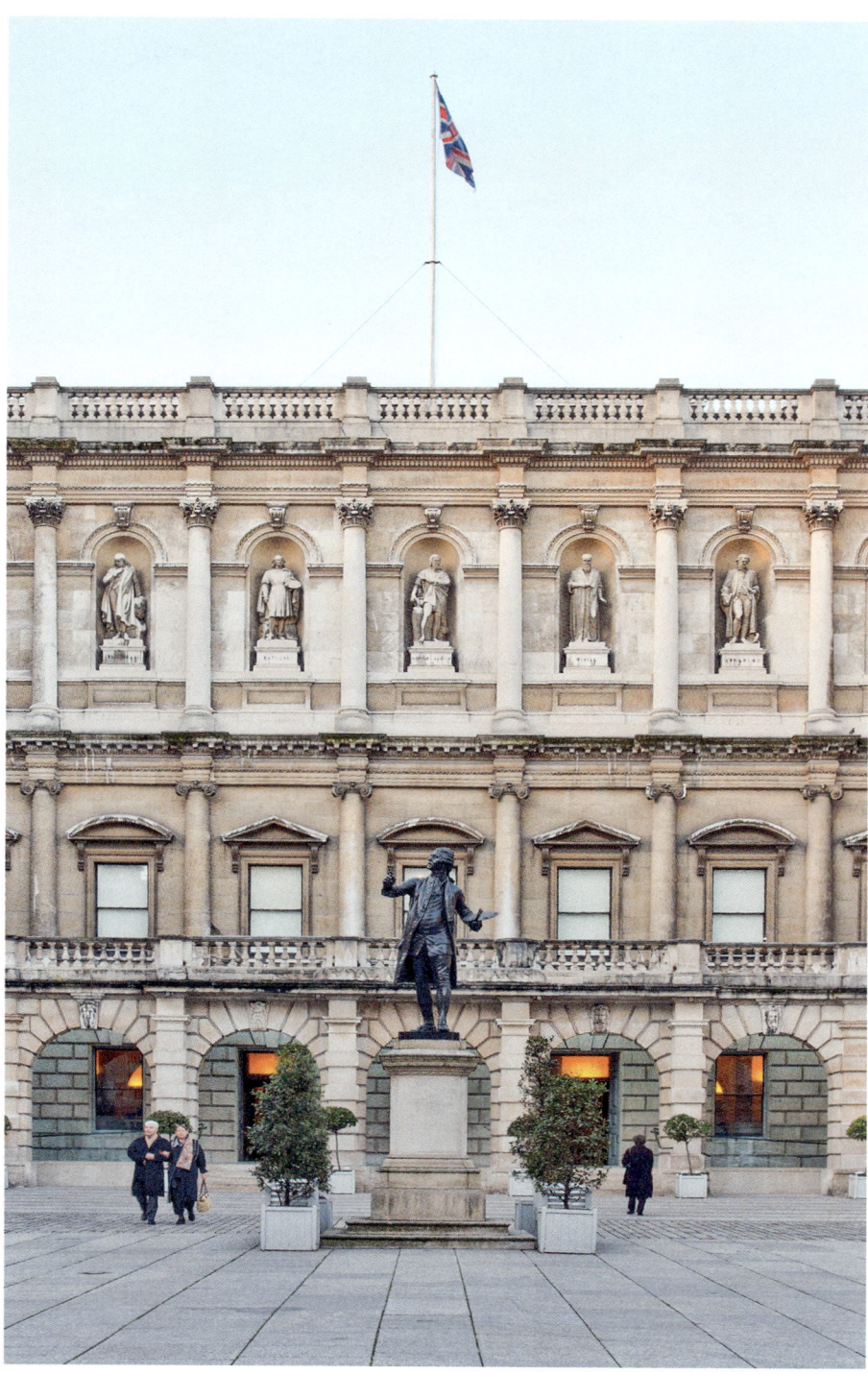

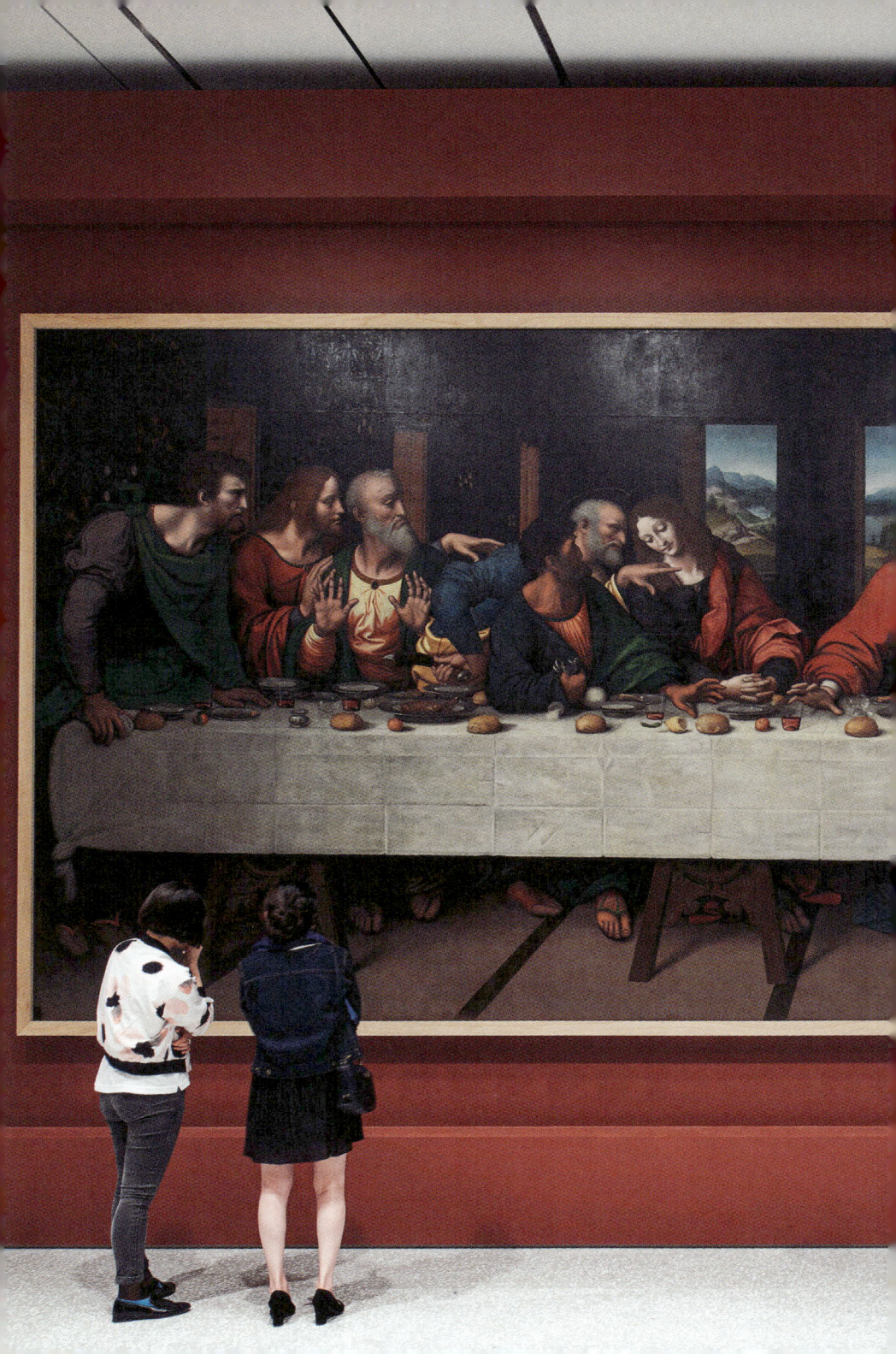

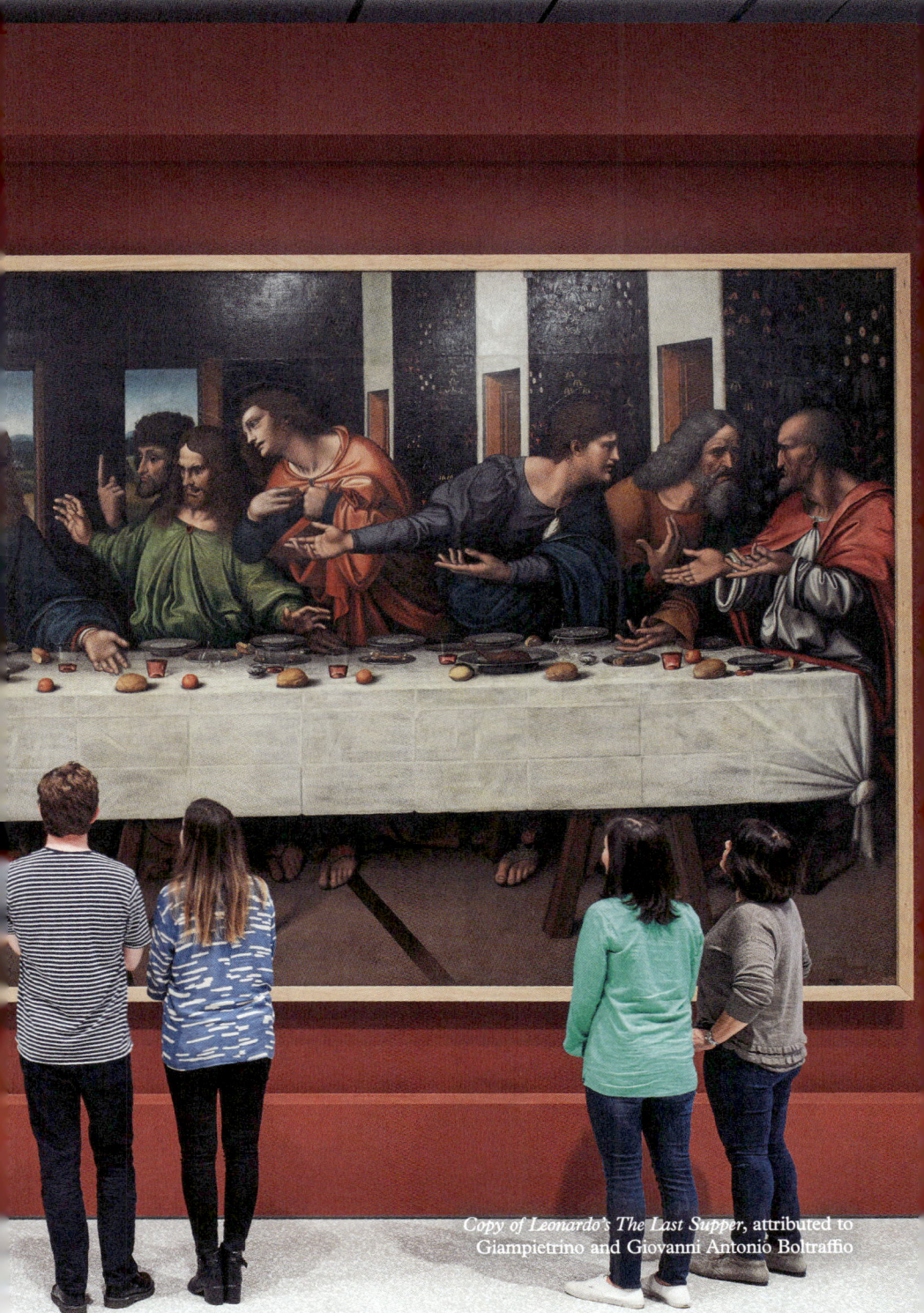

Copy of Leonardo's The Last Supper, attributed to Giampietrino and Giovanni Antonio Boltraffio

NATIONAL GALLERY

Compelling history of Western European art

Nestled in the shadow of Nelson's Column, the National is every inch the Art History student's dream, with its relatively modest (2,300 paintings to the Louvre's 7,500) yet remarkably encyclopaedic collection covering works from the 13th through to the early 20th centuries. While invariably thronged with tourists, the gallery's majestic halls are a joy to peruse, whether you're admiring a Turner sunset, pondering van Eyck's enigmatic *The Arnolfini Portrait* or picturing yourself beside a sun-soaked Seine à la Seurat's *Bathers at Asnières*. The permanent collection is free to enjoy, though the inflated ticket prices for temporary exhibitions are usually worth it, with recent surveys of Raphael, Gentileschi and Monet all proving unmissable. To top it off, newly opened restaurant Ochre boasts a dinner menu worthy of the Masters – best served with a cocktail inspired by the gallery's current touring exhibition – while the more casual Muriel's Kitchen is better suited to a student budget.

Trafalgar Square, London, WC2N 5DN
nationalgallery.org.uk

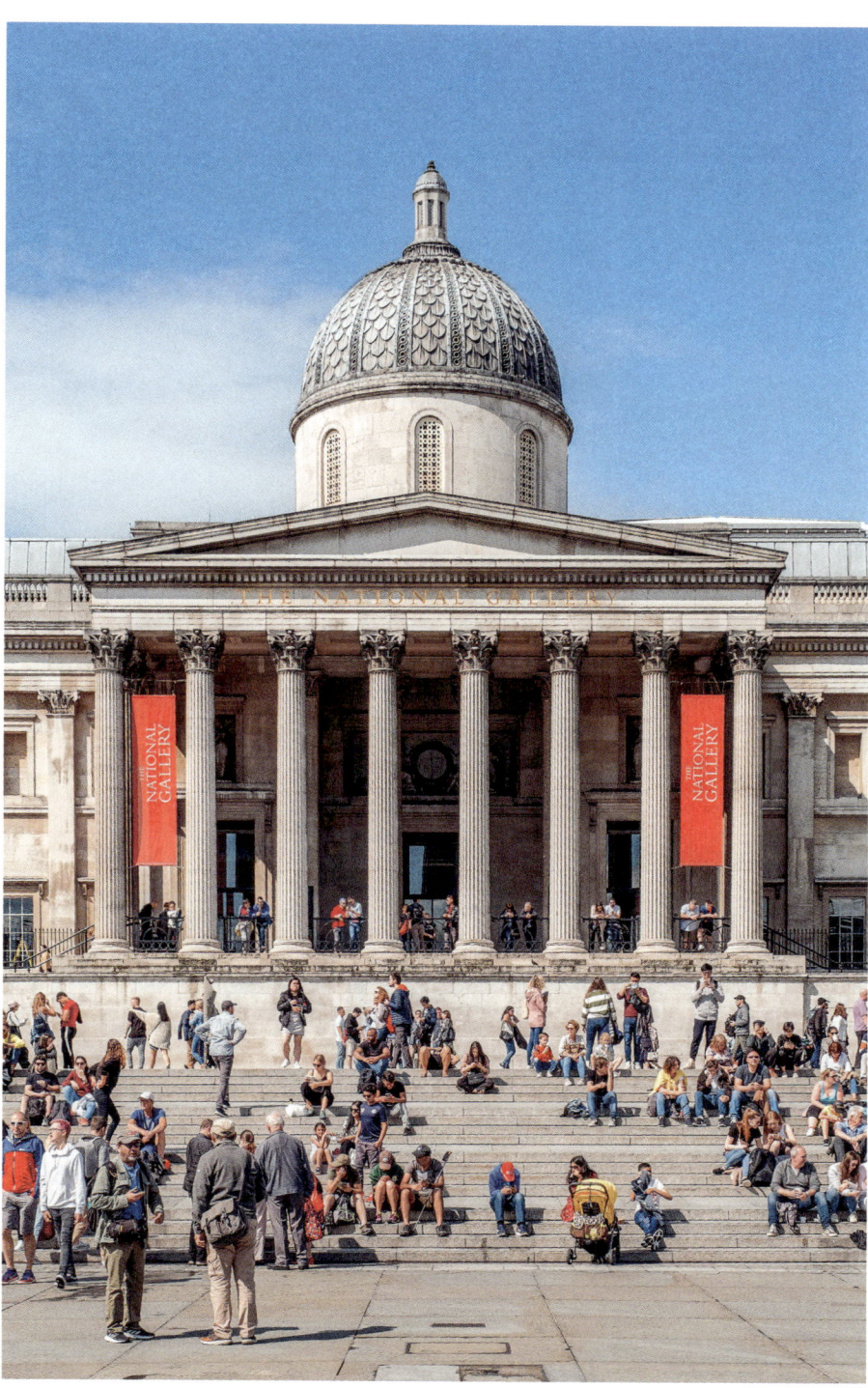

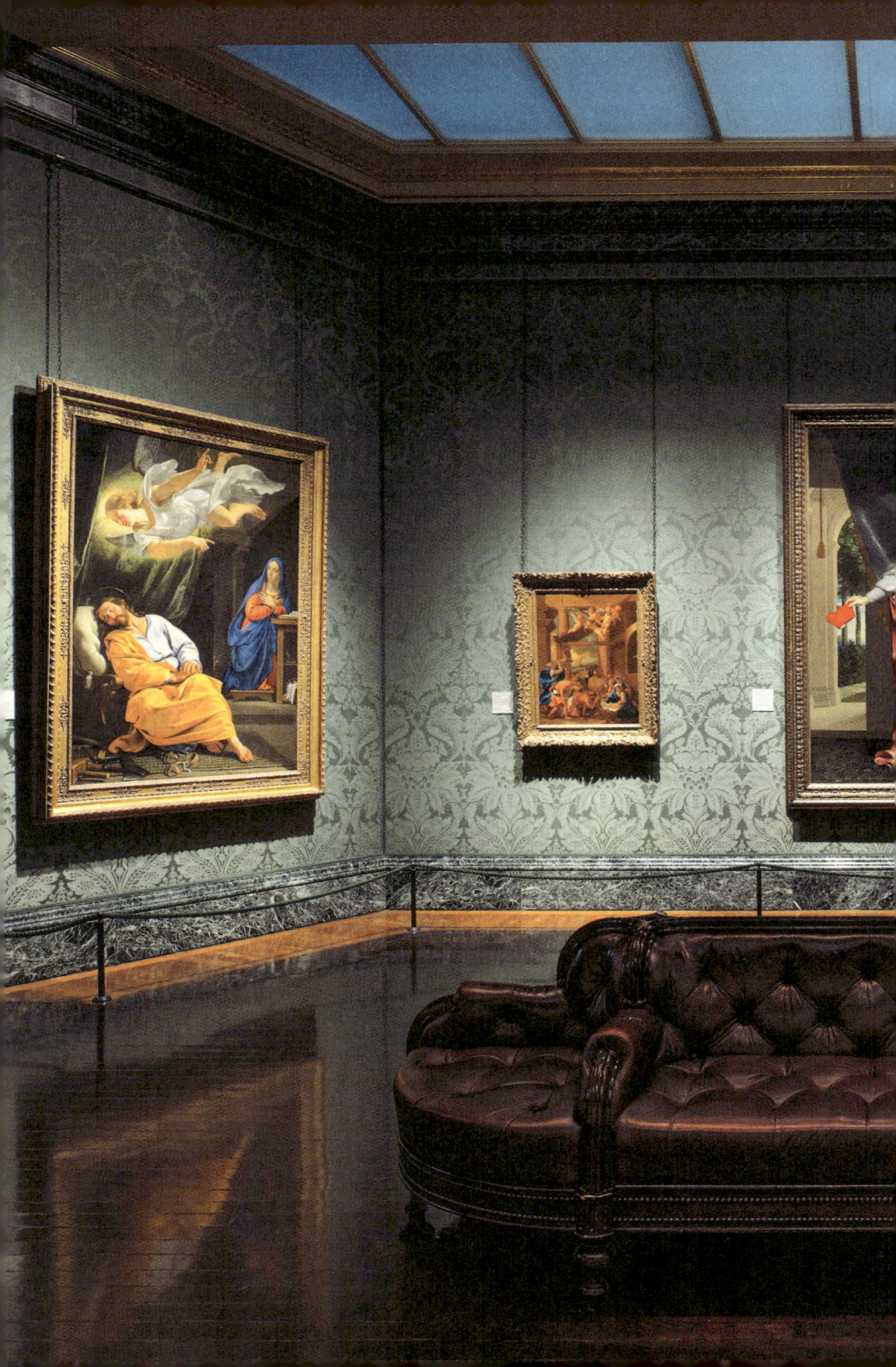

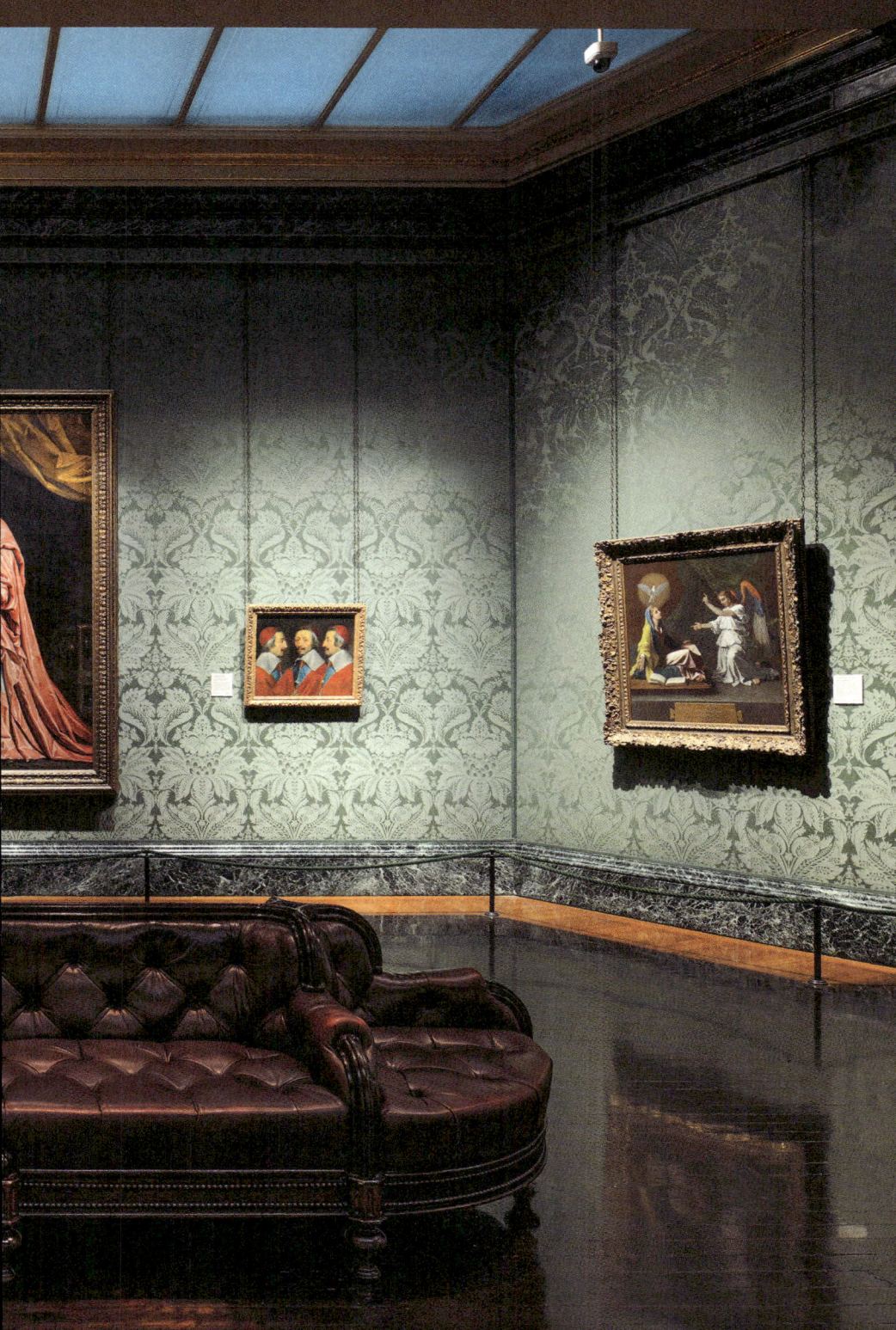

SOUTH LONDON GALLERY

Denmark Hill destination with ever-surprising exhibits

Nestled between the thriving creative hubs of Camberwell and Peckham, any art fan who visits this audacious institution will be handsomely rewarded. Founded by philanthropist William Rossiter in 1891 to 'bring art to the people of south London', the SLG combines the idiosyncrasies of a local gallery with the reputation of a national institution. It's famed worldwide for platforming trailblazing contemporary art, with particular attention to introducing emerging artists who are now household names – their roster includes Tracey Emin, Gavin Turk and Oscar Murillo. Arranged across two architecturally significant but disparate buildings on opposite sides of Peckham Road, it's as much of a destination as its central London counterparts, with a RIBA award-winning Fire Station space, stylish resident cafe South London Louie and endlessly browsable indie art bookshop. Families should time their visits to coincide with the gallery's inspiring artist-led workshops, drawing inspiration from current displays.

65 Peckham Road, London, SE5 8UH
southlondongallery.org

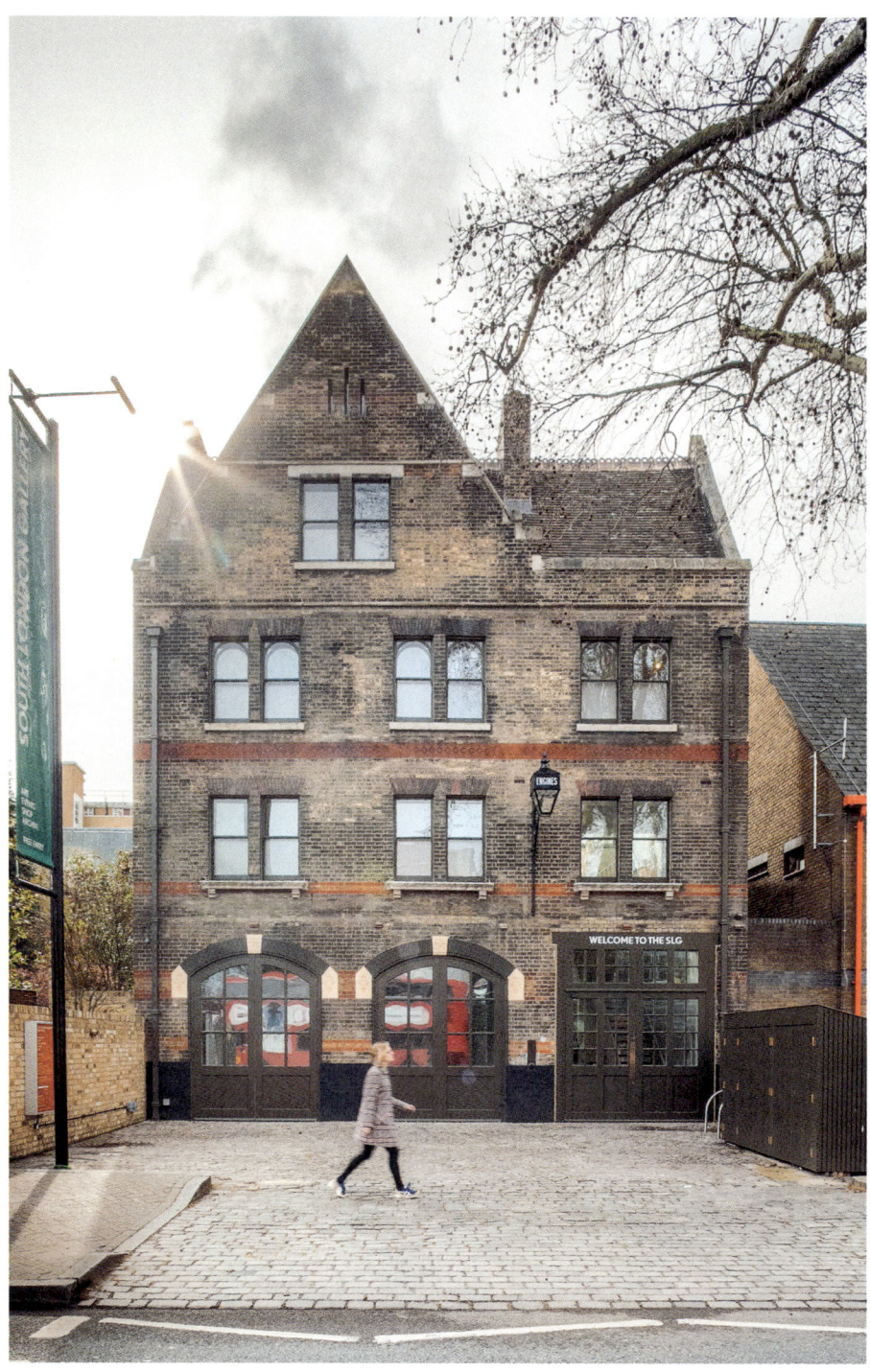

RED HOUSE

William Morris's Arts and Crafts masterpiece

Edward Burne-Jones' account of his friend's Kentish home as 'the beautifullest place on Earth' is probably reason enough to visit it. If it isn't, its standing as the birthplace of the Arts and Crafts movement and a haven for the Pre-Raphaelite Brotherhood definitely is. Since swallowed by suburban London, the Neo-Gothic-inspired Red House is irrefutably beautiful, as well as being the only building ever to have been designed, built *and* lived in by William Morris – if only for five short years. It was here that Morris created his earliest wallpaper designs, though you'll find none of them adorning the walls, which are instead festooned with murals produced collaboratively by the artist and his friends. Alongside these survive jewel-like stained-glass windows, original handmade furniture and one of Red House's most mesmerising features – a glass 'graffiti' screen etched with the signatures of its numerous famous visitors.

Red House Lane, London, DA6 8JF
nationaltrust.org.uk/visit/london/red-house

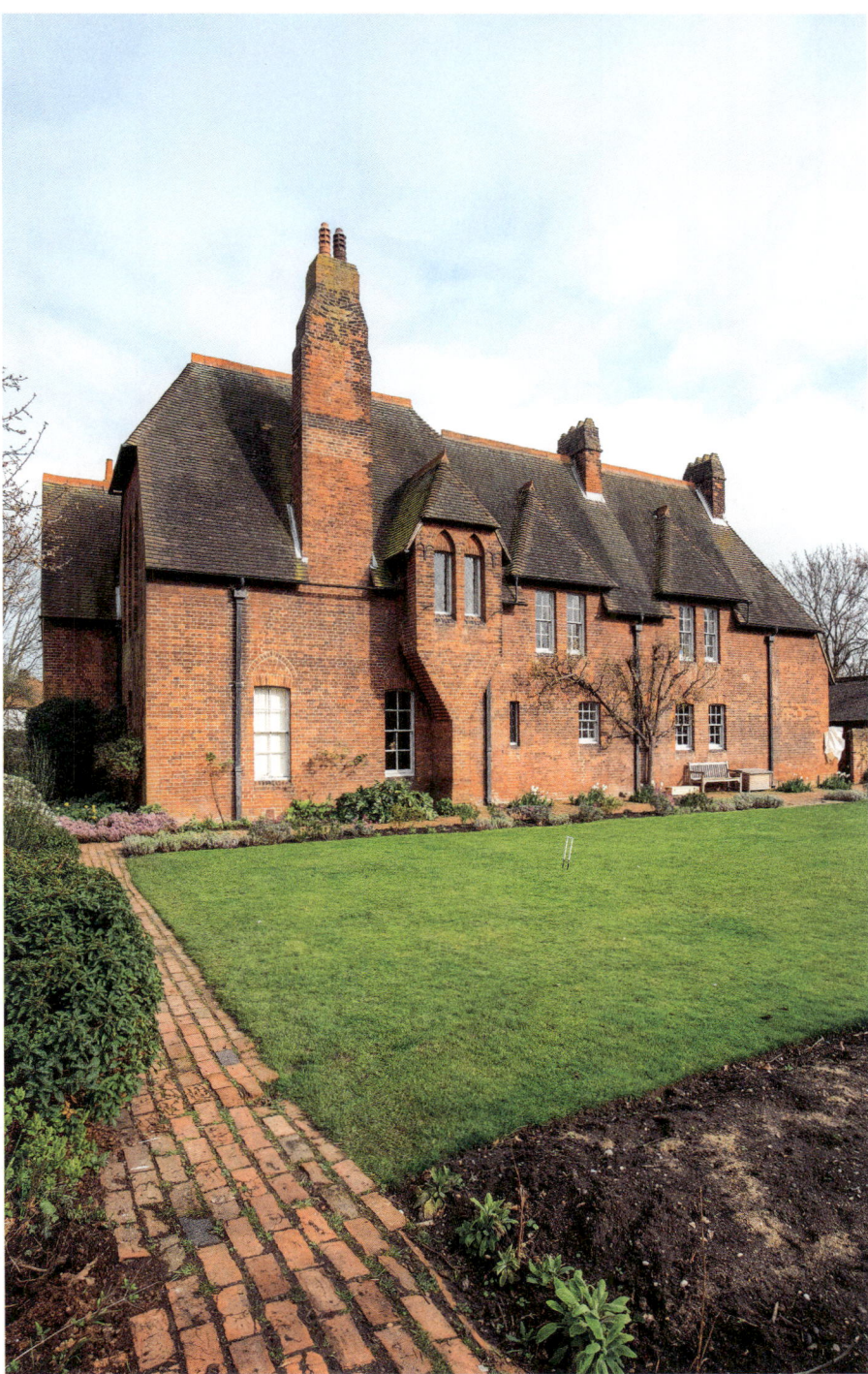

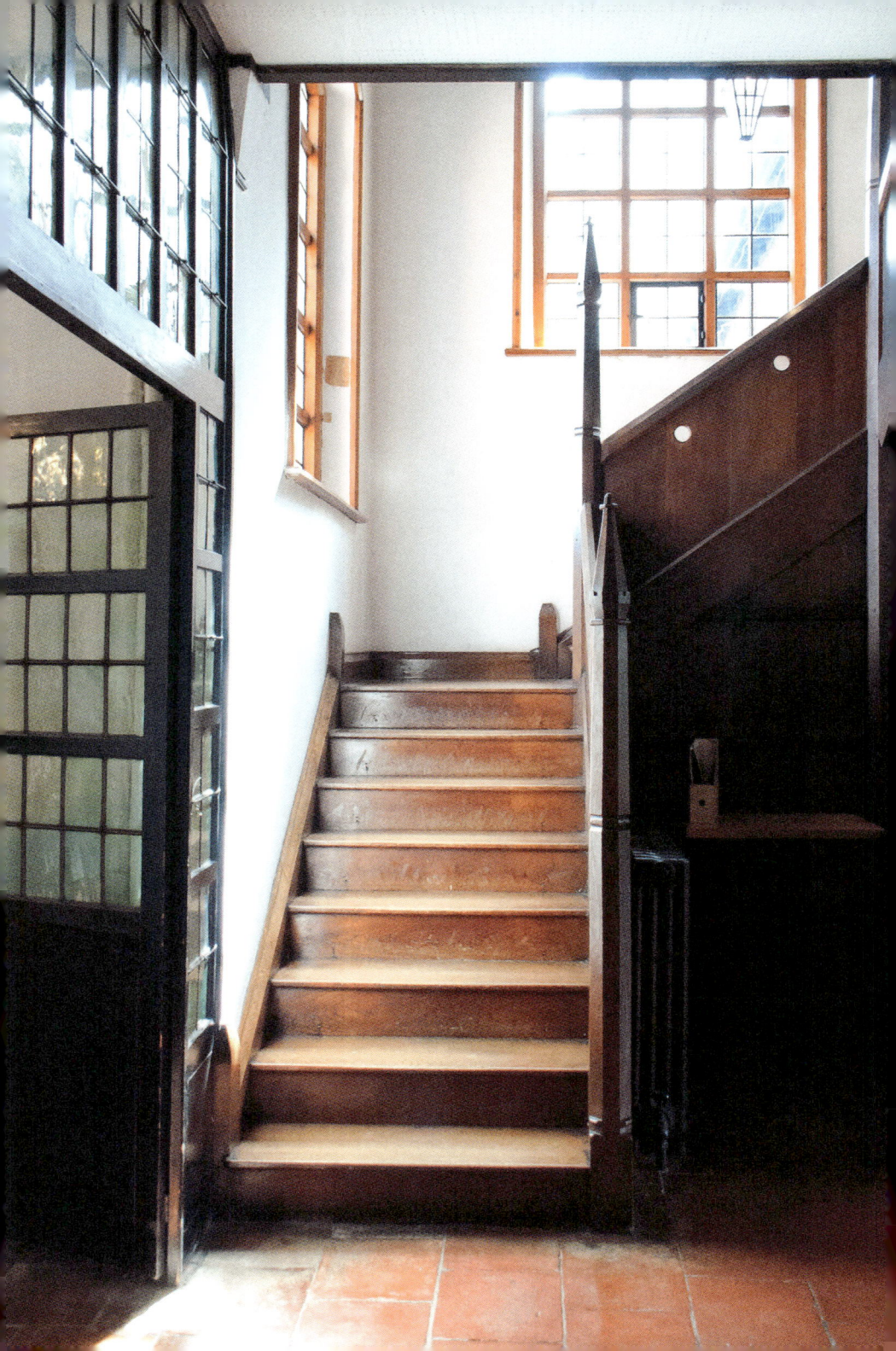

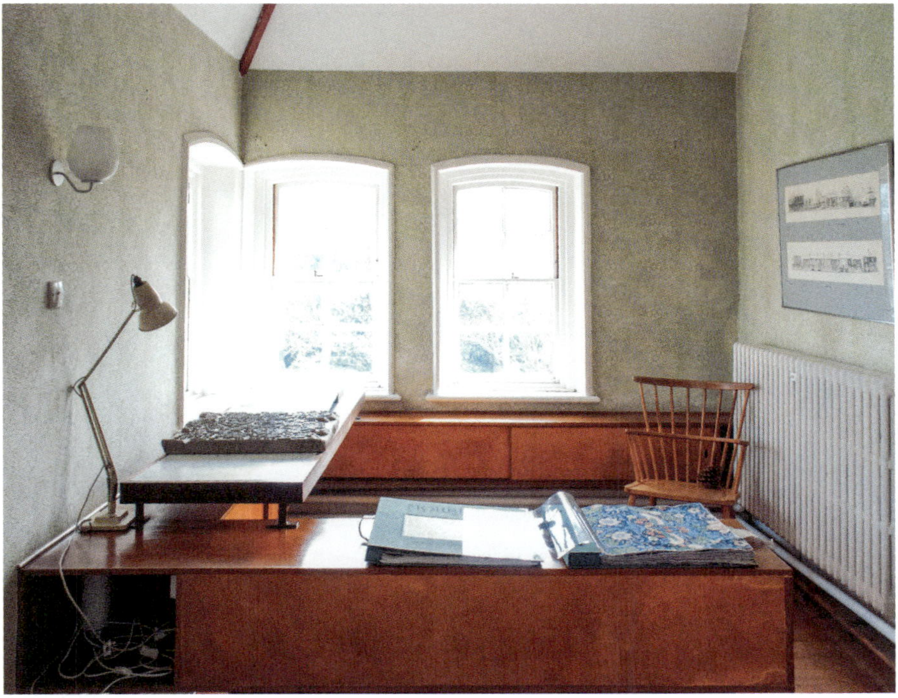

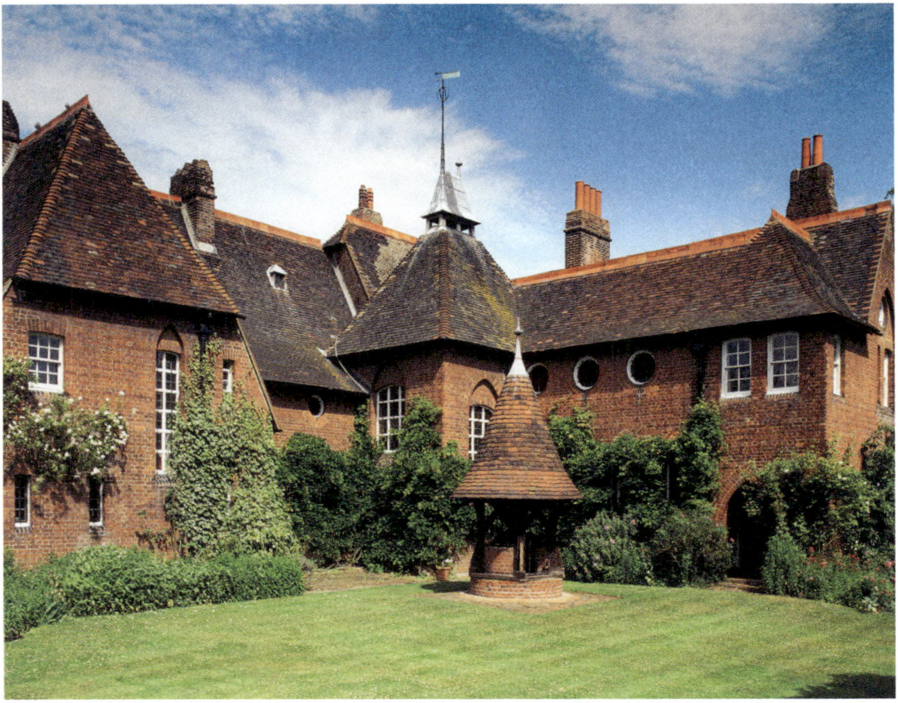

TATE BRITAIN

Iconic institution housing magnificent art

A dizzying crash course in the last 500 years of British art awaits you at this sumptuous palace of creativity, whose hefty collection spans everything from Van Dyck's charismatic court paintings to Francis Bacon's violent triptychs, via the dreamy Pre-Raphaelites. Accessible and comprehensive, Tate Britain is as much famed for its groundbreaking showcases of contemporary artists like Lynette Yiadom-Boakye and Rachel Whiteread as its epic retrospectives spotlighting Turner and Picasso. Then there's its generous family offer, which spans two creative play spaces, a digital drawing studio and a regular line-up of workshops with inspiring children's authors. The main floor's chronological galleries require several hours to digest, but be sure to leave time for the annual Duveen Galleries commission, whose past spectacles have included Hew Locke's procession of 100 life-size human sculptures, Steve McQueen's poignant portraits of 76,000 London schoolchildren and Anthea Hamilton's anthropomorphic *The Squash*.

Millbank, London, SW1P 4RG
tate.org.uk/visit/tate-britain

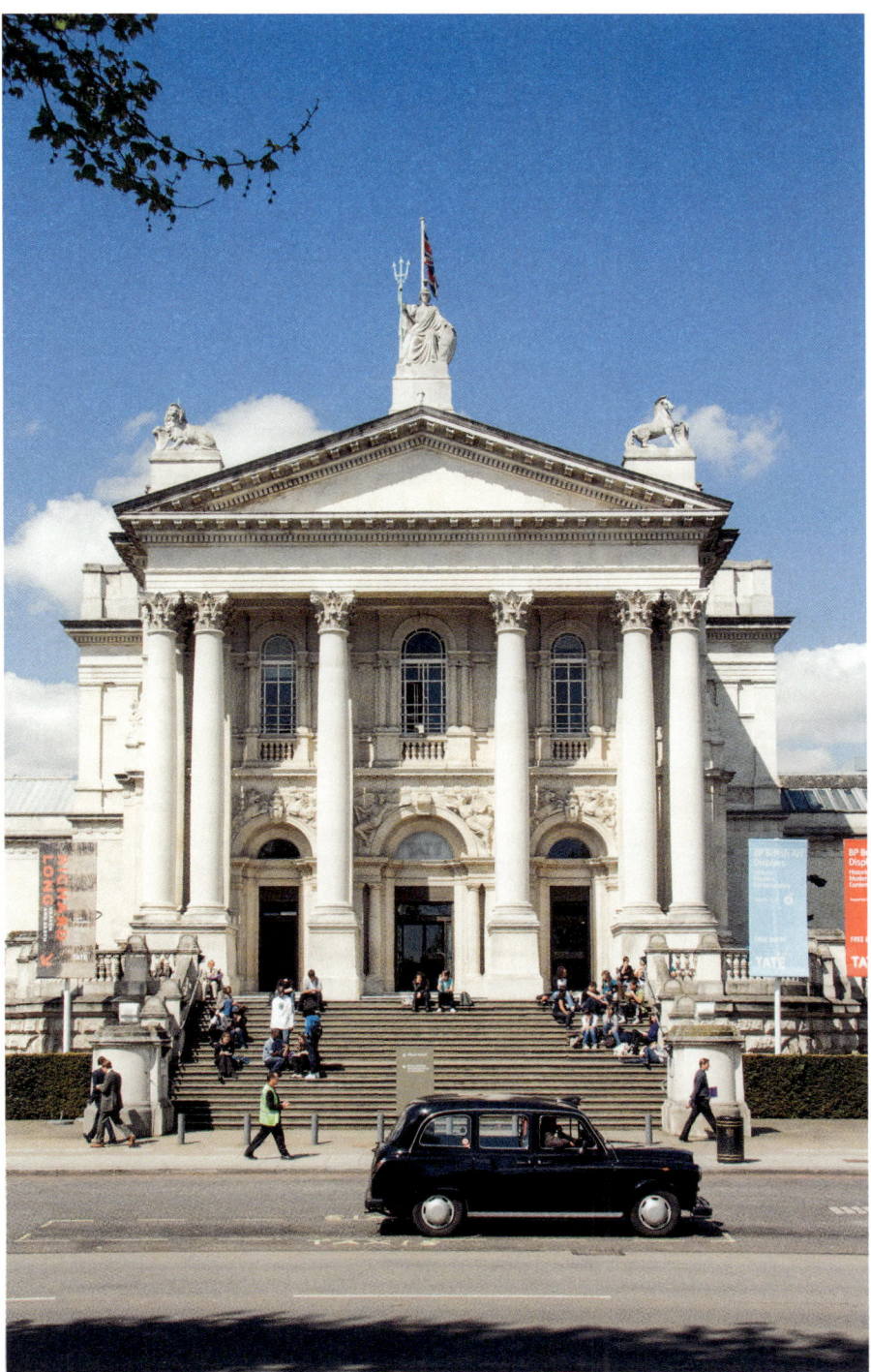

THE ASHMOLEAN

University of Oxford's palace of antiquities

Walter Sickert's pertinent interpretation of the boredom of married life, Michelangelo's preparatory chalk studies for the Sistine Chapel and a Renaissance dish depicting a head composed of penises are just a few of the artistic delights you'll encounter at Britain's very first public museum. Cultivated from the collection that politician Elias Ashmole donated to the University of Oxford in 1677, this dazzling space is home to everything from Egyptian mummies to a tear-shaped jewel made for Alfred the Great – though it's just as celebrated for its millennia-spanning paintings, which include 20th-century works by Henri Matisse and Lucian Freud, and its vast collection of casts taken from monuments and sculptures of the ancient world. Check out the temporary exhibition (recent blockbusters have featured the work of Jeff Koons and William Blake) before heading to the contemplative Pre-Raphaelites gallery in pursuit of Millais' portrait of John Ruskin that led to the latter's divorce. Finally, track down Turner's iconic 1810 depiction of the nearby high street, before heading outside to marvel at how little it has changed.

Beaumont Street, Oxford, OX1 2PH

ashmolean.org

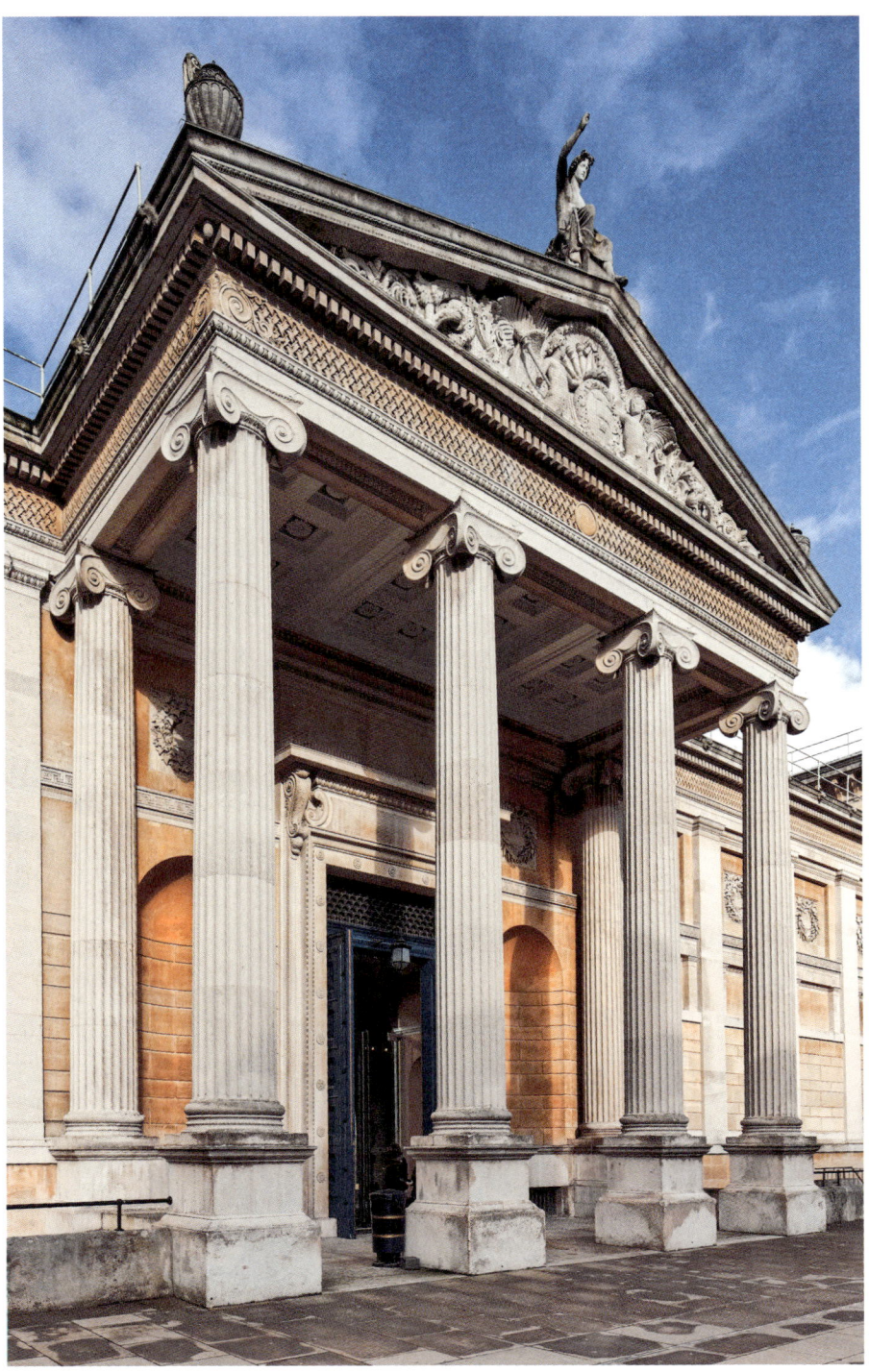

MODERN ART OXFORD

Small but mighty contemporary gallery

Approach this vibrant gallery via its narrow backstreet or tunnel-like side entrances and you'd be conned into thinking it's a somewhat discreet affair. On the contrary, the institution formerly known as MoMA has garnered a robust reputation for its forthright, fearless and radical shows over its six-decade reign – from its early days of experimental, self-generated and participatory exhibitions to Jesse Darling's recent *No Medals No Ribbons*, which earned him the Turner Prize nomination that led to his 2023 win. In between, the old brewery building has borne witness to everything from a Richard Long labyrinth and a Mike Nelson sand dune to Jake and Dinos Chapman's *The Rape of Creativity*, for which the brothers systematically defaced a complete set of Goya's *Disasters of War*. Need a sit-down after all that? Do it in Emma Hart's *Club Together* installation, which has swathed the gallery cafe in a riot of colour.

30 Pembroke Street, Oxford, OX1 1BP
modernartoxford.org.uk

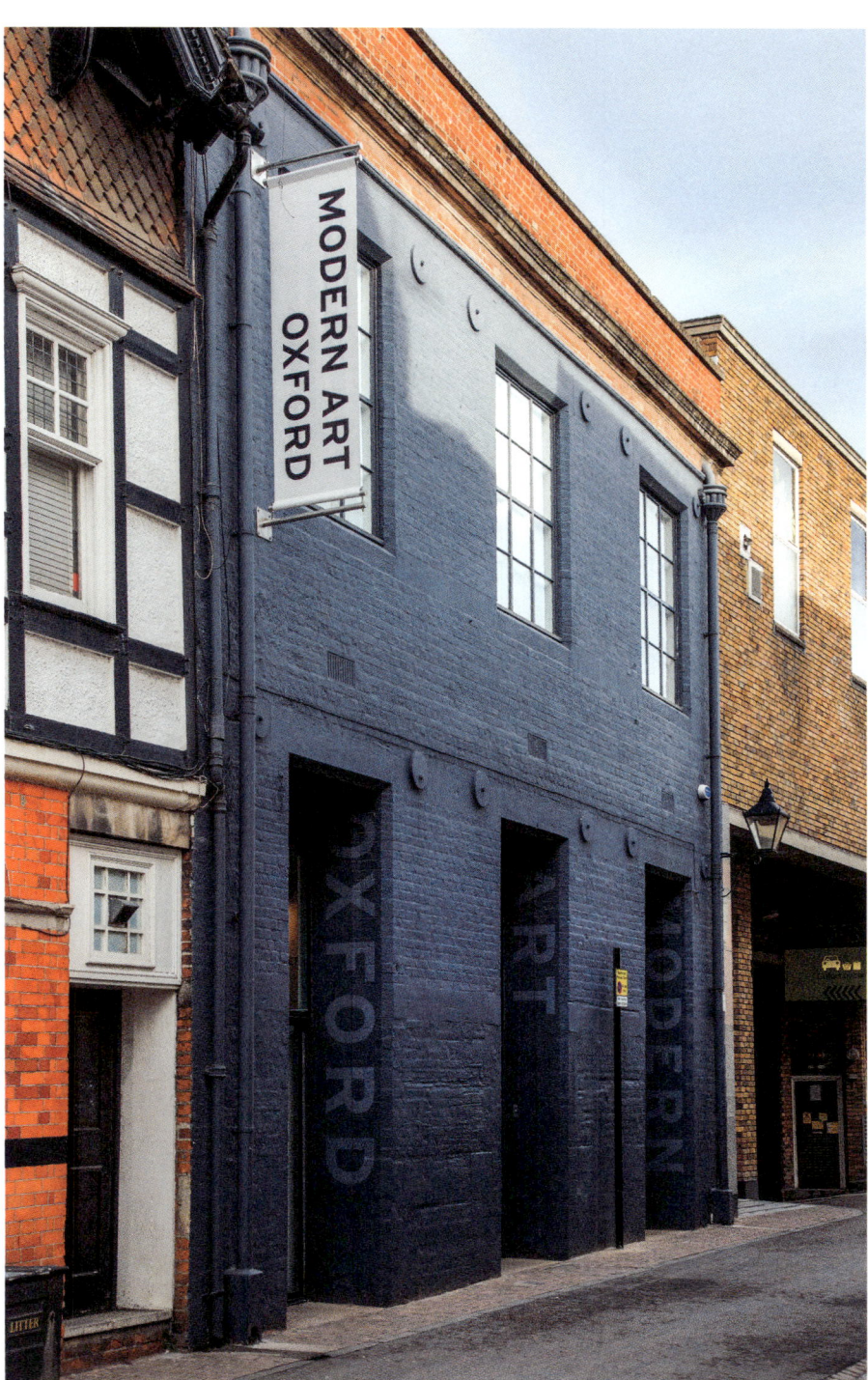

PALLANT HOUSE GALLERY

Idiosyncratic history of modern British art

Its collection of modern British art is often regarded as second only to Tate's (p.46), but this charismatic gallery is a far cry from London's cultural heavyweights, occupying a handsome Queen Anne townhouse and contrasting contemporary extension in Chichester's historic centre. Known affectionately as 'The Dodo House', owing to the curious pair of anatomically incorrect ostriches that flank the entrance, Pallant is appealingly eccentric. It eschews the minimalist White Cube-style presentation often reserved for modern art in favour of a slightly chaotic, maximalist display style that's more in keeping with the domestic setting. Across its intimate rooms, the gallery's 5,000-strong collection hangs side by side and top to tail, recounting the story of British art from 1900 to the present by way of Freud's self-portraits, Caulfield's graphic studies and Blake's collages, to highlight just a handful of must-sees. Keep an eye on the temporary exhibition programme for deep dives into the worlds of Pallant's most celebrated artists.

8-9 North Pallant, Chichester, PO19 1TJ

pallant.org.uk

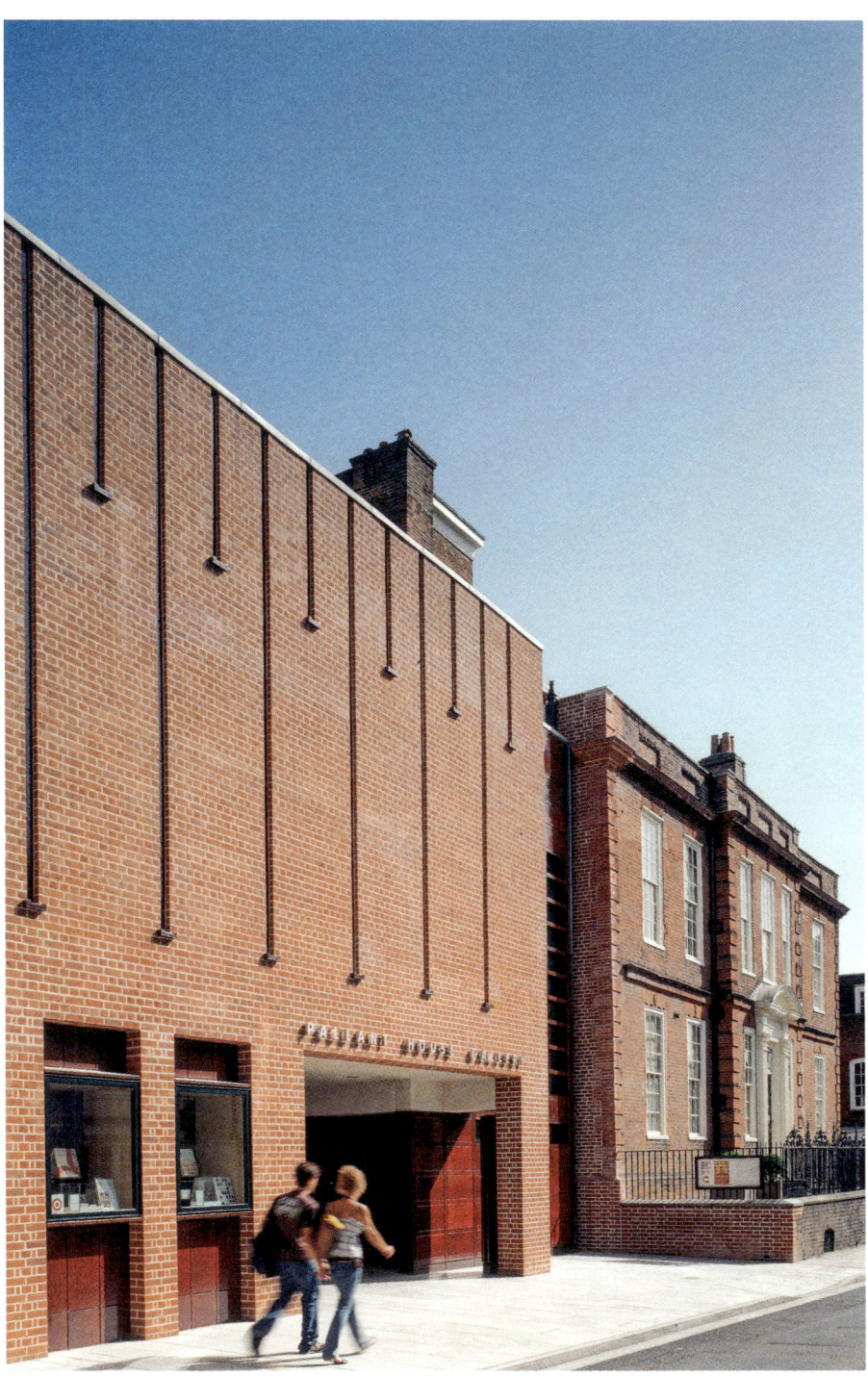

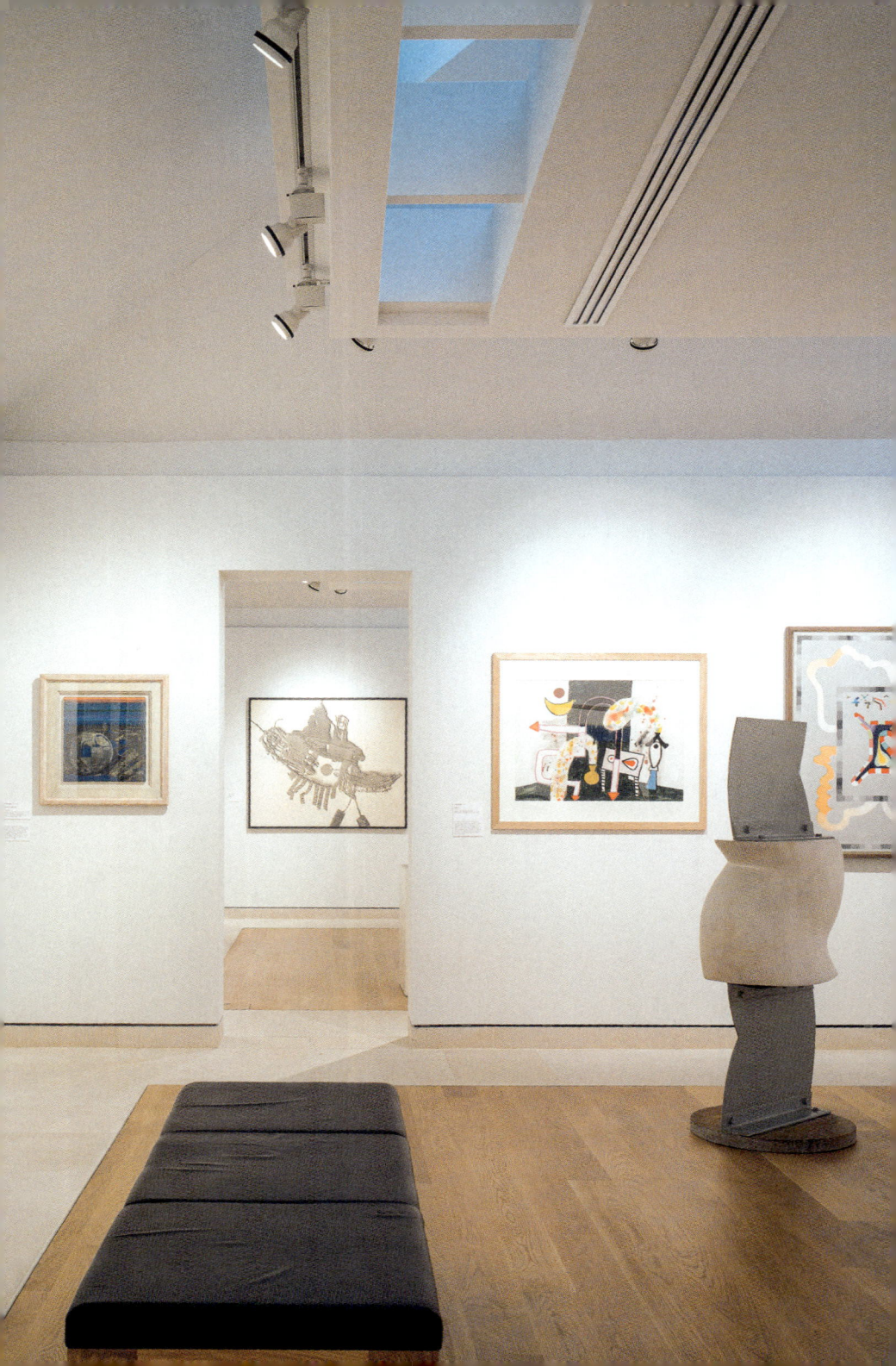

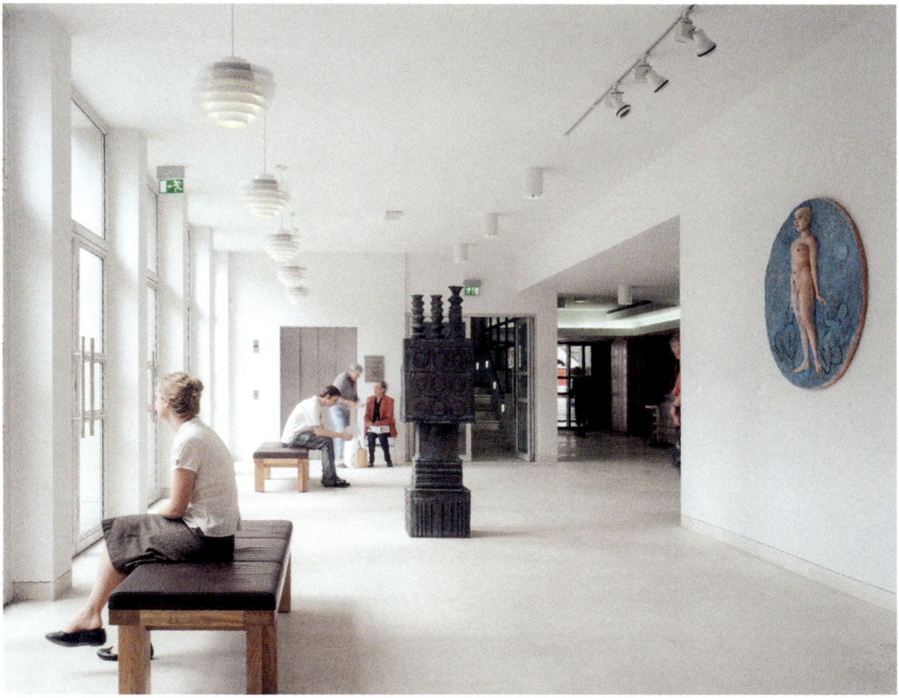

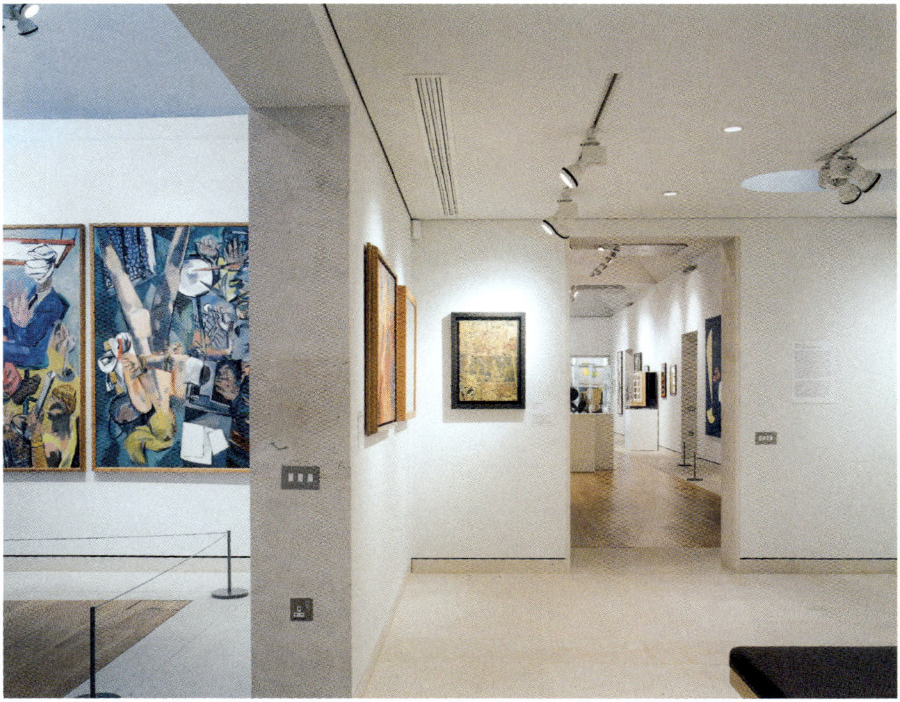

TOWNER EASTBOURNE

Colourful coastal gem

Like a pot of pure gold at the end of Lothar Götz's geometric rainbow, Towner is one of the South Coast's richest artistic treasures. Founded in 1923 with a bequest from its namesake, local benefactor John Chisholm Towner, the gallery moved to its current home – a concrete monolith designed to emulate the nearby Beachy Head cliffs – in 2009. Along with touring exhibitions, which have included local artist showcases and the 2023 Turner Prize exhibition, the Towner regularly rotates its display of work from its vast permanent collection. Along with pieces by Olafur Eliasson, Vanessa Bell and Pablo Picasso, the gallery is home to the world's largest hoard of works by Eric Ravilious, the local artist known for his dreamy South Downs landscapes. Elevate your visit by prebooking an illuminating behind-the-scenes tour of the purpose-built Art Store – and a table at stylish on-site Scandi restaurant, Light.

Devonshire Park, 82 College Road, Eastbourne, BN21 4JJ
townereastbourne.org.uk

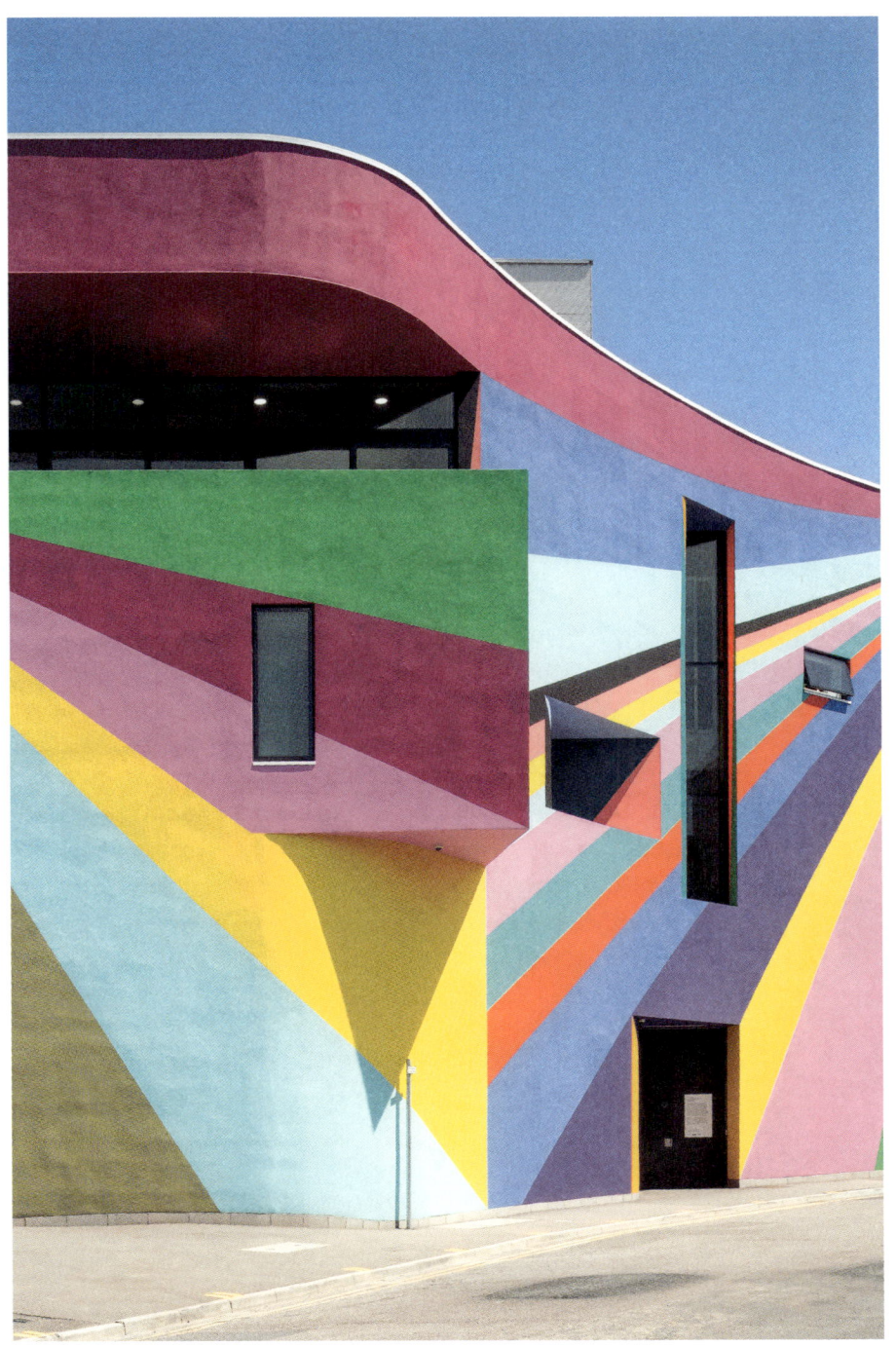

Dance Diagonal, Lothar Götz

A HOUSE FOR ESSEX

Grayson Perry's immersive abode

Ever wondered what it would be like to enter Grayson Perry's brain? This madcap Essex holiday let is the closest you'll come to doing just that – before spending the night (or two). Commissioned as part of Alain de Botton's Living Architecture scheme, which allows ordinary people to stay inside extraordinary buildings, this fairytale folly was conceived as a shrine to the fictional Julie Cope, dreamt up by Perry as an 'Essex everywoman'. Inside, the artist's intricate tapestries, ornate ceramics, life-size effigies and elaborate mosaics sumptuously illuminate Julie's comfortingly conventional life story, from birth to divorce and, ultimately, her premature death at the hands of the delivery motorbike that hangs from the ceiling. Chapel-like in shape, with pseudo-religious iconography throughout, A House for Essex affords a darkly comedic yet almost spiritual experience for Perry fans, who should be duty-bound to make the pilgrimage at least once in their lifetime.

Black Boy Lane, Wrabness, Manningtree, CO11 2TP
living-architecture.co.uk/the-houses/a-house-for-essex

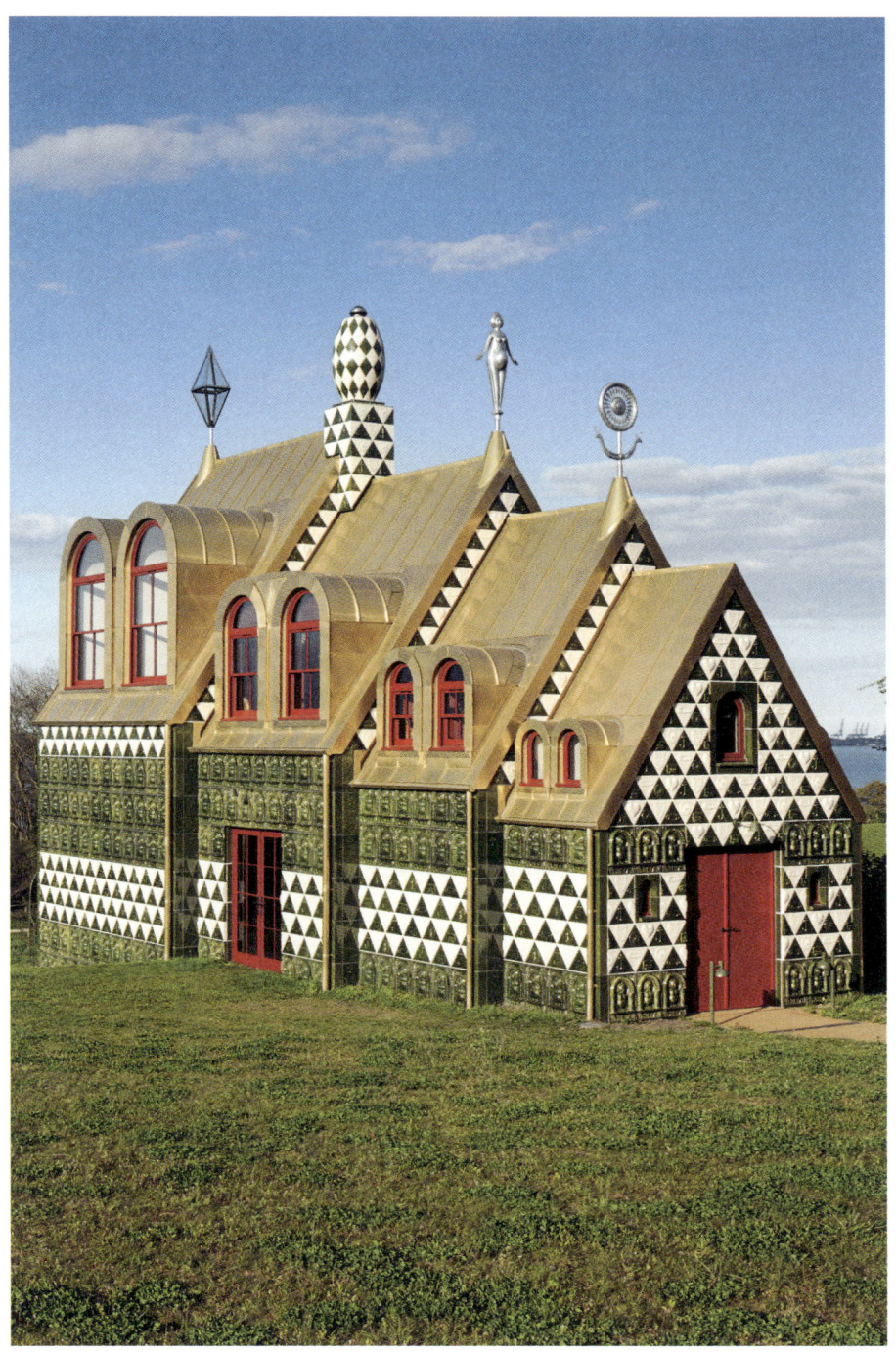

A House for Essex, Grayson Perry

FARLEYS HOUSE & GALLERY

Lee Miller's fanciful farmhouse

There's something appropriately dreamlike about visiting Farleys – the Sussex home of photographer Lee Miller and her Surrealist artist husband Roland Penrose – and being assigned their son Tony as your personal tour guide. Known as 'The Home of the Surrealists', the idiosyncratic farmhouse was once a popular meeting place for leading 20th-century artists, whose eclectic works, amassed by Miller, cover the brightly painted walls. In the kitchen, a hand-painted Picasso tile hangs nonchalantly above the Aga, while elsewhere paintings by Man Ray and Dorothea Tanning are interspersed with Penrose's own distinctive works. Beyond the house, two expertly curated galleries host a dynamic rota of exhibitions, while a captivating sculpture garden offers visitors the chance to experience the views that Miller and Penrose adored. There's a dizzying amount to see, but even more should you book onto the exclusive private tour, featuring sneak peeks of ordinarily out-of-bounds upstairs rooms.

Muddles Green, Chiddingly, BN8 6HW
farleyshouseandgallery.co.uk

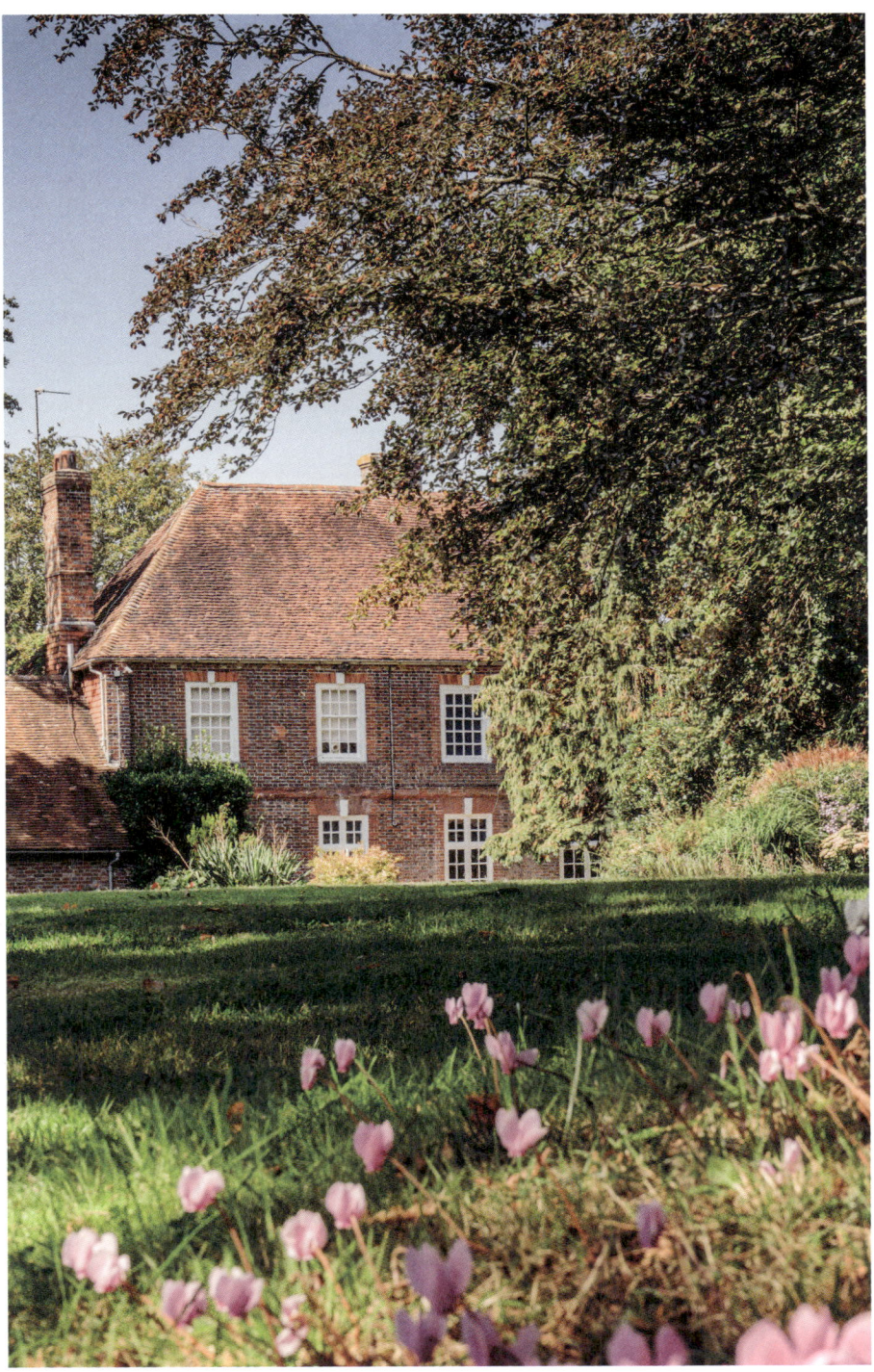

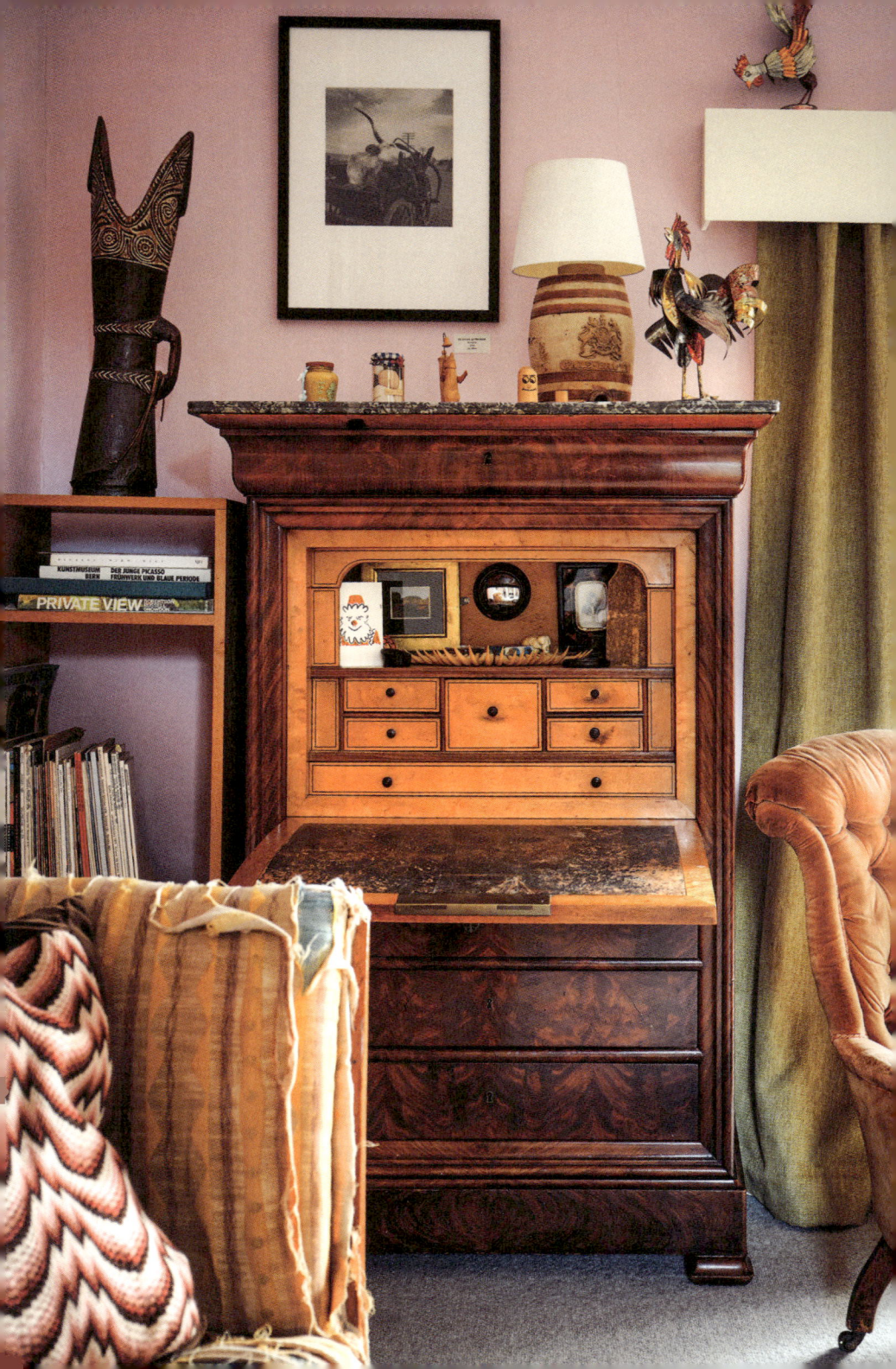

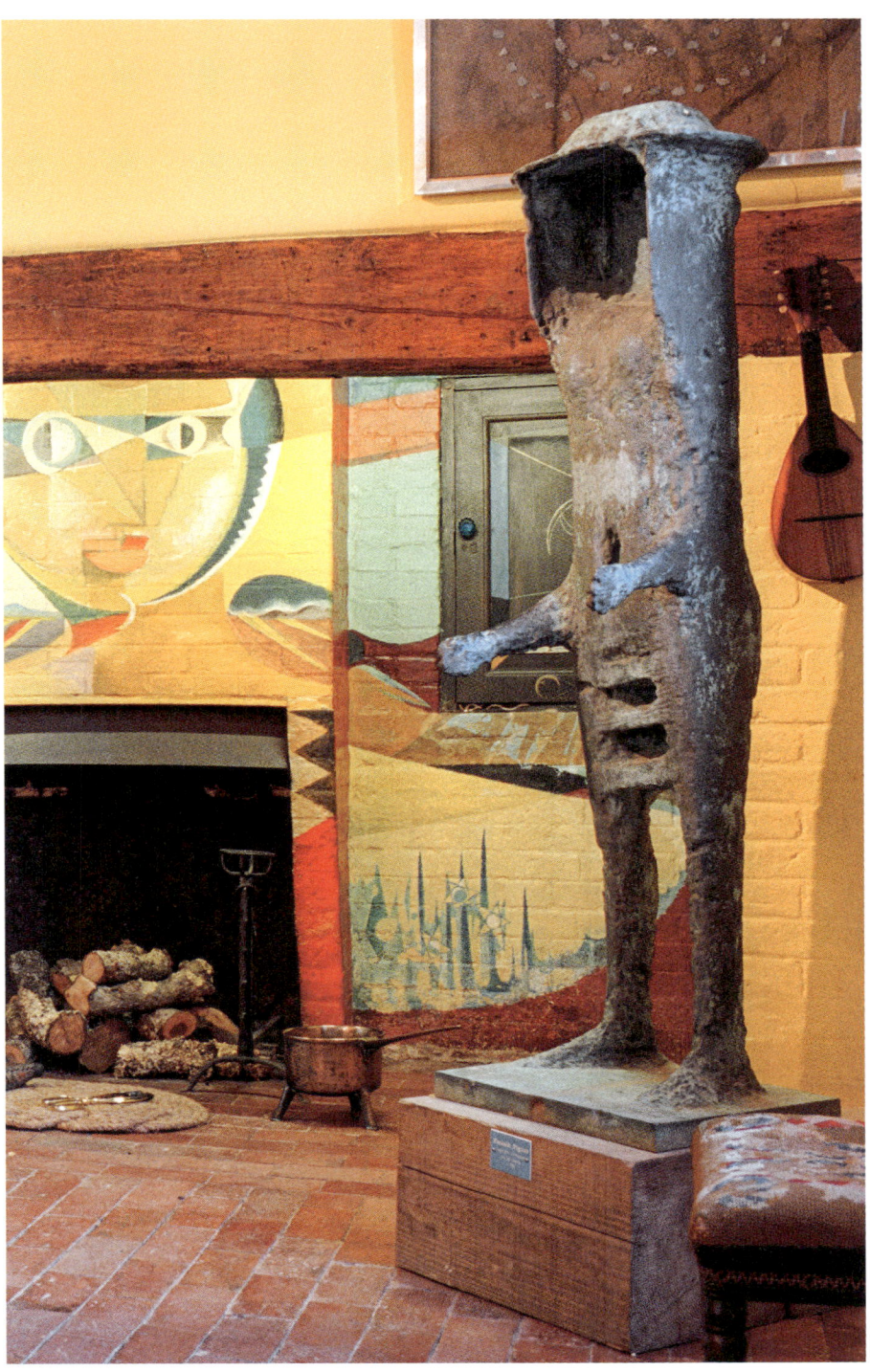

WATTS GALLERY – ARTISTS' VILLAGE

Symbolist painter's chocolate-box treasure

The home of George Frederic Watts, the artist hailed as 'England's Michelangelo', is a startlingly little-known attraction. Dismissed for years as an oddity – his work being unaffiliated with any particular movement – Watts became internationally recognised as 'the greatest painter since the Old Masters' by the end of the 19th century. Established in the leafy Surrey Hills a few months before his death in 1904, this charming gallery offers a bewitching stage for more than 100 of Watts's works, its opulent jewel-toned walls and skylights bringing them dramatically to life. Peruse Watts' celebrity portraits, allegorical paintings and vast white sculptures before discovering the pleasures of his enchanting on-site home, Limnerslease. Don't miss the atmospheric burial ground, just a short walk offsite and home to Watts' remains and his wife Mary's exquisitely decorated Arts and Crafts mortuary – stunning enough to rival the Sistine Chapel.

Down Lane, Compton, GU3 1DQ
wattsgallery.org.uk

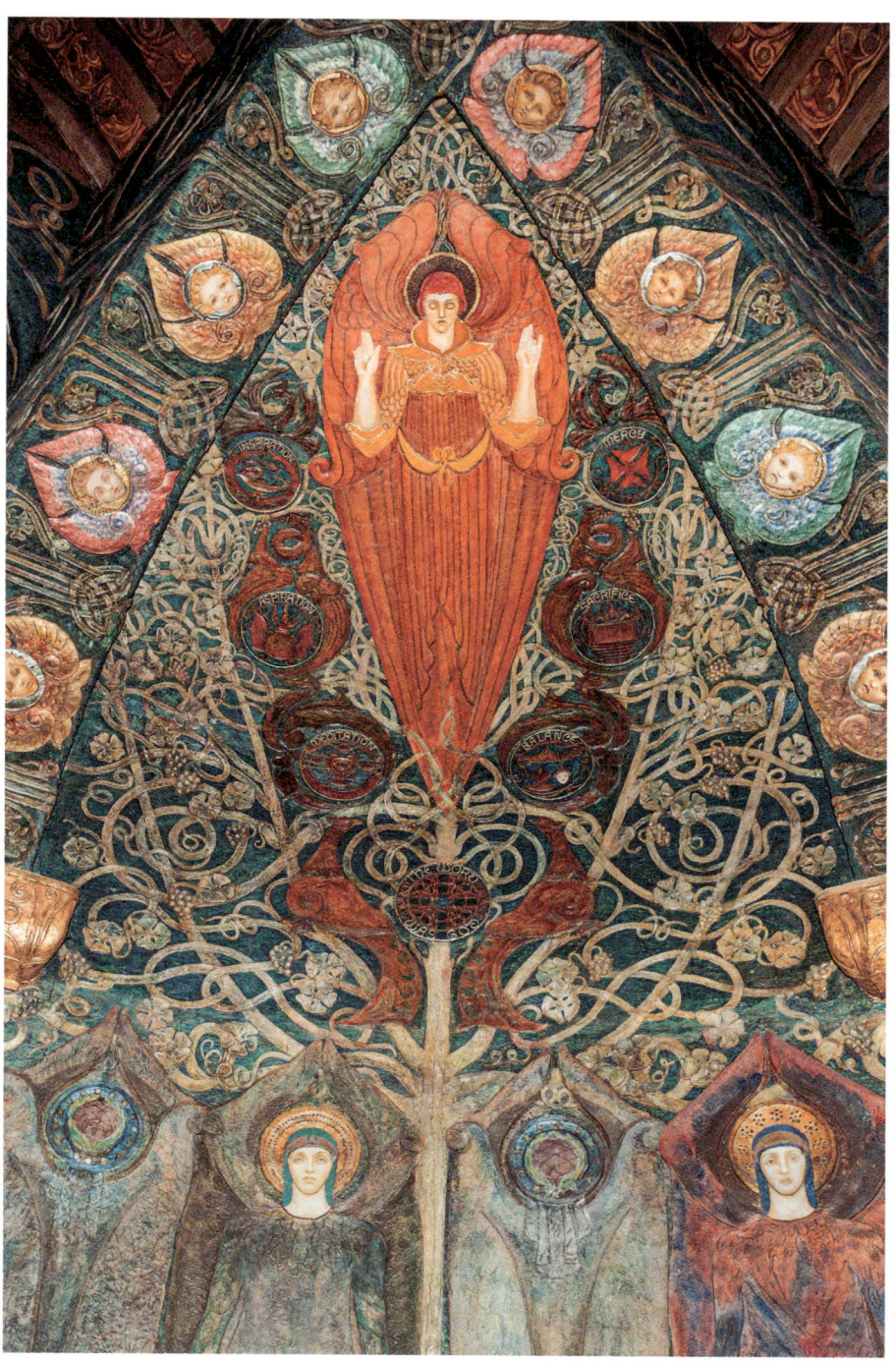

Watts Cemetery Chapel interior, Mary Watts

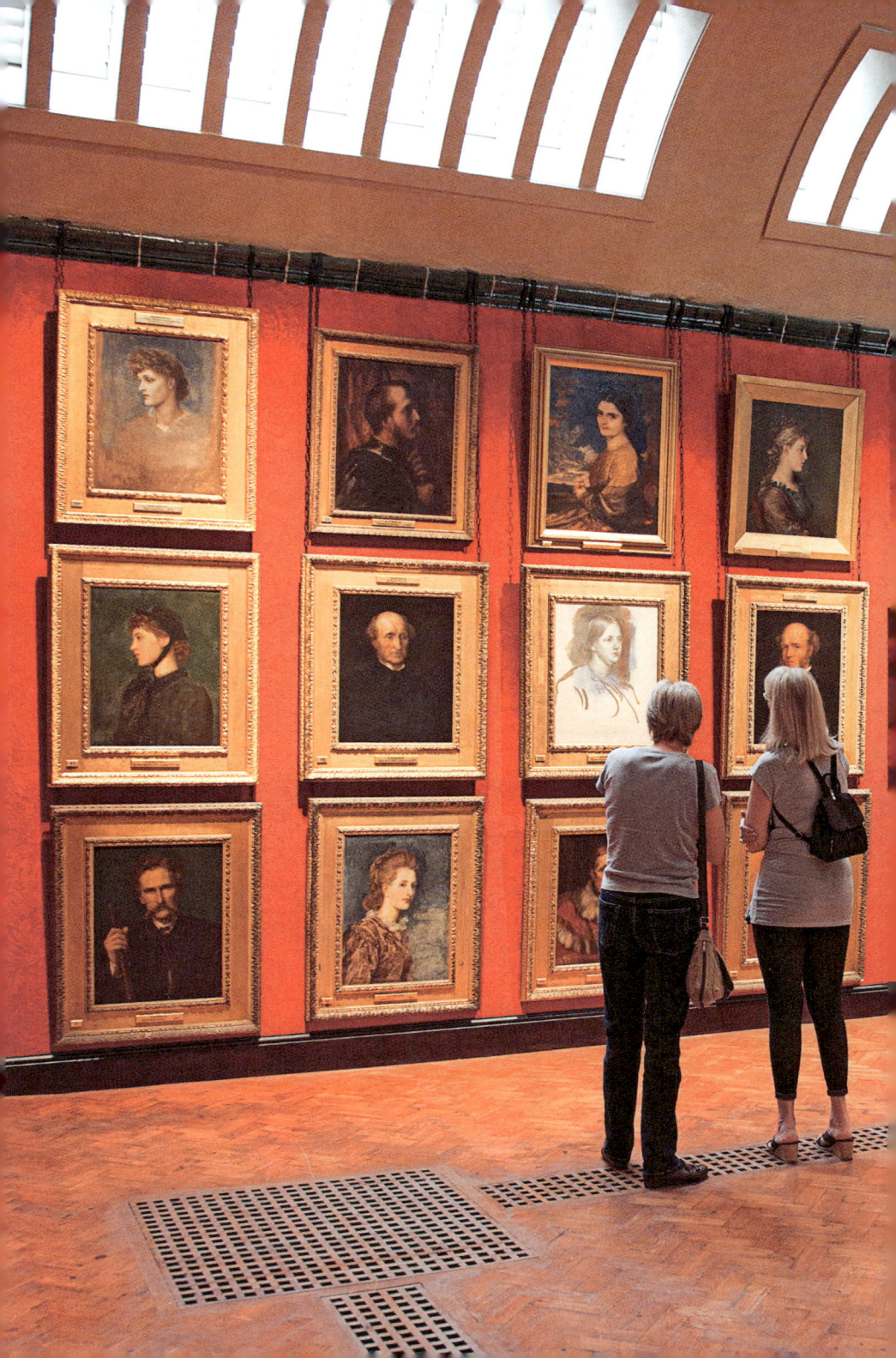

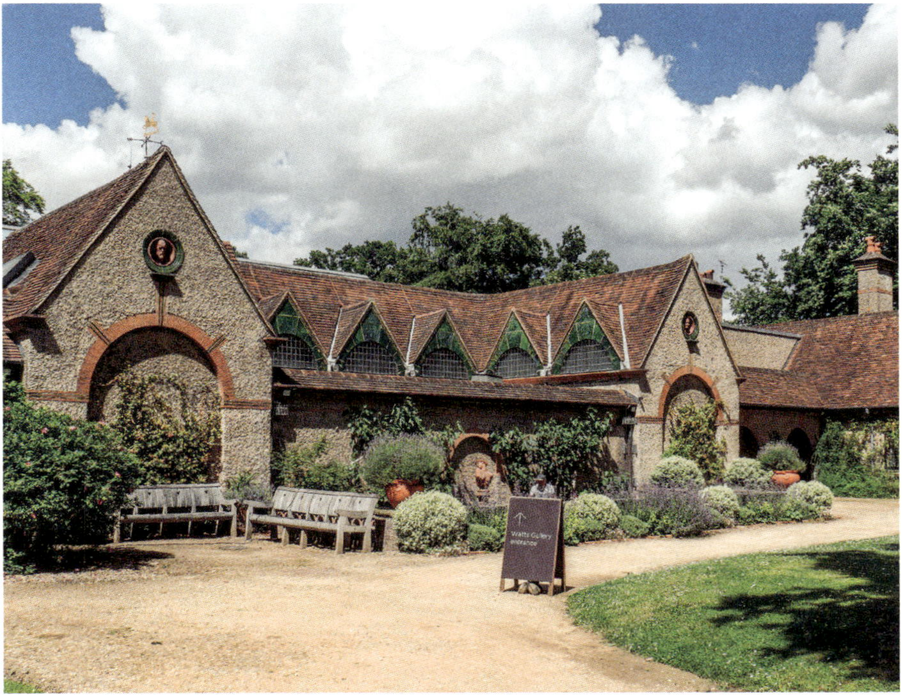
Watts Gallery
entrance

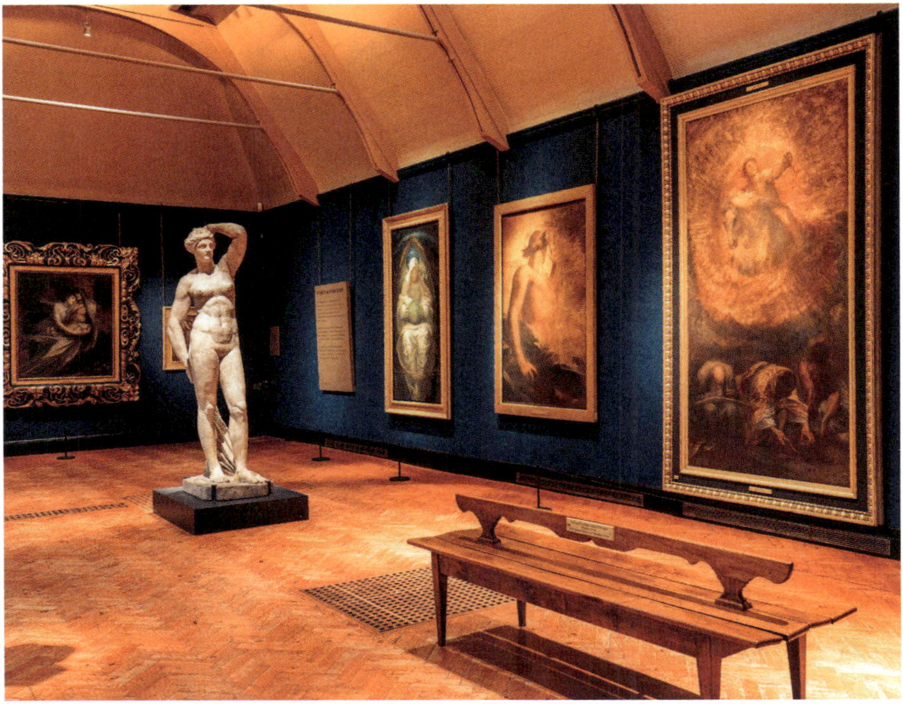

CHARLESTON HOUSE

Vanessa Bell's charismatic country cottage

Ponder the great works of the Bloomsbury group, and Virginia Woolf's *Mrs Dalloway* or E.M. Forster's *A Passage to India* might spring to mind. Perhaps the group's most remarkable legacy, though, is Charleston – the Sussex home and studio of Woolf's sister, Vanessa Bell, and her friend and co-parent, fellow artist Duncan Grant. A long-time gathering place for some of the 20th century's most radical thinkers, the house pulses with character. Richly layered with hand-painted panels, vintage textiles and ceramics, alongside the couple's own works on canvas, it exists as a glorious work of art in its own right. Beyond the house, whose delights visitors are permitted to absorb at their own pace, is a revolving programme of contemporary art exhibitions which uphold the group's modernist ideals. Be sure to catch Bell and Grant's epic *Famous Women Dinner Service*, a tribute to esteemed women throughout history, and the verdant walled garden that inspired the pair's work.

Firle, Lewes, BN8 6LL
charleston.org.uk

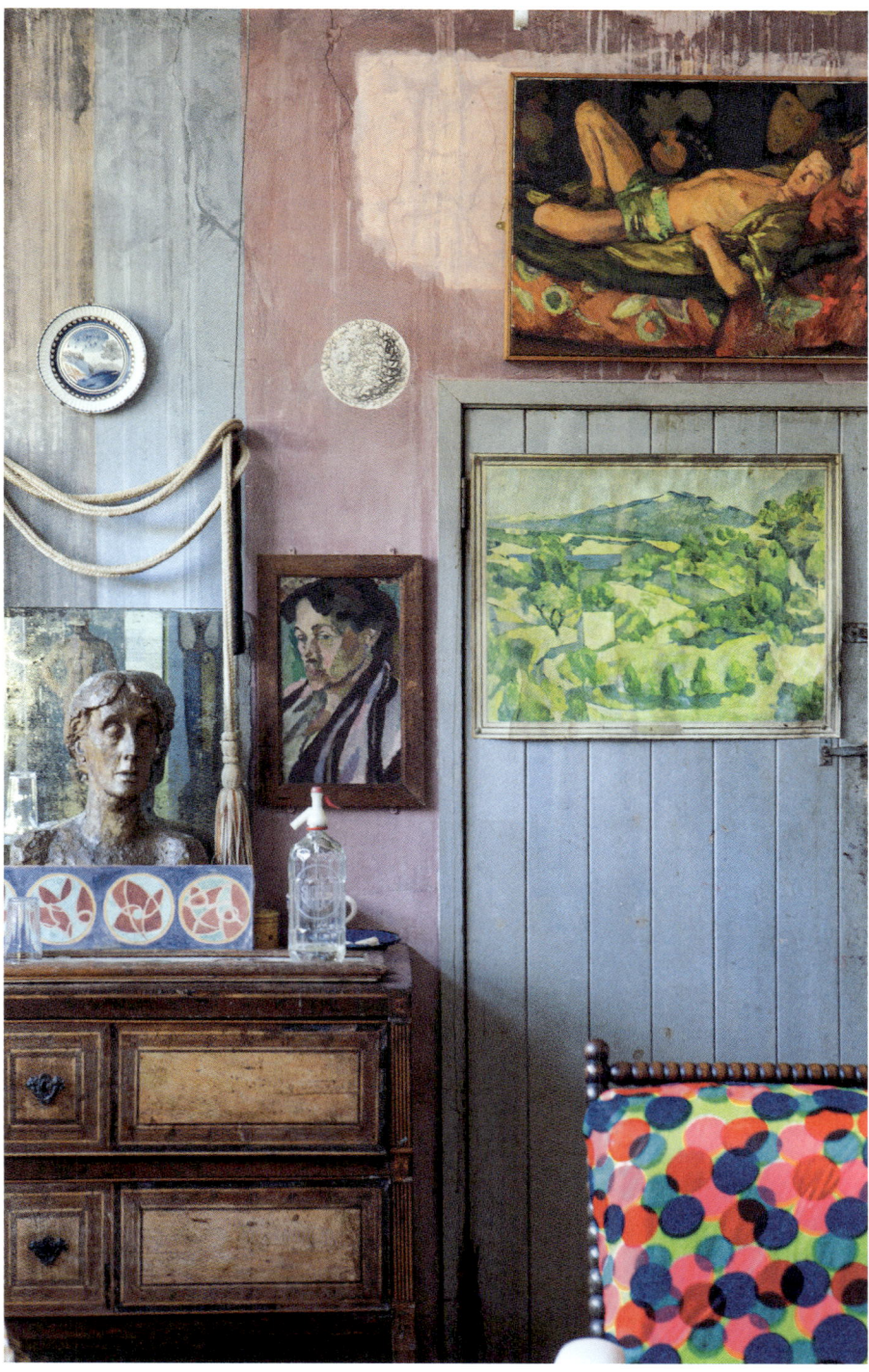

TURNER CONTEMPORARY

Coastal gallery with ever-changing programme

Turner fans take note: this breezy seaside gallery might share its name with the Romantic painter – and occupy the very spot where his Margate lodgings once stood – but you won't find much of his work within its angular walls. Credited as the catalyst for the town's cultural renaissance, this sun-drenched space made its name with exhilarating contemporary exhibitions, showing work by everyone from seaside snapper Martin Parr to local icon Tracey Emin. True, you might not find a Turner seascape, but you can gaze upon the views that inspired them from the gallery's vast picture windows – and, if the tide is low, see if you can catch a glimpse of Antony Gormley's hypnotic *Another Time* sculpture. Round off your trip with a scenic lunch at resident cafe Louie on Sea before cruising the hip gift shop for original art and prints, as well as luxury toiletries made from local seaweed by the brand Formerly Known As Haeckels.

Rendezvous, Margate, CT9 1HG
turnercontemporary.org

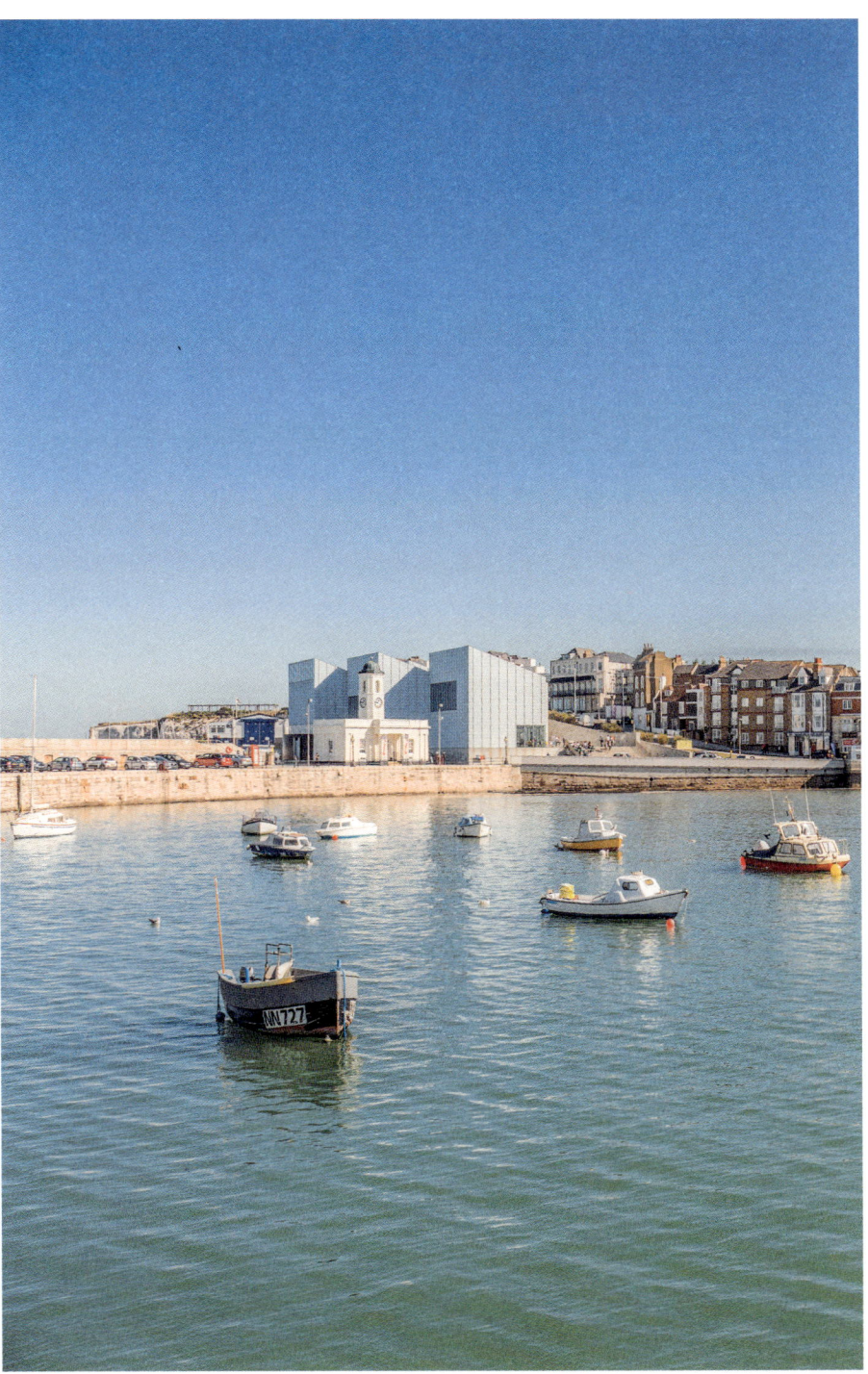

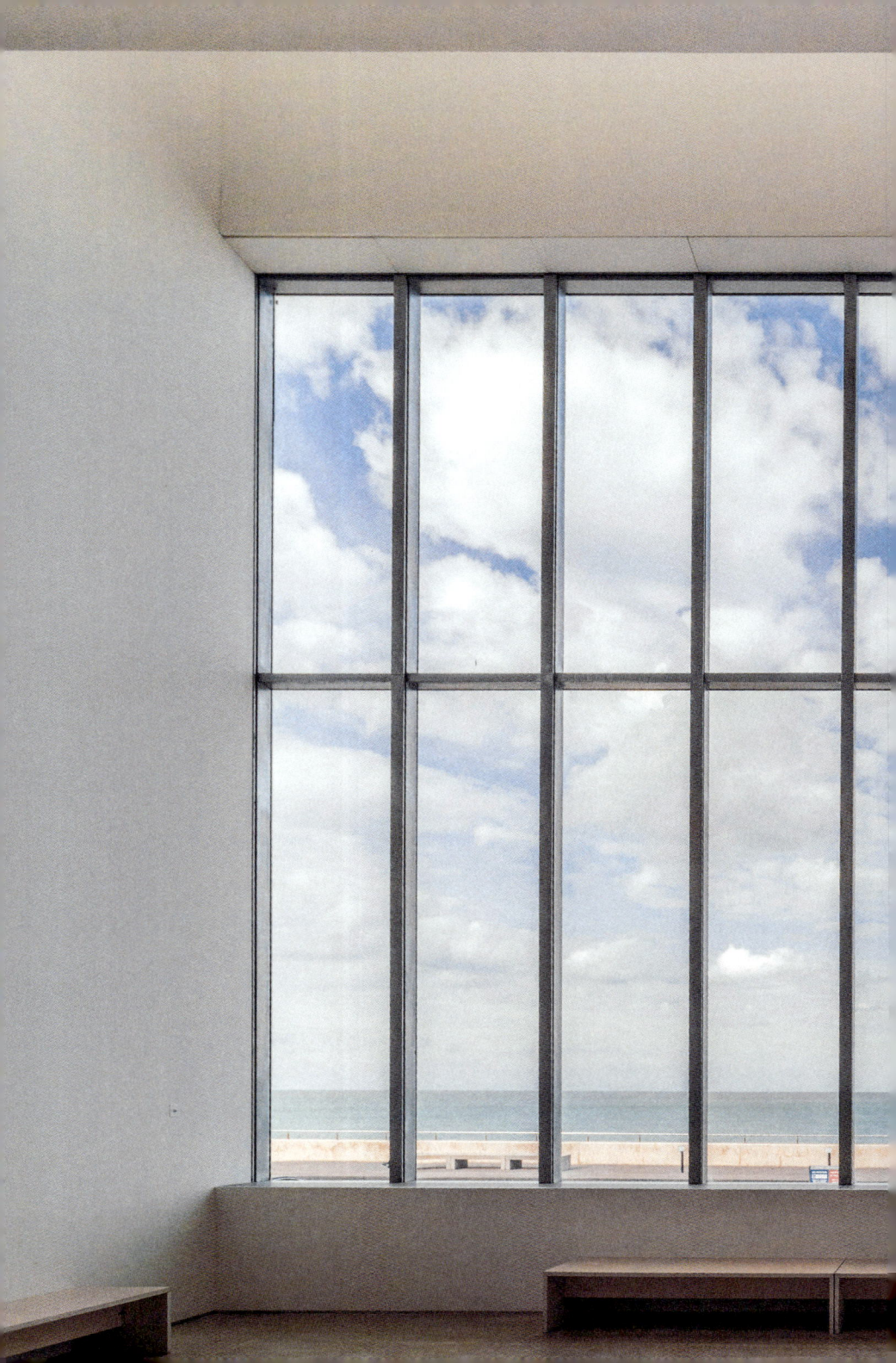

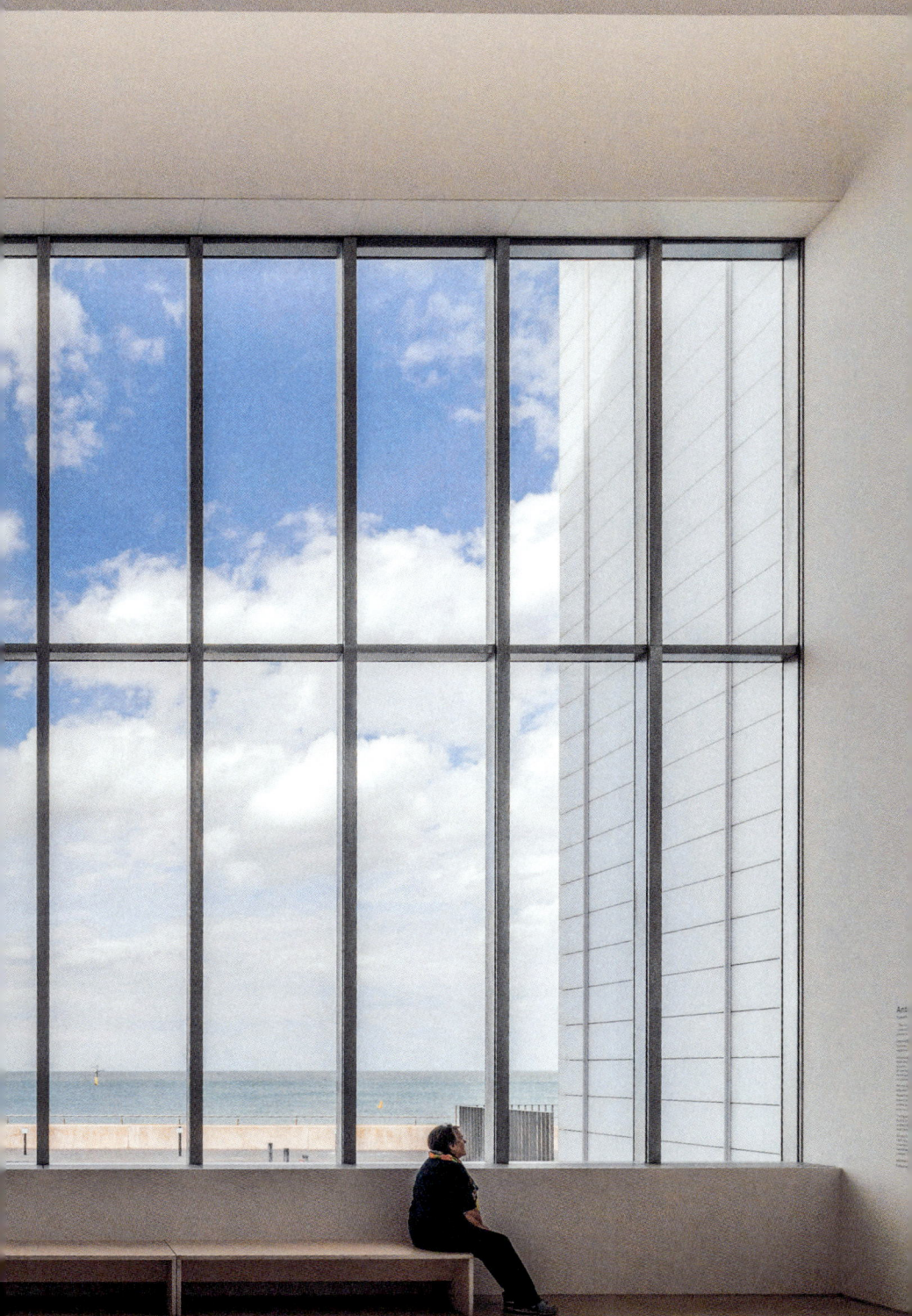

CREATIVE FOLKESTONE ARTWORKS

Sprawling coastal art trail

'Folkestone is an Art School' proclaims a hand-painted sign at the seaside town's train station. To the uninitiated, it might look like just another piece of trackside graffiti scrawled by – albeit studious – teenagers, but the cheerful notice is actually the work of British artist Bob and Roberta Smith, and marks the beginning of the UK's largest outdoor exhibition of contemporary art. Created by 46 artists – a number that grows every three years as permanent works are commissioned for the Folkestone Triennial – the nonlinear trail's 74 artworks are largely site specific and personal to the town, from Cornelia Parker's *The Folkestone Mermaid*, which was cast from the body of a local resident and references Copenhagen's iconic *The Little Mermaid*, to Amalia Pica's *Souvenir*, which elevates decorative seashells by casting them in bronze. Choose from one of the four trail clusters – or go rogue and explore them all.

Quarterhouse, Mill Bay, Folkestone, CT20 1BN
creativefolkestone.org.uk/folkestoneartworks

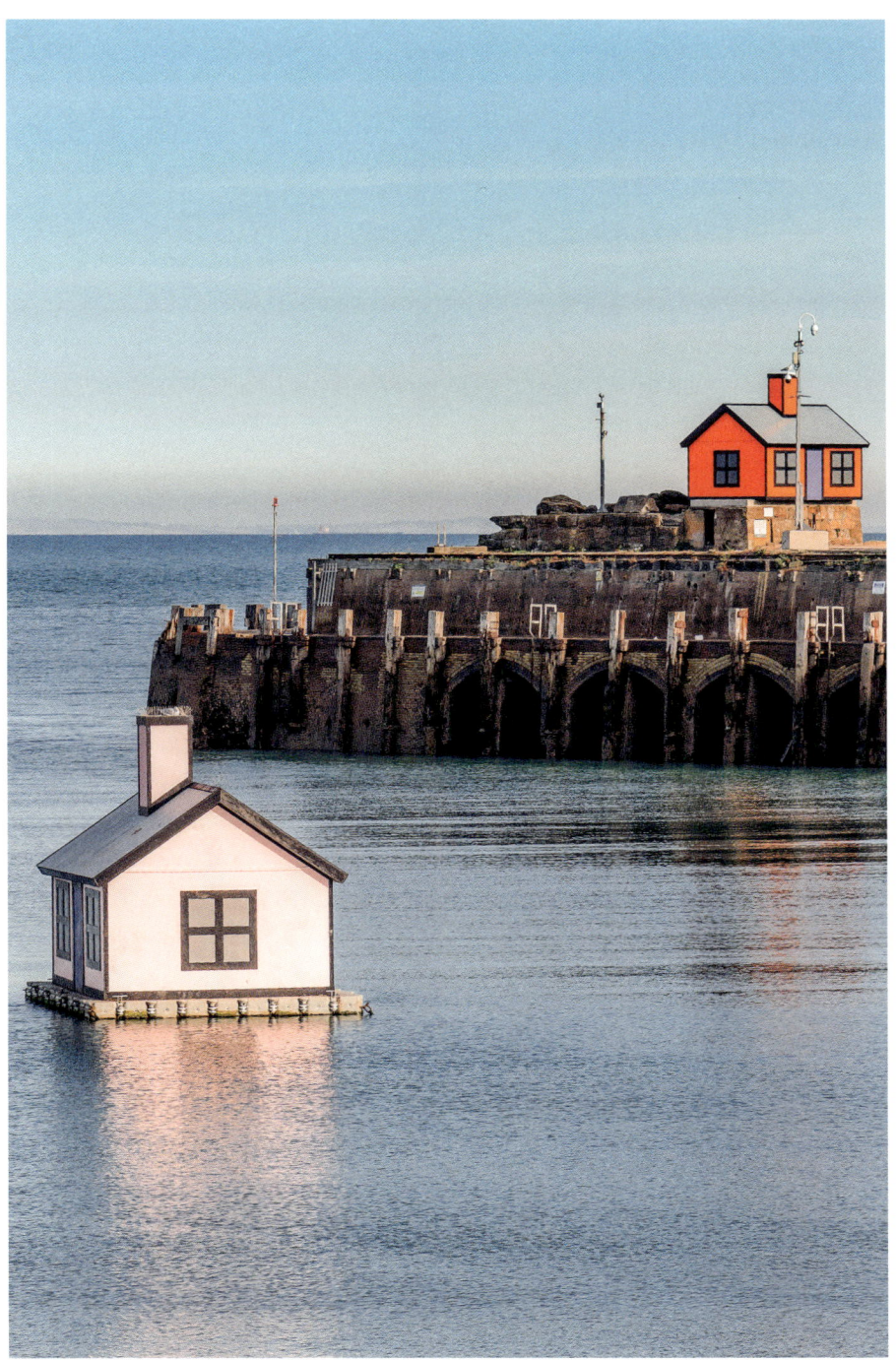

Holiday Home, Richard Woods

PROSPECT COTTAGE

Derek Jarman's seaside sanctuary

Visiting Derek Jarman's house is a little how you might imagine it feels to visit the Moon. A site of pilgrimage since the artist, filmmaker and gay rights activist died in 1994, the distinctive fisherman's hut and its surrounds are like nowhere else on Earth, set among the arid shingles of Dungeness with little but a defunct nuclear power station for company. Jarman's otherworldly scheme of rainbow-hued blooms and driftwood sculptures have long lured visitors to the Prospect Cottage garden, but it's only recently that the house itself has opened to the public, thanks to a 2020 campaign. Across four atmospheric main rooms, you'll find a portrait of Jarman by Maggi Hambling; a charcoal drawing of his companion, Keith Collins, by Robert Medley; and numerous works by Jarman himself, from humorous assemblages like *He-Man clutches a classical plaster cast* to more thought-provoking pieces such as *One Day's Medication* – a visual record of the daily drugs needed to treat HIV.

1 Dungeness Road, Romney Marsh, TN29 9NE
creativefolkestone.org.uk/prospect-cottage

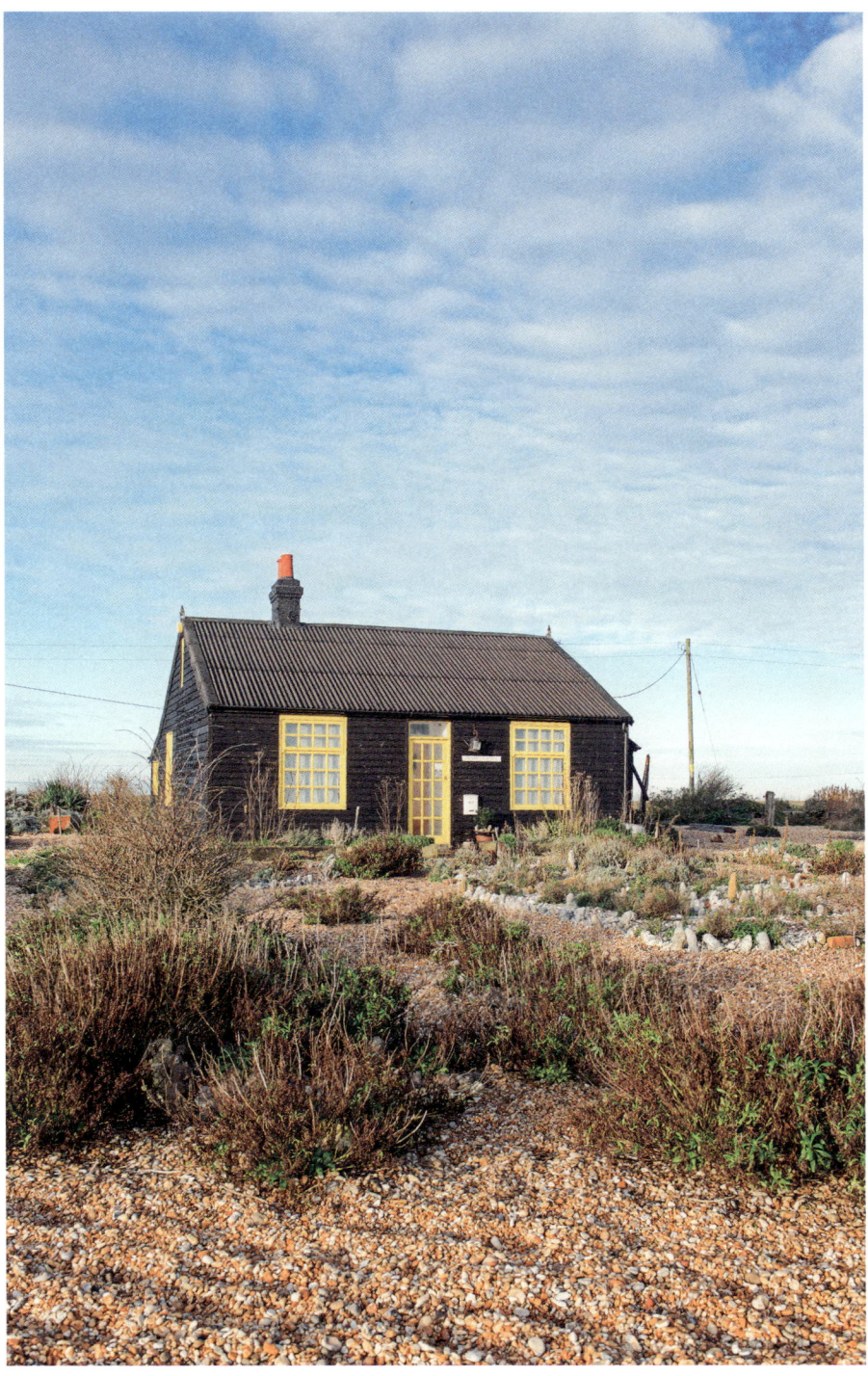

ALBION BARN & FIELDS

Audacious gallery-without-walls

The cultural desert that was the coronavirus lockdown gave rise to a multitude of temporary sculpture trails – though few were as impressive as Albion Fields' inaugural exhibition, which showcased epic works by the likes of Erwin Wurm and Jeppe Hein. Occupying art dealer Michael Hue-Williams' 50-acre Oxfordshire estate, the ever-evolving line-up of bold and often humorous contemporary artworks (think Ai Weiwei's deceptively solid marble sofas and Wim Delvoye's neo-Gothic cement truck) contrasts brilliantly with the wild, formerly agricultural landscape, with sculptures often partially concealed among trees or long grass. To the east of the park, the 3000-square-foot Barn hosts biannual indoor exhibitions of less weather-hardy works by artists such as Max Lamb and Richard Woods, whose 2025 exhibition took its cues (and its medium) from a tree felled in a nearby forest.

Church Hill, Little Milton, Oxford, OX44 7QB
albionbarn.com

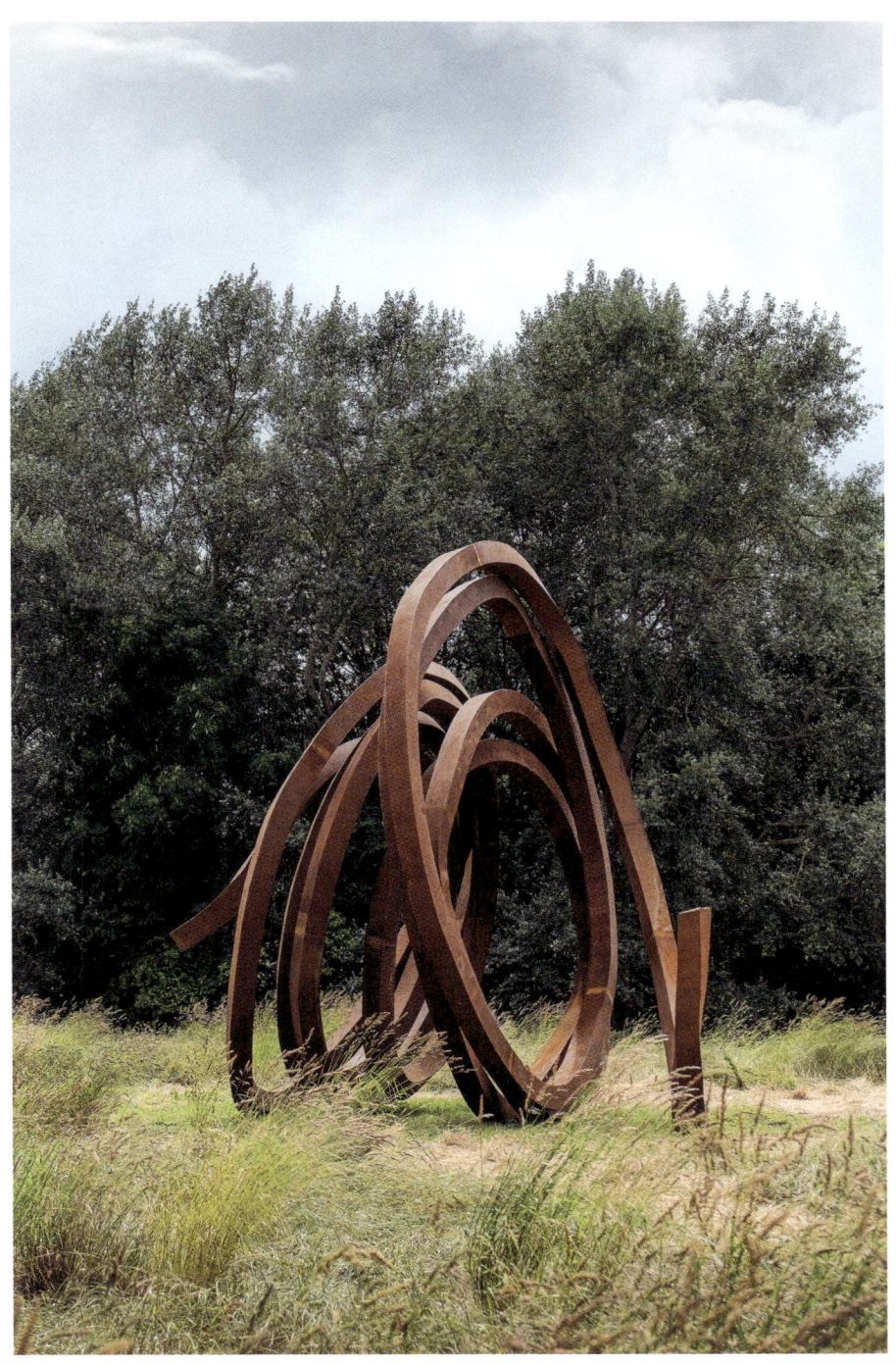

Indeterminate Line, Bernar Venet

DE LA WARR PAVILION

Modernist arts centre by the sea

Dominating the Bexhill seafront like a washed-up ocean liner, this gleaming concrete edifice might look like a relic of the town's seaside-holiday heyday, but the spirit of De La Warr remains as innovative as the day it launched 90 years ago. Originally conceived as a 'People's Palace' for events and culture, the building was re-established as a contemporary arts centre in 2005 but remains devoted to its diverse community through its exhilarating programme of family activities, workshops and annual free exhibitions of contemporary art. Memorable moments from recent years have included Richard Wilson's 2012 recreation of the final scene of 1969 film *The Italian Job*, for which the artist precariously suspended a full-sized bus from the pavilion's roof, and in 2023, when over 300 volunteers came together to clean artist Tschabalala Self's vandalised sculpture of a Black female figure. DLWP seldom stages a show that doesn't linger in your mind.

Marina, Bexhill-on-Sea, TN40 1DP
dlwp.com

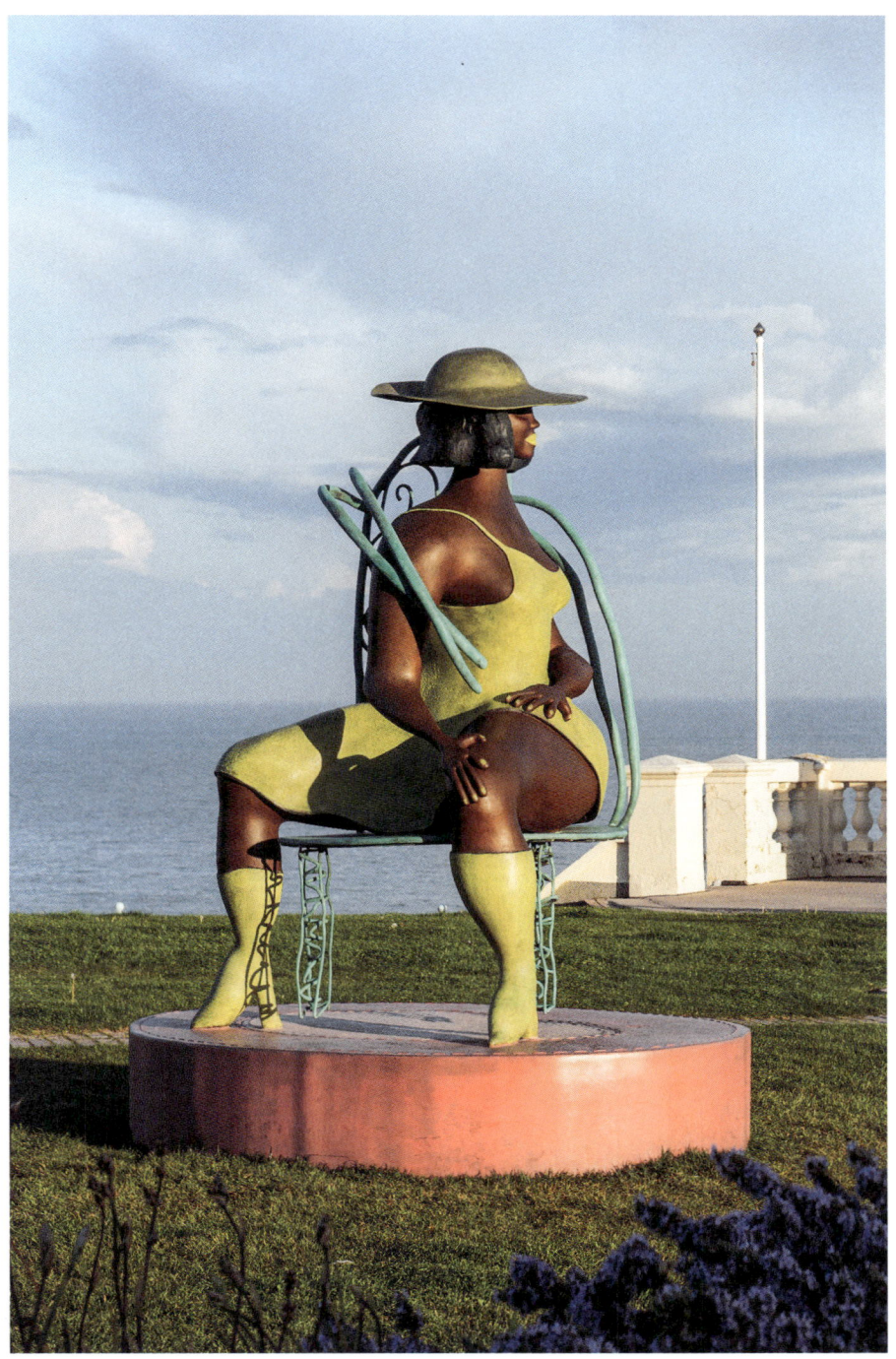

Seated, Tschabalala Self

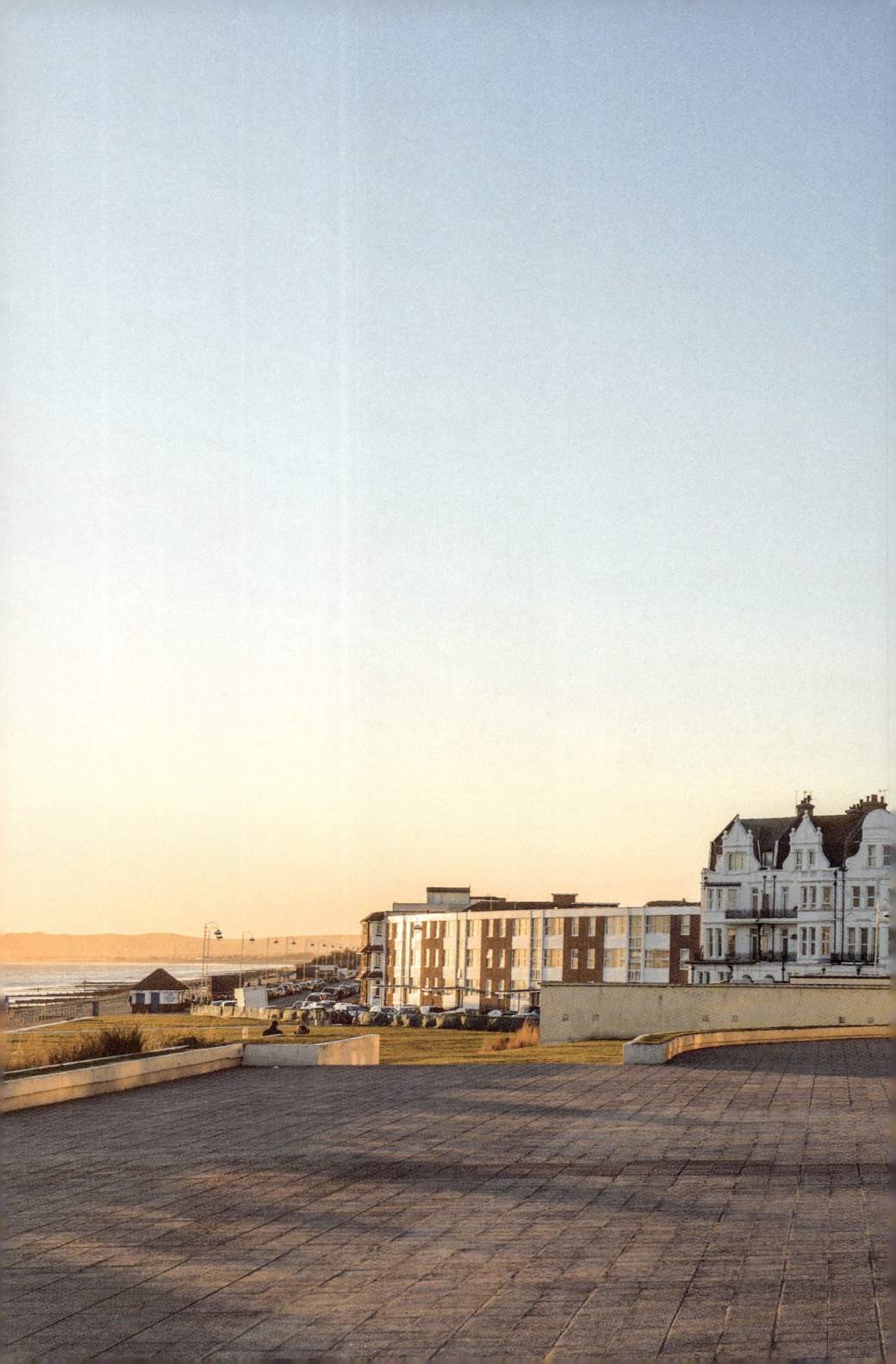

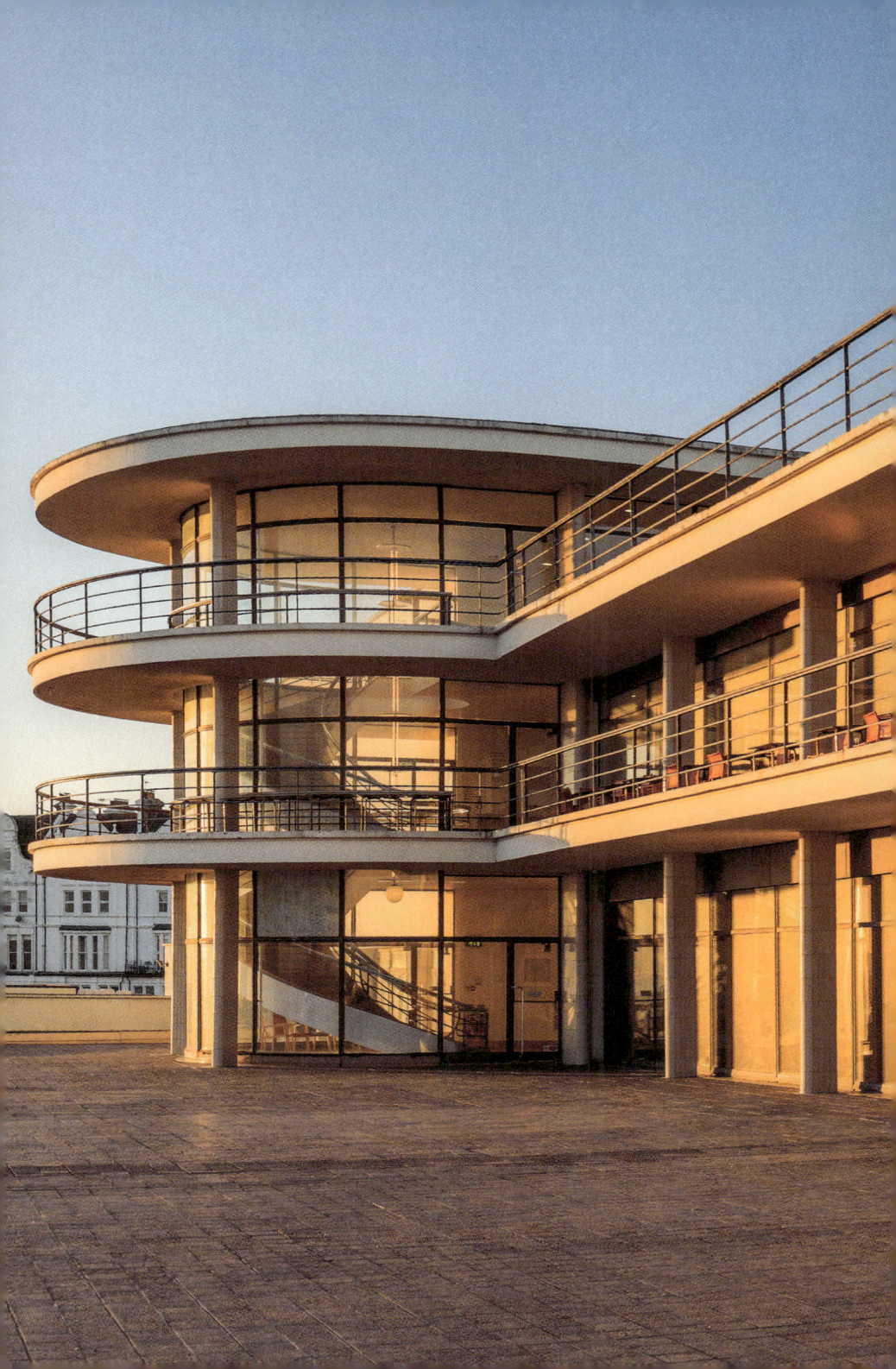

SAINSBURY CENTRE

Progressive gallery on university grounds

That you're not just allowed, but *encouraged* to 'hug a Henry Moore' is reason enough to visit this Norman Foster-designed gallery, which sits at the southwestern edge of University of East Anglia's 360-acre campus. The world's first art museum to formally recognise art as being 'alive', the Sainsbury recently unveiled a permanent 'Living Art' display dedicated to arty interactions that include admiring an Alberto Giacometti from the comfort of a hammock and recalling childhood hugs while embracing Moore's *Mother and Child*. Along with its unconventional policy on touching, the gallery employs radical practices such as a pay-what-and-if-you-can entry system and an open-plan layout with flexible partitions, rendering it more akin to an exhibition centre than a formal art gallery. Its 1,400-artwork collection boasts drawings by Picasso and portraits by Bacon, along with sculptures by Elisabeth Frink and Lynn Chadwick in the surrounding parkland. Perfect for those seeking a more laid-back art encounter.

Norfolk Road, Norwich, NR4 7TJ
sainsburycentre.ac.uk

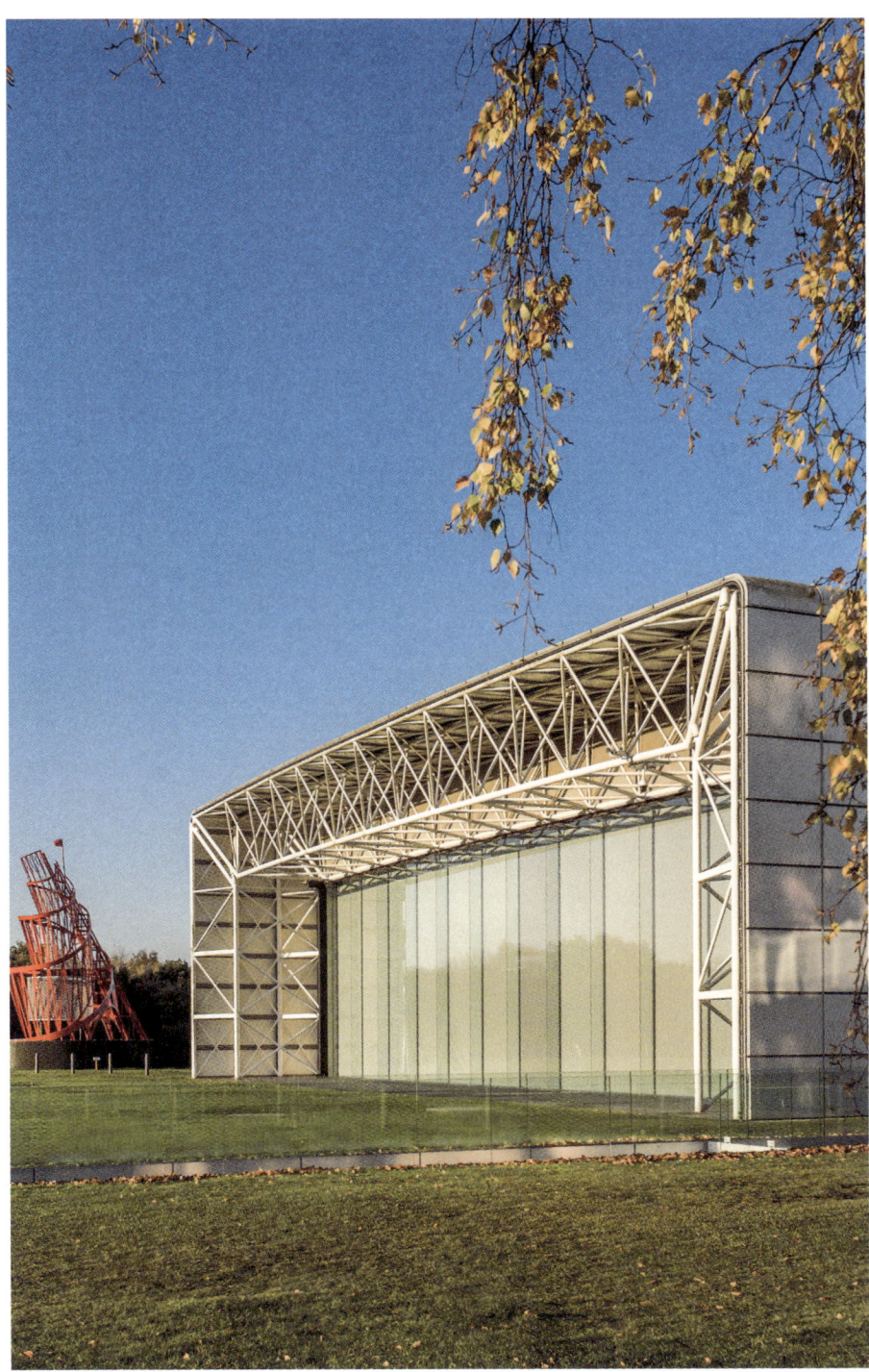

HENRY MOORE STUDIOS & GARDENS

Sculptor's bucolic home and studios

'I think we may stay here for some time,' mused Henry Moore upon moving to this tranquil patch of rural Hertfordshire – a sentiment you'll likely echo on arrival. The sculptor ended up staying until his death in 1986, and even today his painstakingly preserved studios give the sense that the artist has merely stepped out momentarily. As you roam the 70 acres Moore called home for more than half his life, a palpable sense of peace pervades, whether you're poking about in the studios, catching an intimate glimpse of his personal life in his sympathetically restored family home, Hoglands, or experiencing the powerful presence of his monumental works in the magnificent setting that inspired them. Hoglands recces are via guided tour only, but the gardens and their two-dozen artworks are best surveyed solo – albeit with the assistance of the handy map and sculpture guide.

Dane Tree House, Perry Green, Much Hadham, SG10 6EE
henry-moore.org/studios-and-gardens

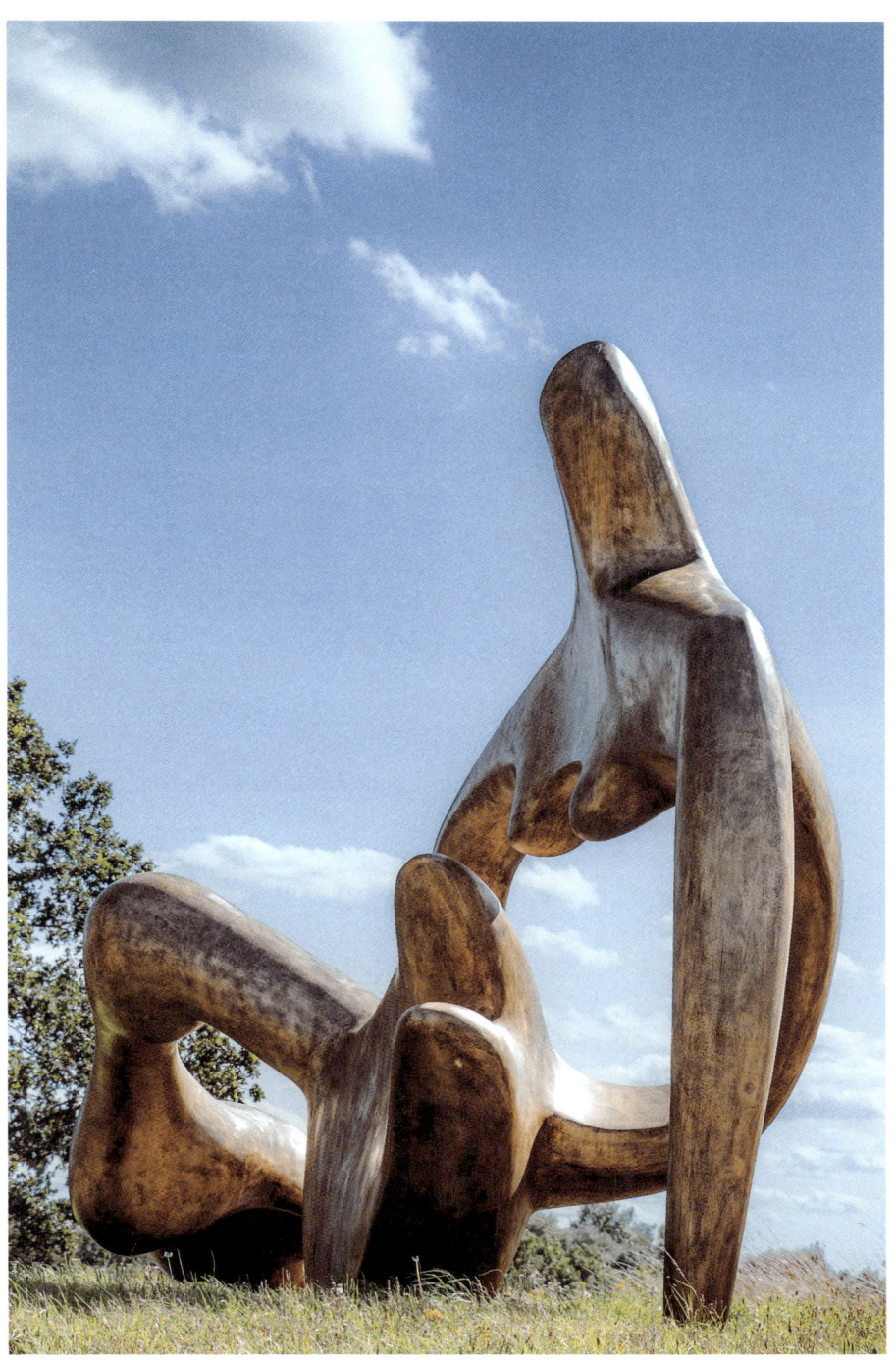

Large Reclining Figure, Henry Moore

HOUGHTON HALL

Neoclassical mansion with annual sculpture show

Once home to the legendary Walpole Collection – an Old Masters-heavy hoard amassed by its original occupant, first British Prime Minister Robert Walpole – this Palladian pile is better known today for the contemporary works and impressive temporary exhibitions championed by its current owner, the 7th Marquess of Cholmondeley. Houghton's grounds alone are home to myriad modern delights, from the Brutalist structures of artists Sean Scully and Rachel Whiteread to the much-loved annual exhibition, which has seen the site infiltrated by a 100-strong army of Antony Gormley figures and a tongue-in-cheek Richard Woods installation whose footprint dwarfed the house. Far from stopping at the door, these temporary takeovers have seen Houghton's Gainsboroughs and Reynoldses swapped for Damien Hirst's colourful spot paintings, and its Stone Hall's marble busts traded for Anish Kapoor's mirrored discs – crushing any inkling that this is just your average stately home in the process.

Bircham Road, King's Lynn, PE31 6TY
houghtonhall.com

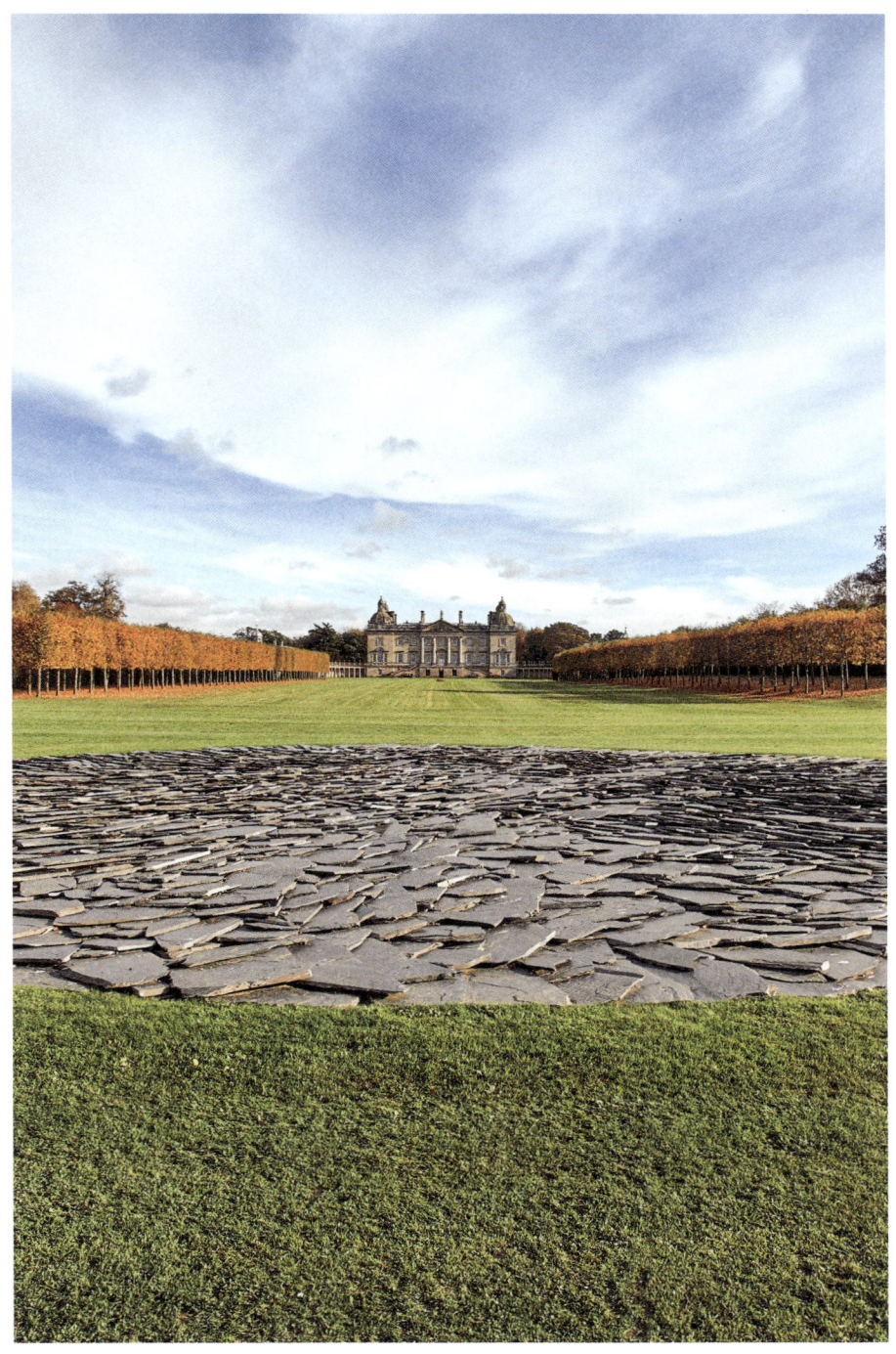

Full Moon Circle, Richard Long

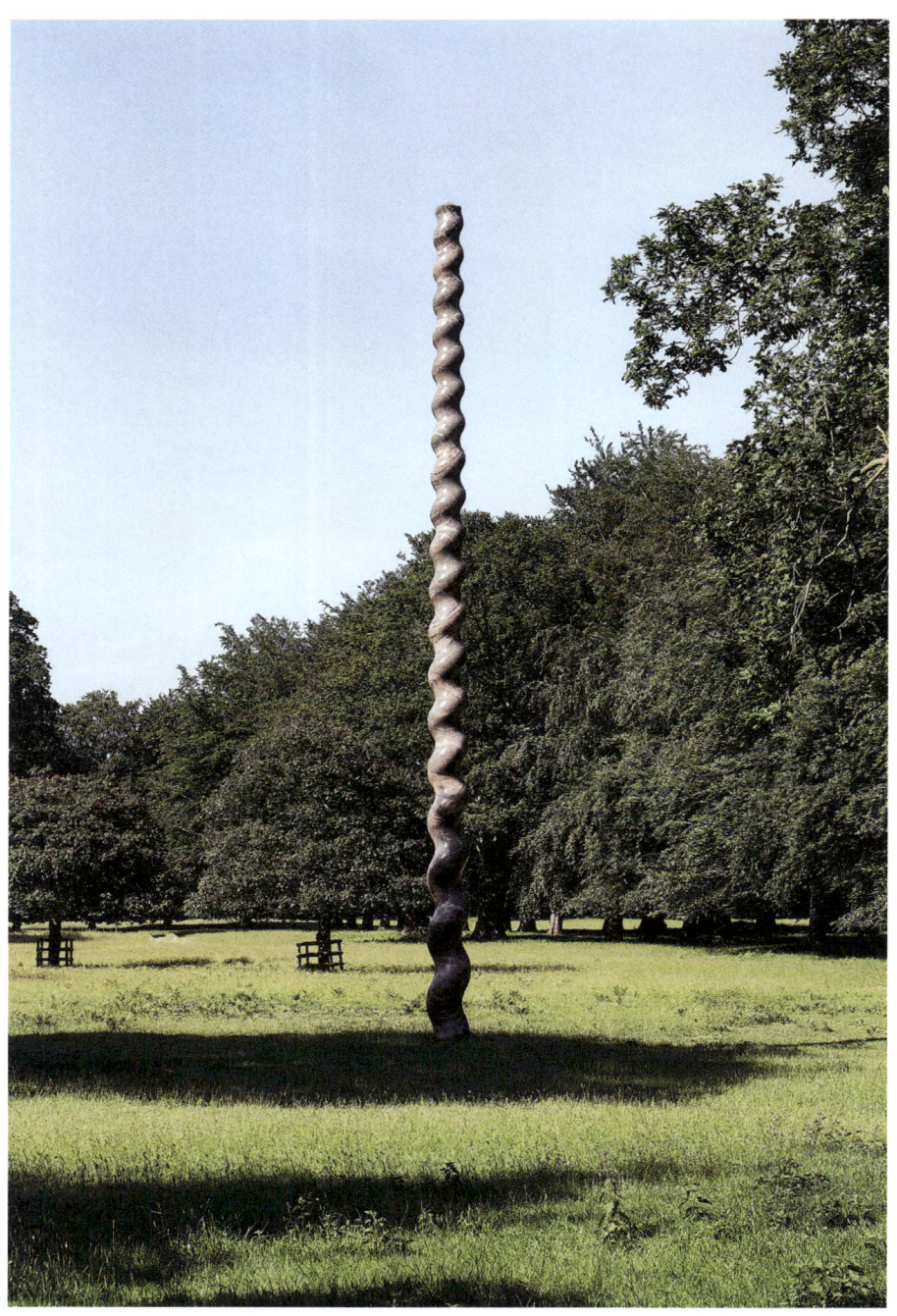

Above: *Axis of the World*, Claudio Parmiggiani
Opposite above: *Houghton Hut*, Rachel Whiteread
Opposite below: *Houghton Cross*, Richard Long

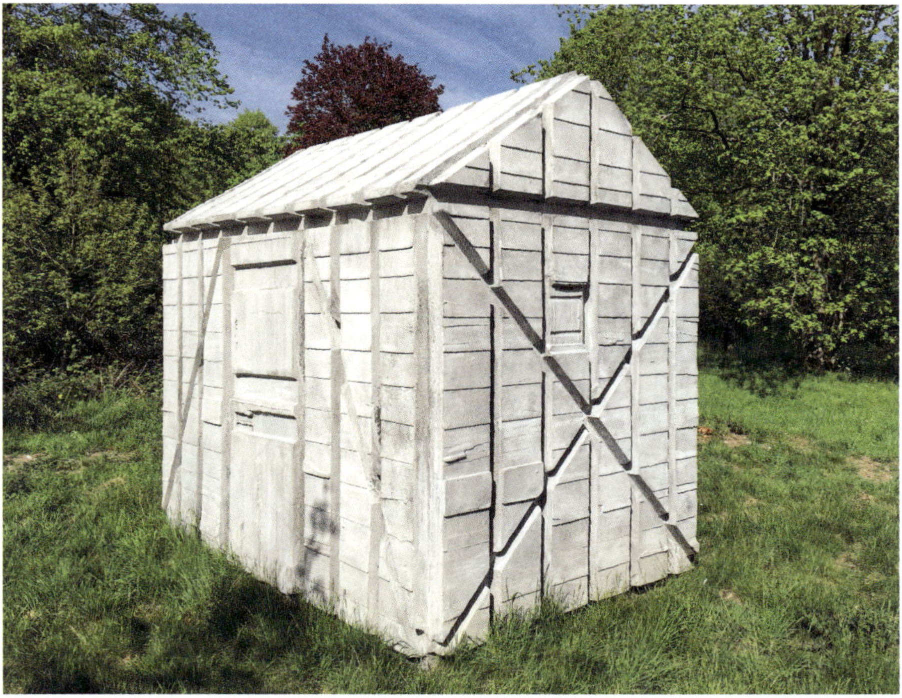

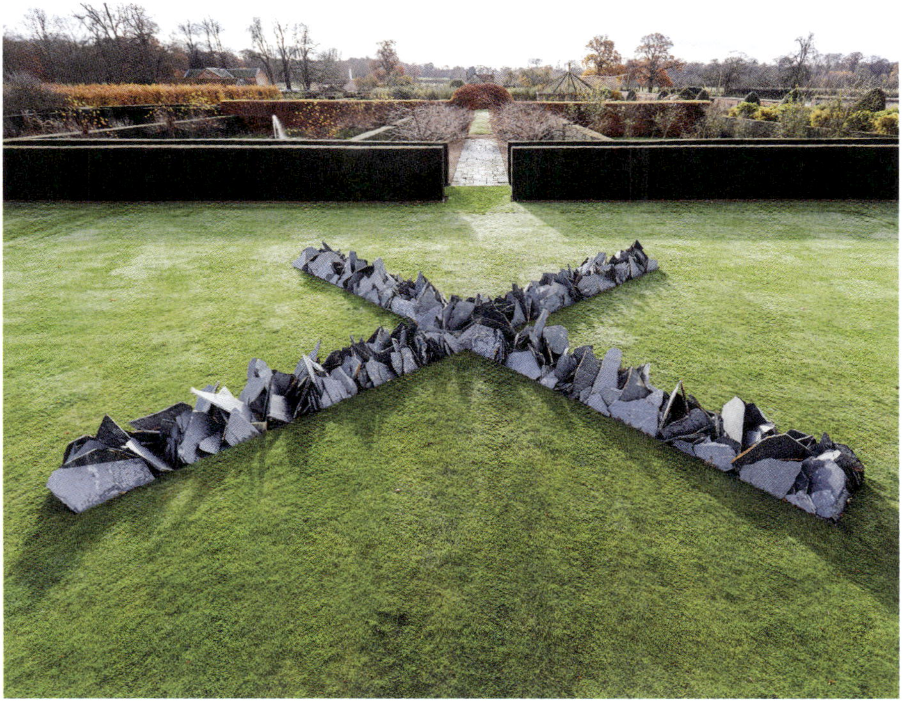

KETTLE'S YARD

Remarkable modern art in intimate setting

A poke around the charismatic Cambridge home of Jim and Helen Ede feels wickedly nosey. Preserved exactly as the curator–collector and his wife left it when they relocated in 1973, this quaint cluster of cottages is home to an entrancing cornucopia of early 20th-century art spanning Constantin Brâncuşi heads, a Christopher Wood self-portrait and Henri Gaudier-Brzeska's *Sleeping Fawn*, all frozen in time – as per Ede's instructions. But while he was exacting when it came to the conservation of his house, the collector was far from private, maintaining an open-door policy for every afternoon that he lived there, before bequeathing the house and its contents to the University of Cambridge. Today, a tour of the home can be followed with a browse of the adjoining modernist gallery, whose past shows have spotlighted the work of unknown and migrant artists, those prominently featured in Ede's collection, and even homages to Ede himself.

Castle Street, Cambridge, CB3 0AQ
kettlesyard.cam.ac.uk

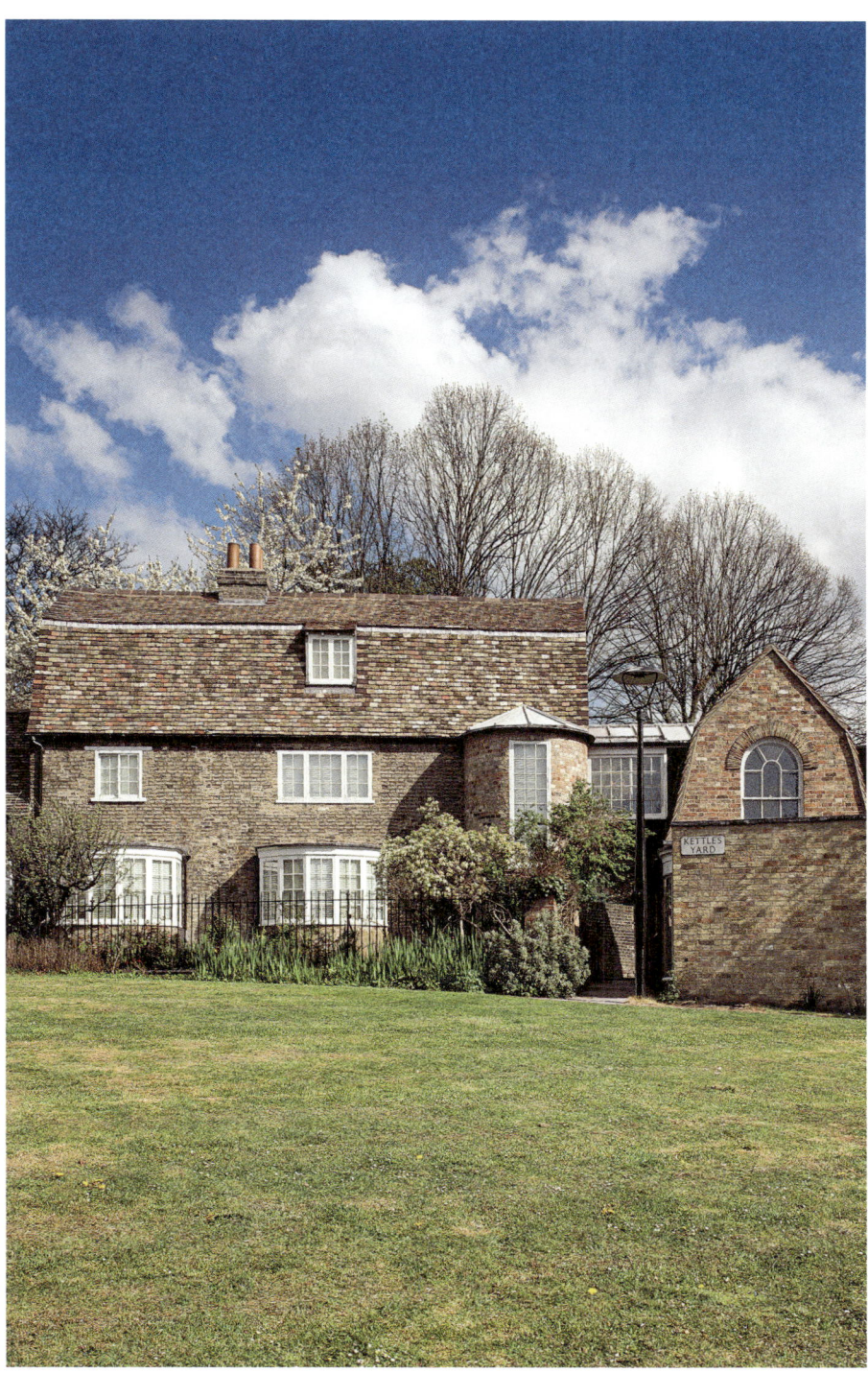

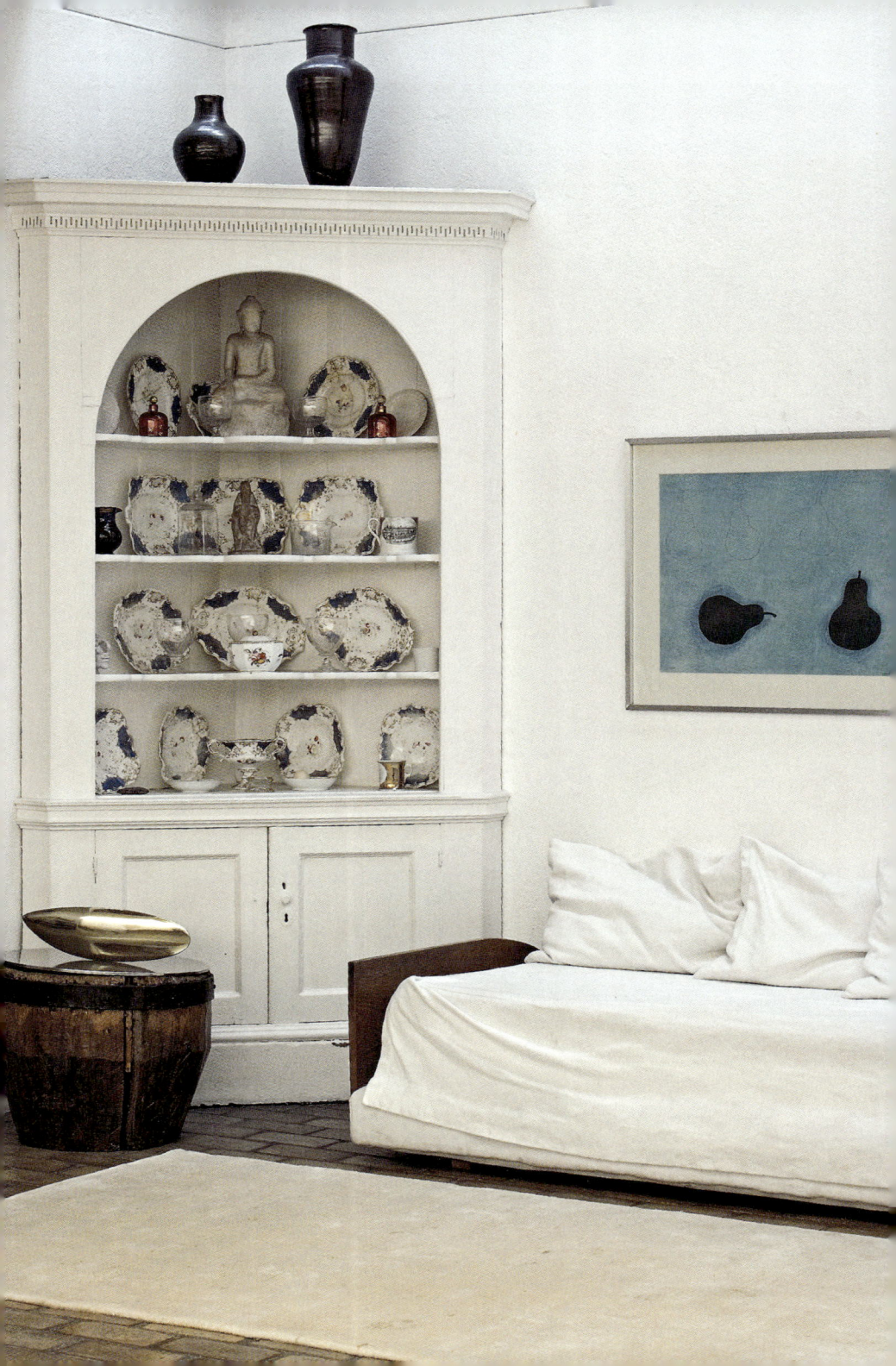

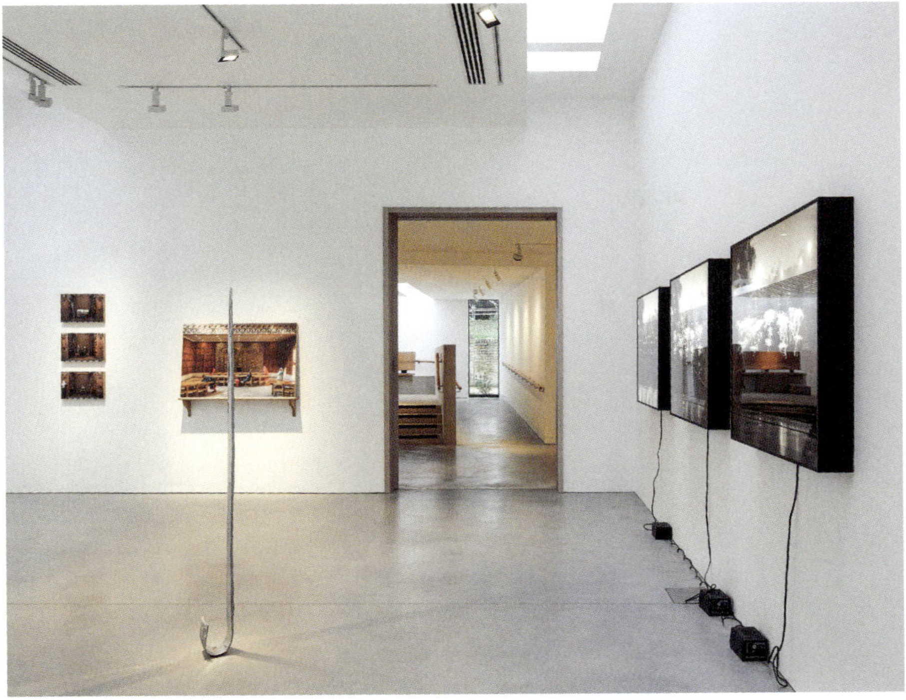

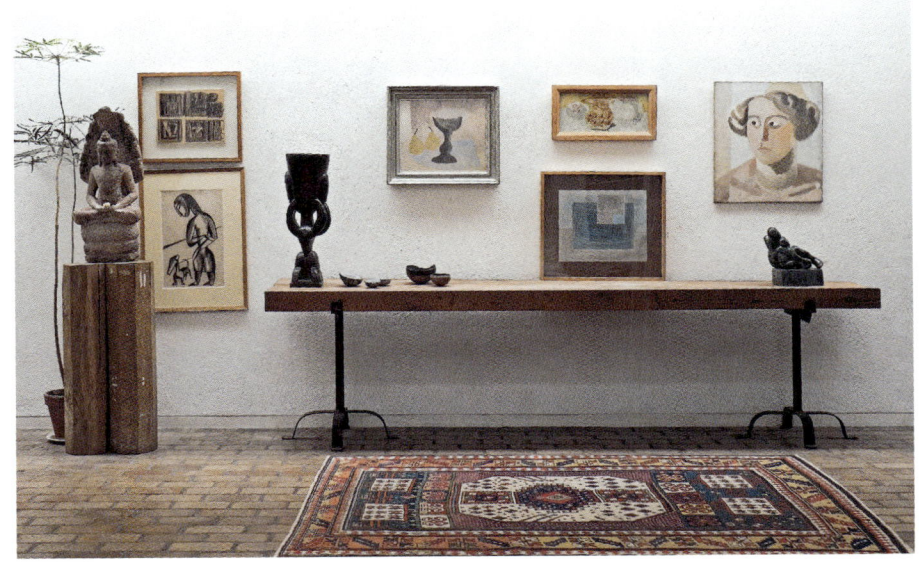

HAUSER & WIRTH SOMERSET

Awe-inspiring art on sweeping site

When Iwan and Manuela Wirth converted a derelict farm on the outskirts of the tiny Somerset town of Bruton into a gallery, they wondered if anyone would come. They needn't have worried. While breathtakingly rural, the colossal site vibrates with life, enticing culture vultures from miles around with its world-class exhibitions, Piet Oudolf-designed gardens, sophisticated Italian restaurant, well-stocked farm shop and vibrant bar – itself an immersive art installation. Exhibitions vary from multimedia group shows to major retrospectives that extend across the site's various galleries and outdoor spaces, with notable past presentations spotlighting the work of Phyllida Barlow, Thomas J Price, Don McCullin and Franz West. Make time for a poke around Smiljan Radić's fibreglass folly, a former Serpentine Gallery pavilion that looks uncannily like a marooned spaceship.

Durslade Farm, Dropping Lane, Bruton, BA10 0NL
hauserwirth.com

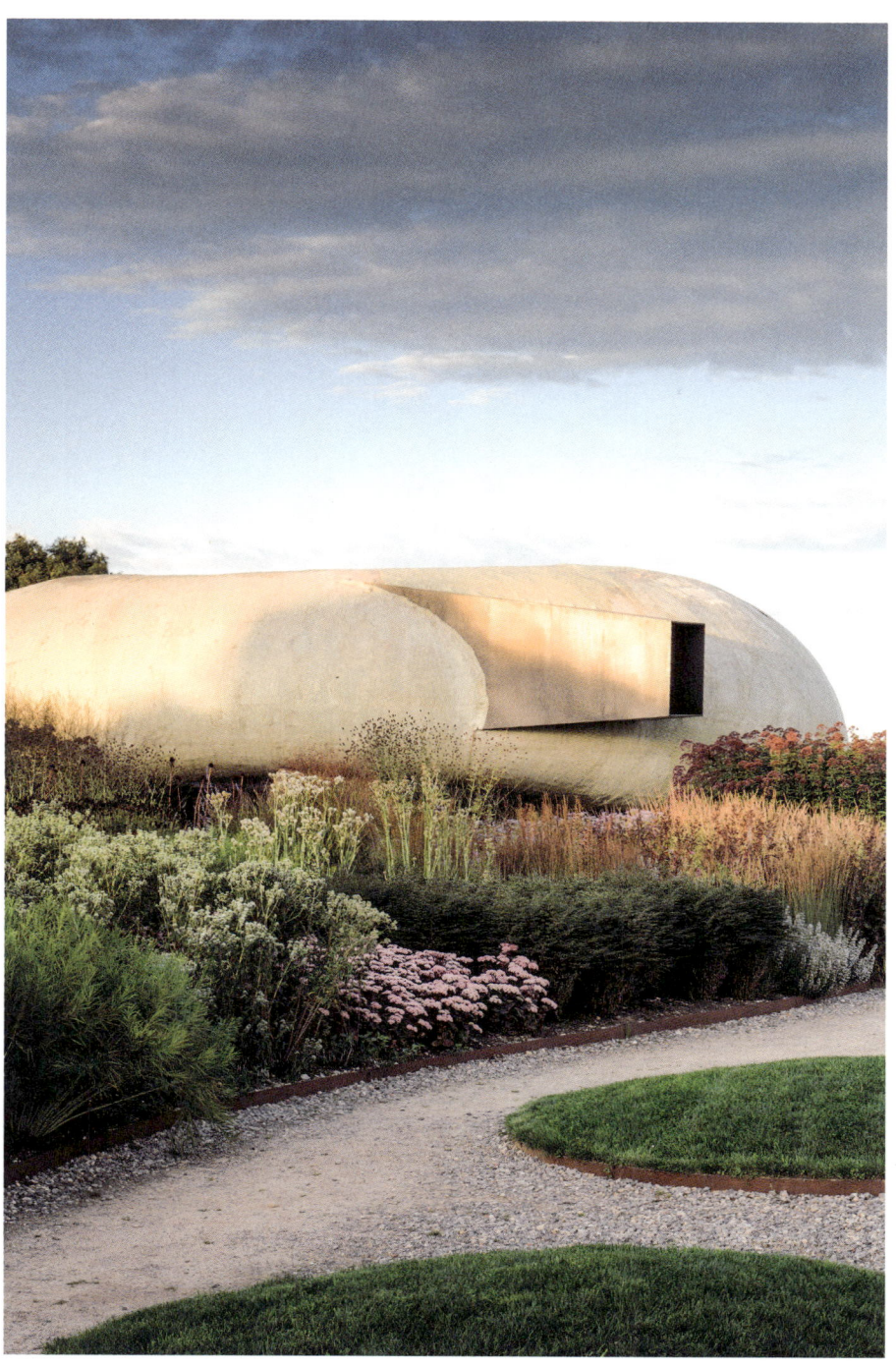

Radić Pavilion, Smiljan Radić

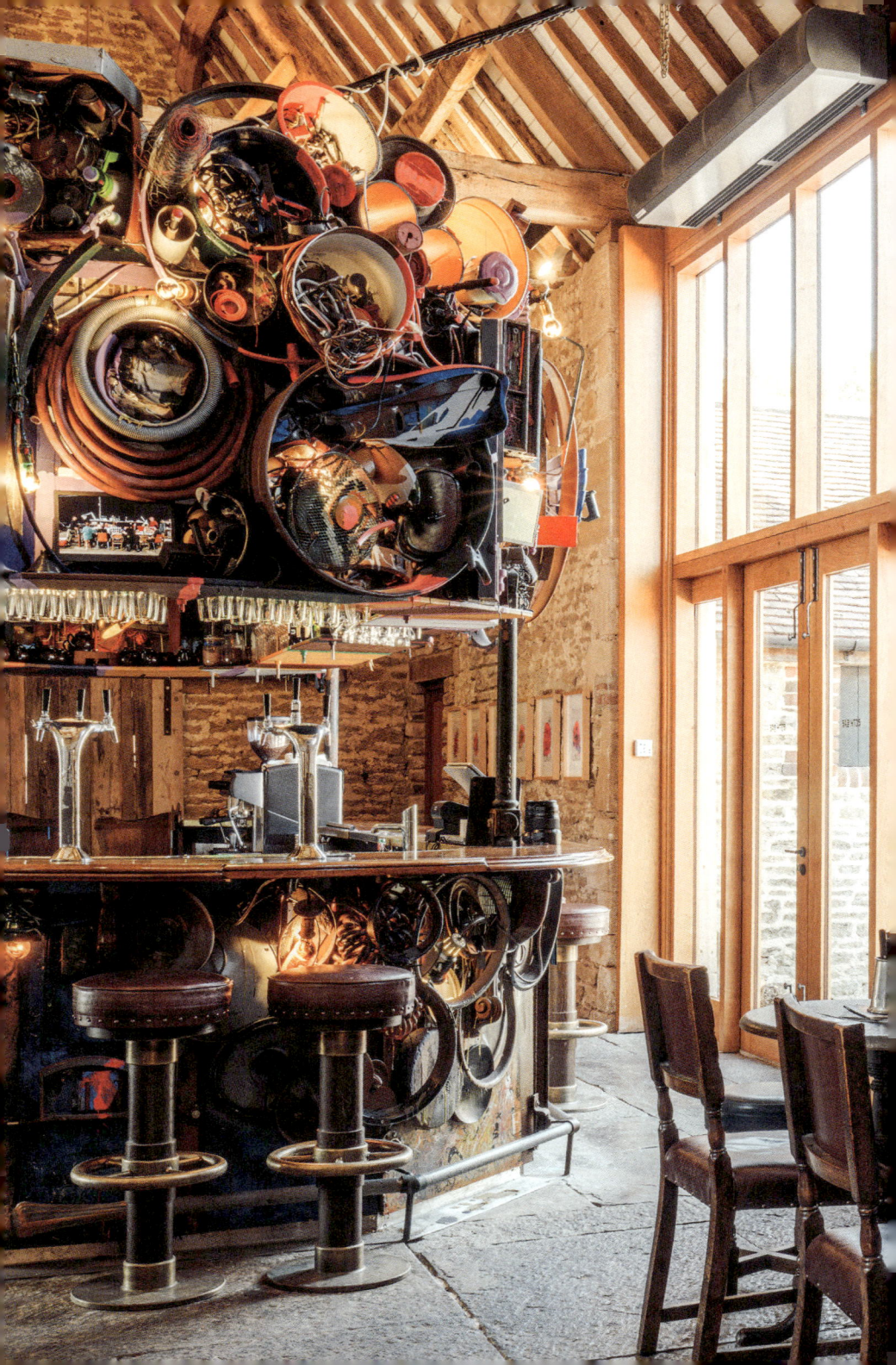

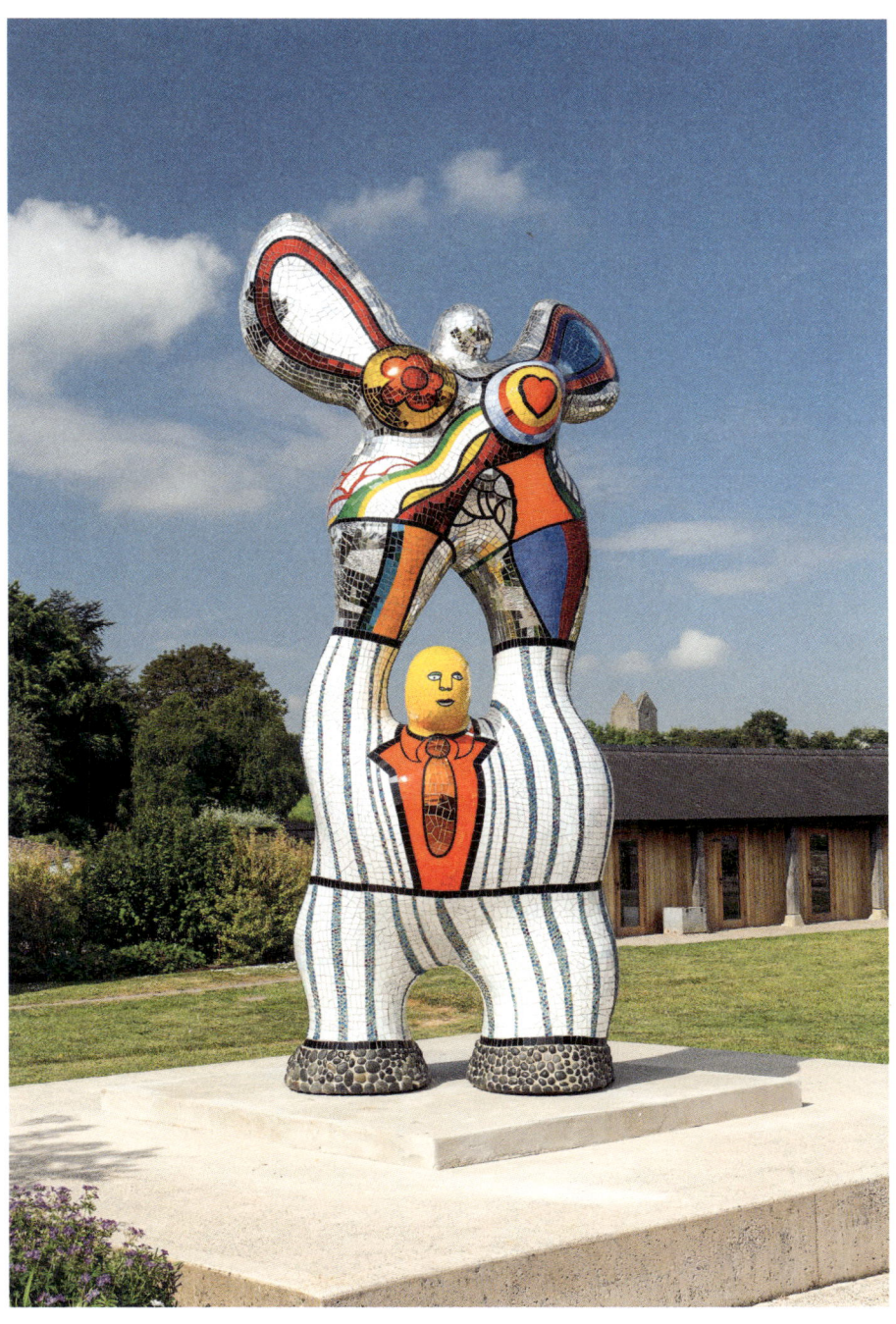

Above: *Le Poète et sa Muse*, Niki de Saint Phalle
Opposite: The Roth Bar

COTSWOLD SCULPTURE PARK

Offbeat attraction with holiday lets

Its attention-grabbing artwork and awe-inspiring views offer reason enough to swing by the Cotswold Sculpture Park, but there's much more to this ten-acre wonderland than meets the eye. Founded and landscaped by scrap-metal sculptor David Hartland, whose whimsical works are scattered throughout, this verdant oasis is part commercial gallery, part holiday hotspot, with almost every sculpture for sale and on-site Airbnbs in the form of three intimate shepherds' huts and a surprisingly cosy converted water tower. Sculptures number between 150 and 200 and tend to err on the wackier side – with Hartland's towering tree sculpture composed entirely from old car parts with the shell of a Morris Minor caught in its upper 'branches' – setting the tone. Catch it in the grounds of the delightful Poppin Tearoom, where you can fuel up on satisfying hunks of cake and door-stop sandwiches in preparation for your arty amble.

The Paddocks, Somerford Keynes, Cirencester, GL7 6FE
cotswoldsculpturepark.co.uk

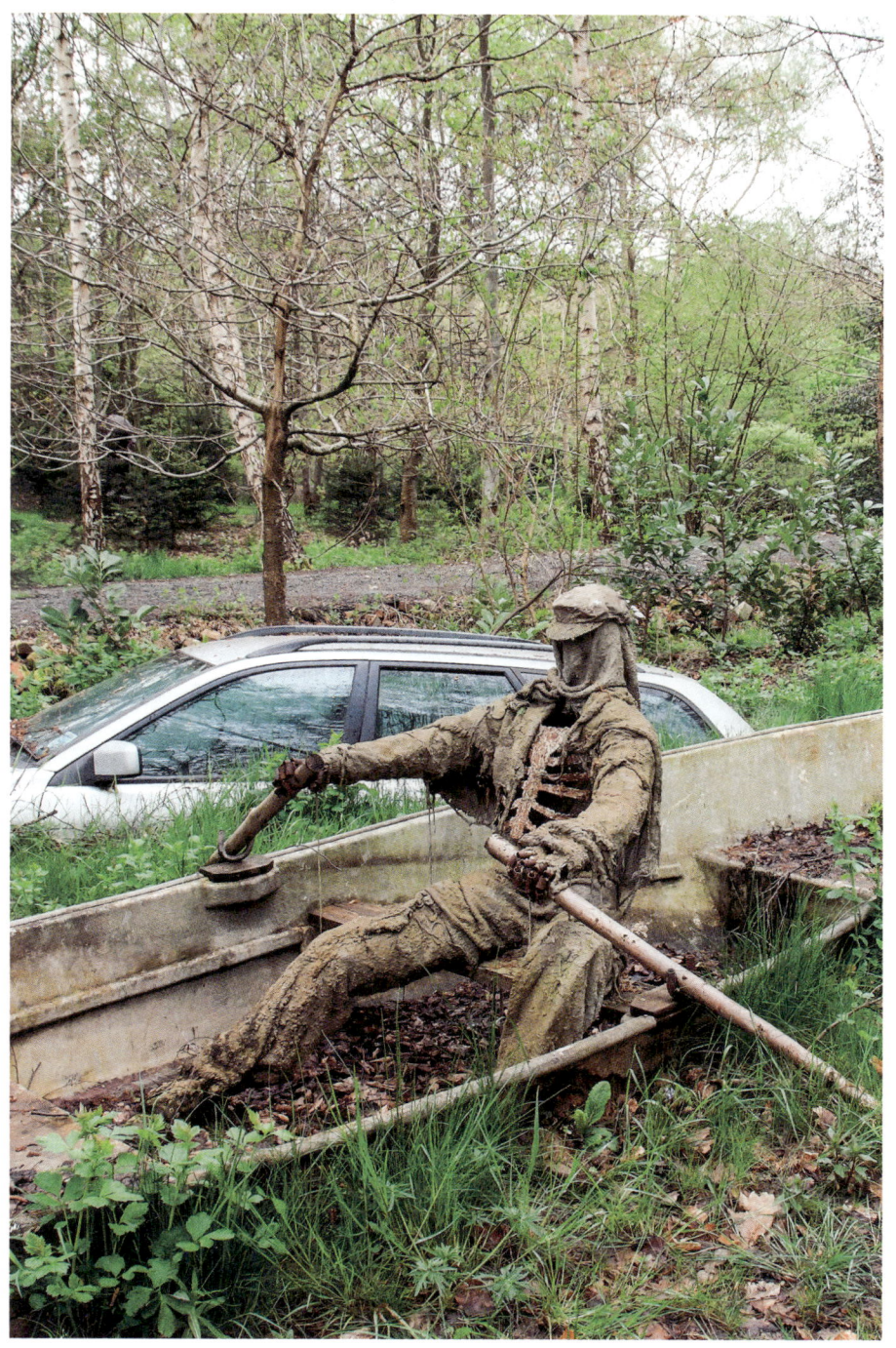

Ostrich, David Hartland

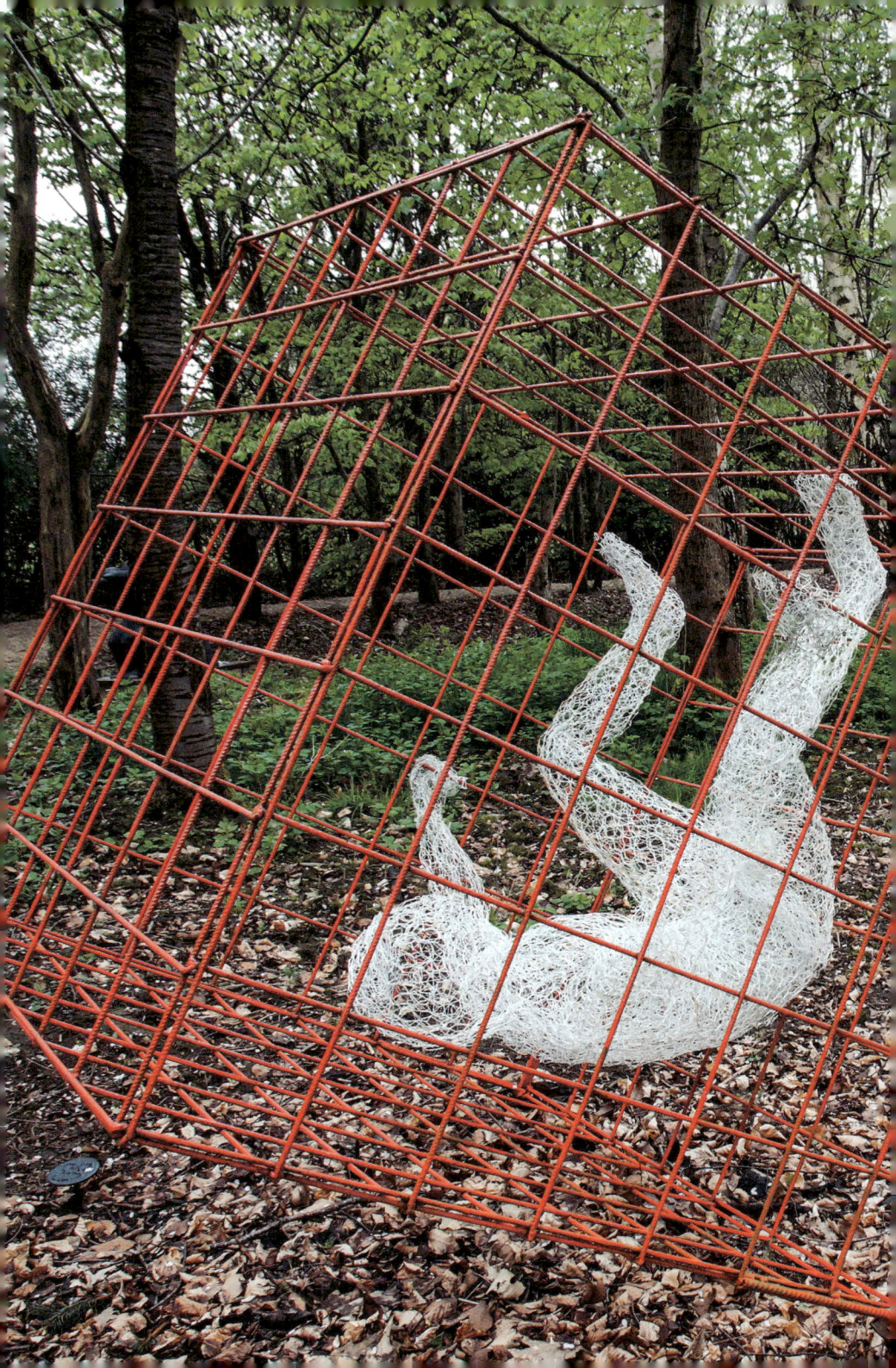

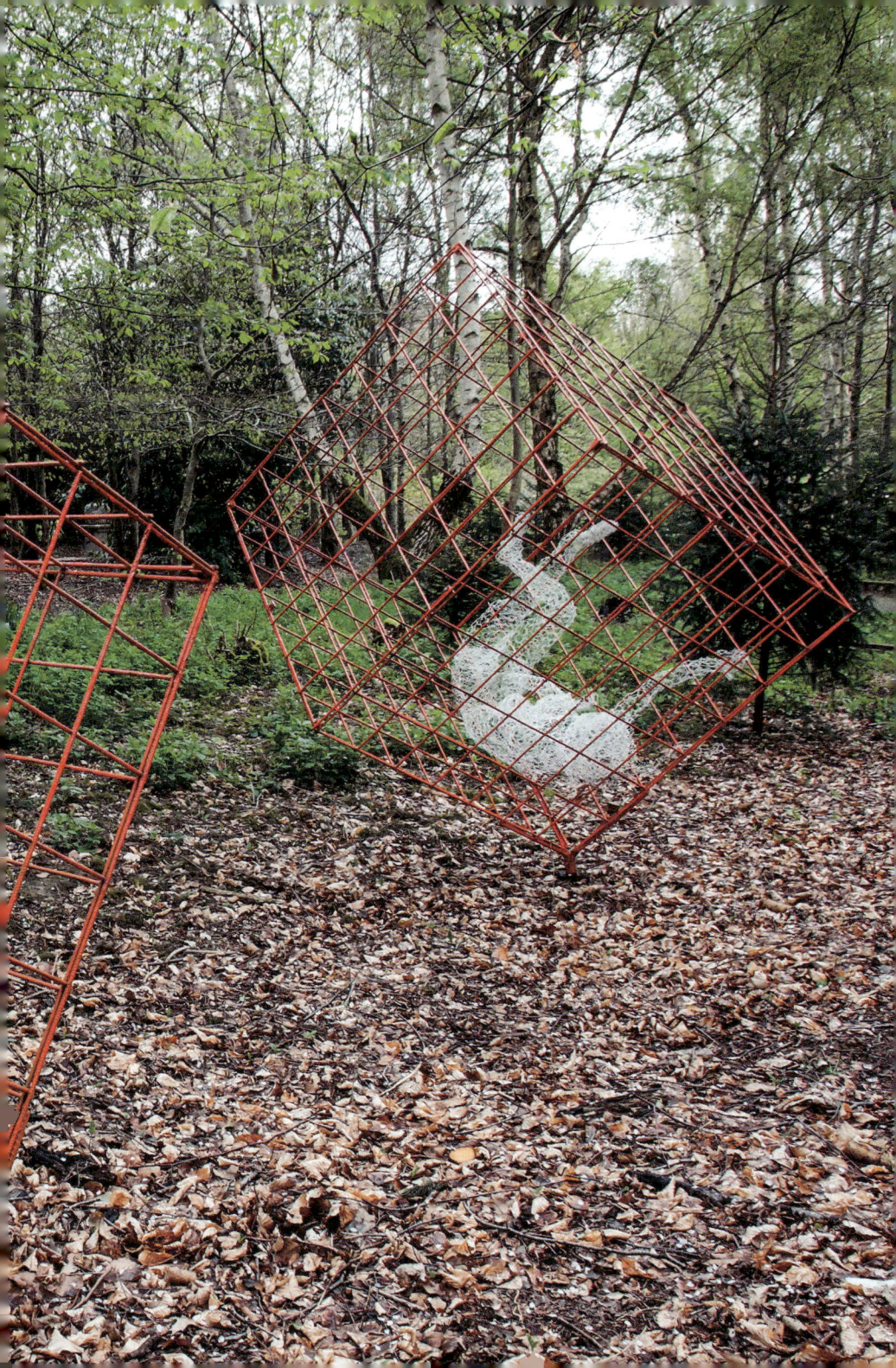

FOREST OF DEAN SCULPTURE TRAIL

Otherworldly gallery among the trees

From inspiring J.R.R. Tolkien's imaginary worlds to standing in for *Doctor Who's* Weeping Angel-infested woodland and *Star Wars'* planet Tokodana, the Forest of Dean has to be one of Earth's *least* earthly locations. Stretching 4.5 miles, this 18-sculpture trail renders the spot even more enigmatic with its site-specific works, among them a disappearing path of railway sleepers and an elfin house on stilts. Conceived in partnership with Bristol's Arnolfini (p.122) in 1986, the trail was one of the first to open in the UK and is composed entirely of works created in response to this inimitable landscape. Kristina Veasey's *Meander*, for example, draws its inspiration from conversations the artist had with local people whilst offering them a place to rest, while Kevin Atherton's colossal stained-glass window draws on the analogy of the forest as a cathedral – an idea that feels especially apt in this ethereal setting.

Speech House Road, Coleford, GL16 7EL
forestofdean-sculpture.org.uk

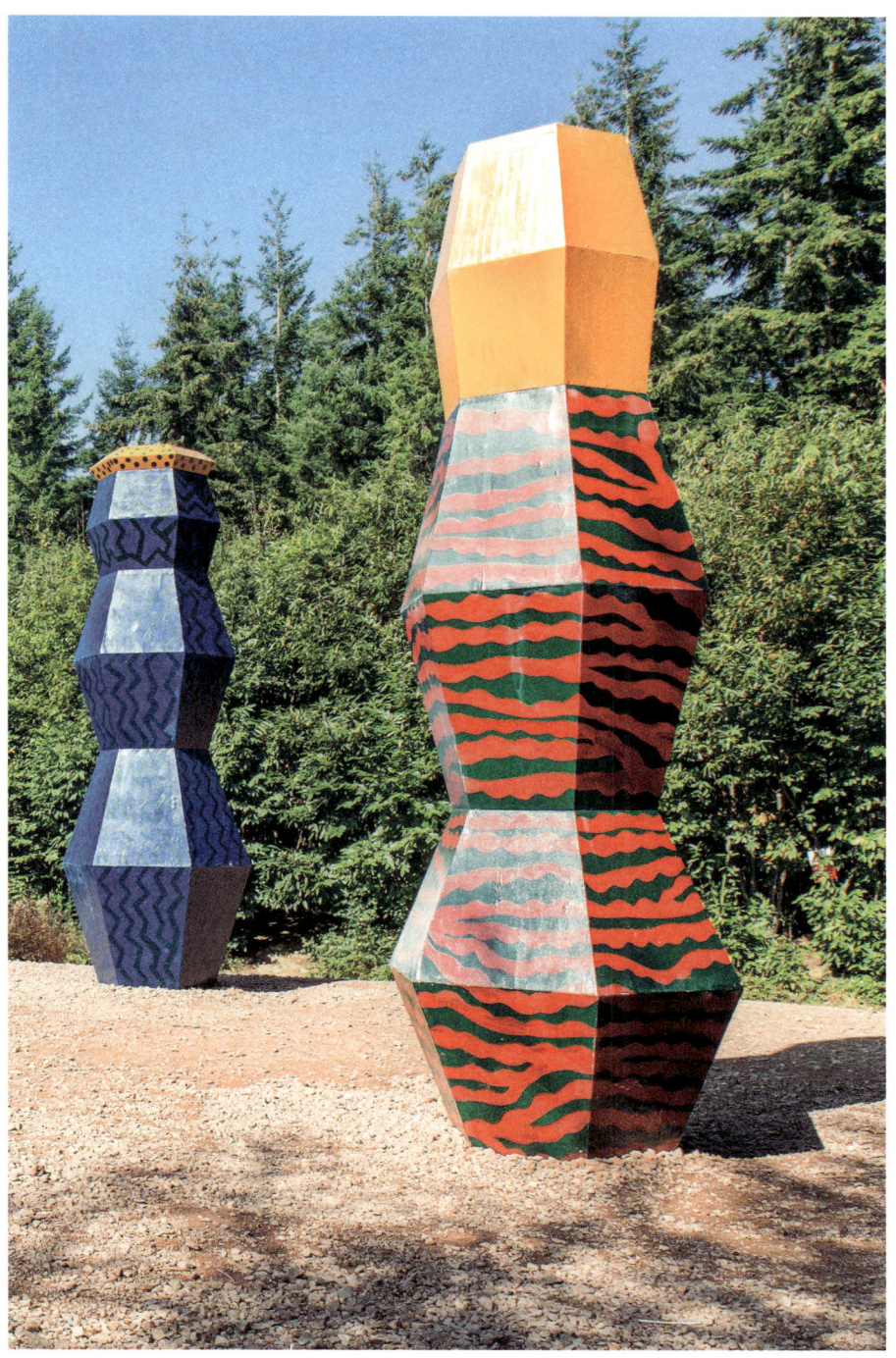

Totemy, Alicja Biała

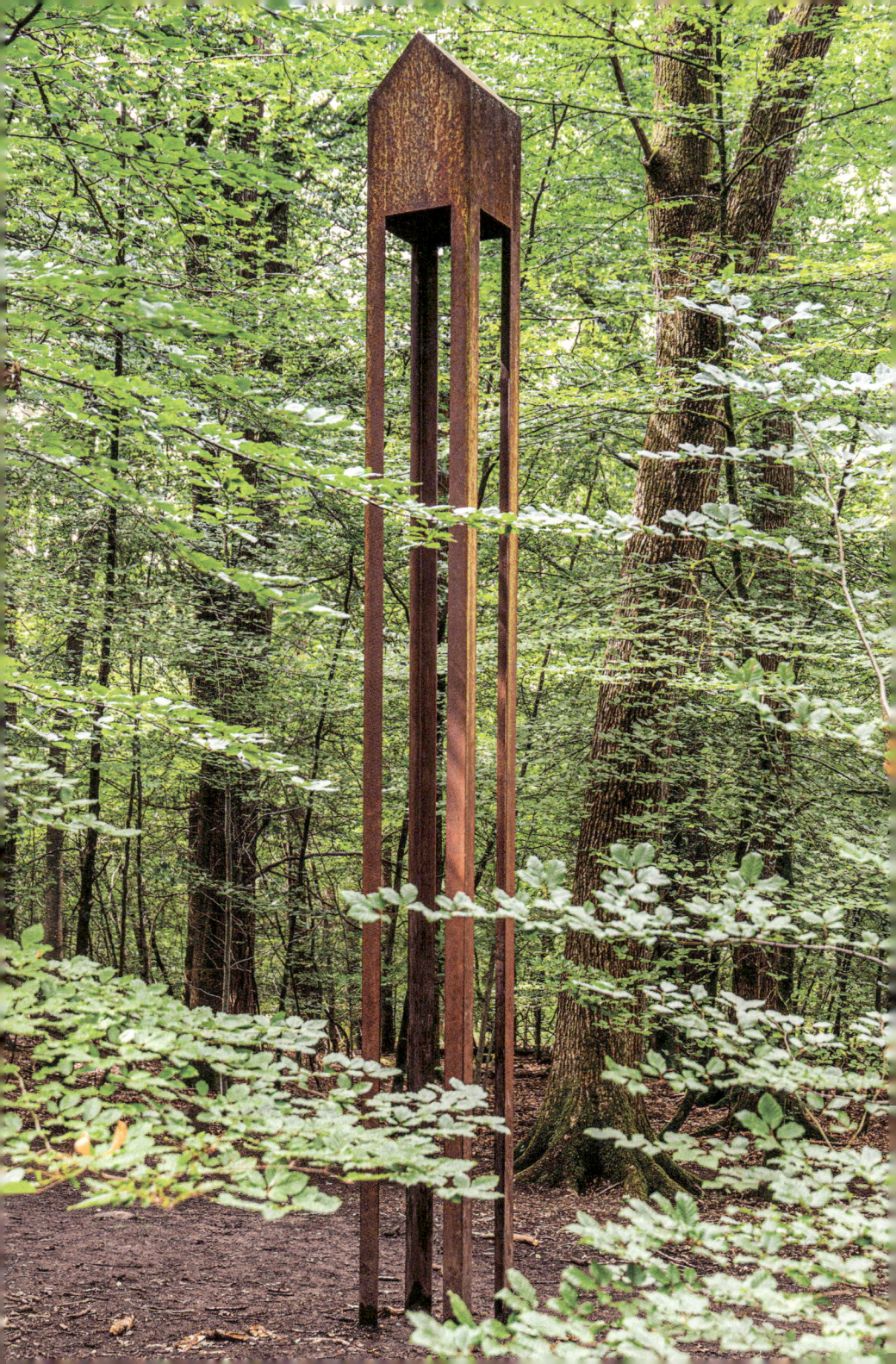

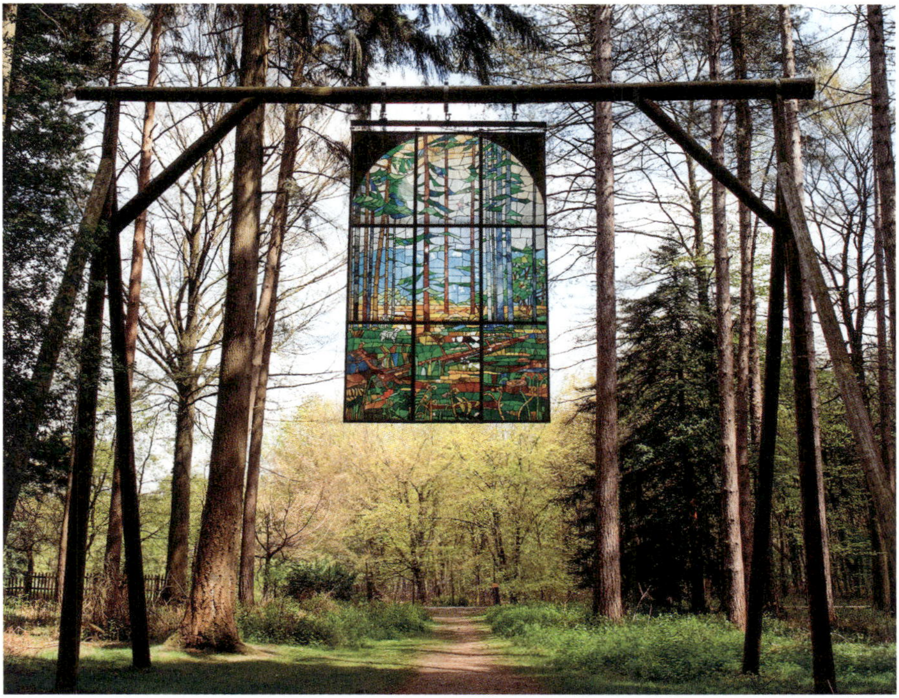

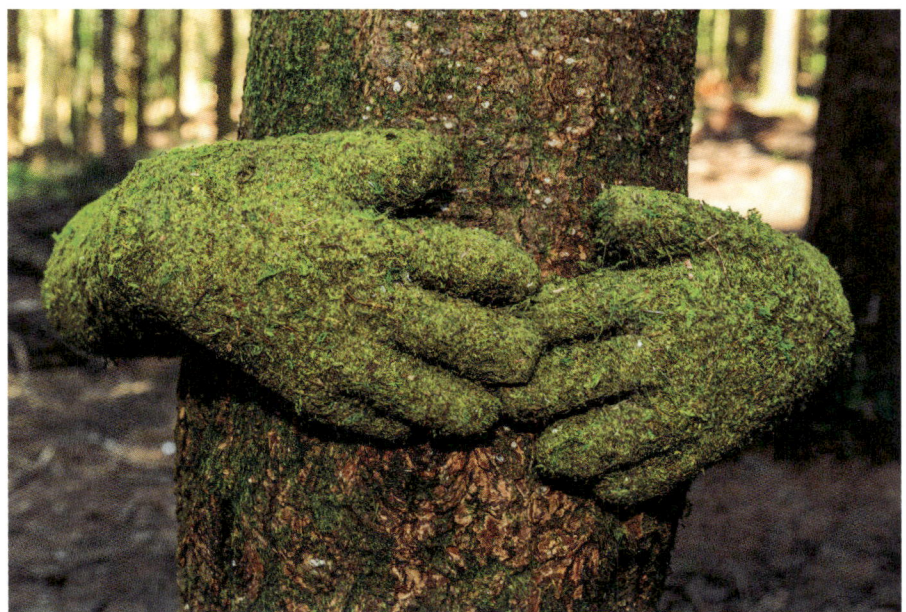

Opposite: *House*, Miles Davis
Above: *Cathedral*, Kevin Atherton
Below: *Tree Hug*, Monsieur Plant

ROCHE COURT SCULPTURE PARK

Contemporary works in charming countryside

Anthony Caro's *Palanquin* stands in a clearing like a distorted Wendy house. Nearby, Laura Ford's trio of bronze poodles reimagine Sir Joshua Reynolds' *The Ladies Waldegrave* as Crufts entrants, while Michael Craig-Martin's steel outline of a purple umbrella lies abandoned by a wall. Surprises await around every corner of this leafy sanctuary, with more than 100 sculptures arranged across more than 60 magnificent acres. Originally a London gallery, the New Art Centre decamped to Wiltshire in 1994, shunning four walls in favour of open sky and grazing cows – as per the yearnings of founder Madeleine Ponsonby, Countess of Bessborough. The countess was certainly onto something, though Roche Court encompasses indoor galleries too, from the domestic-style Design and Artists houses to the Gallery, whose displays – recently featuring work by Edmund de Waal and Gary Hume – can be viewed through full-height windows. There's no set way to explore the sculpture-studded grounds, but grabbing a map on arrival should ensure you don't miss a thing.

East Winterslow, Salisbury, SP5 1BG
sculpture.uk.com

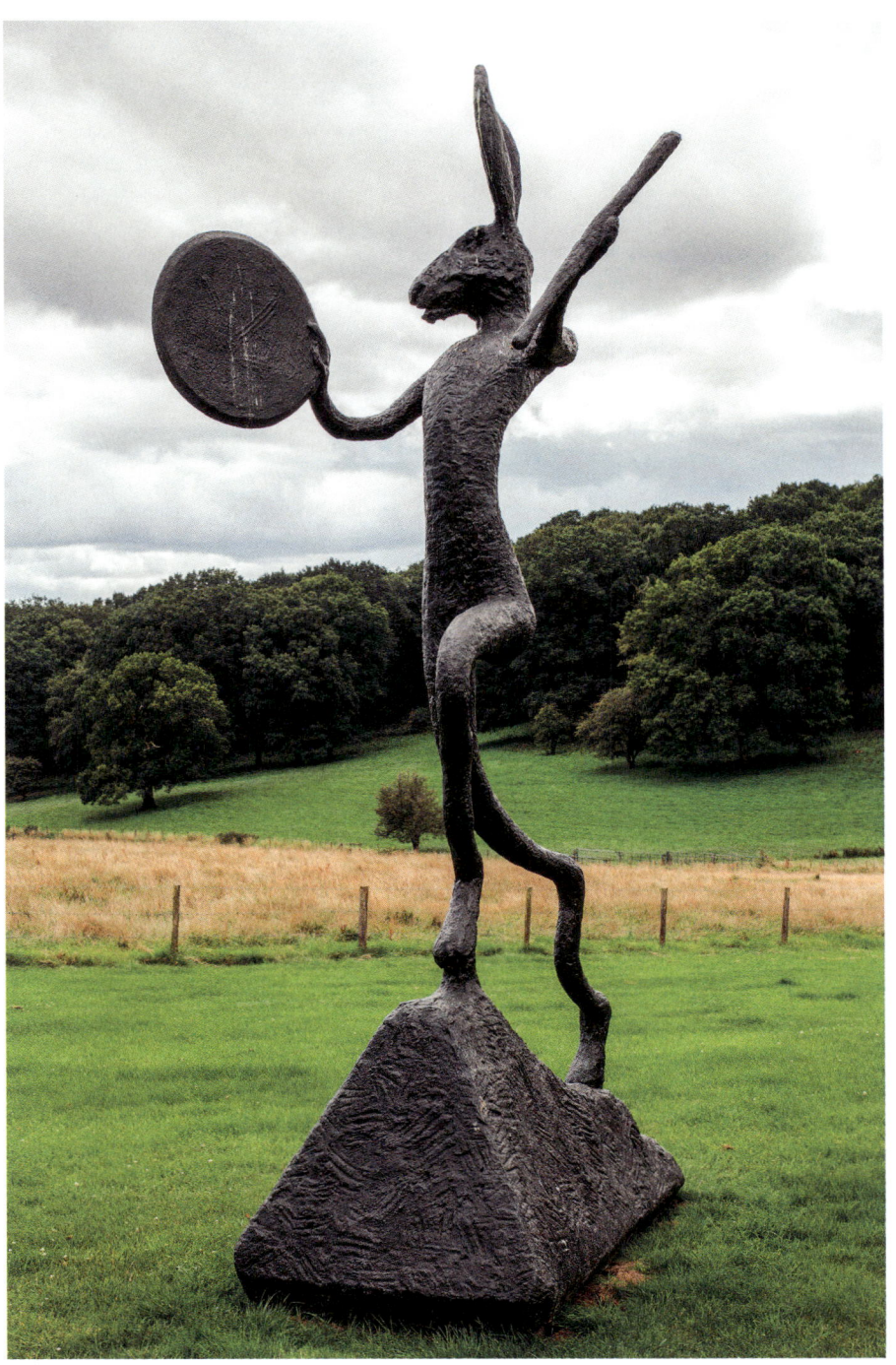

Large Left-Handed Drummer, Barry Flanagan

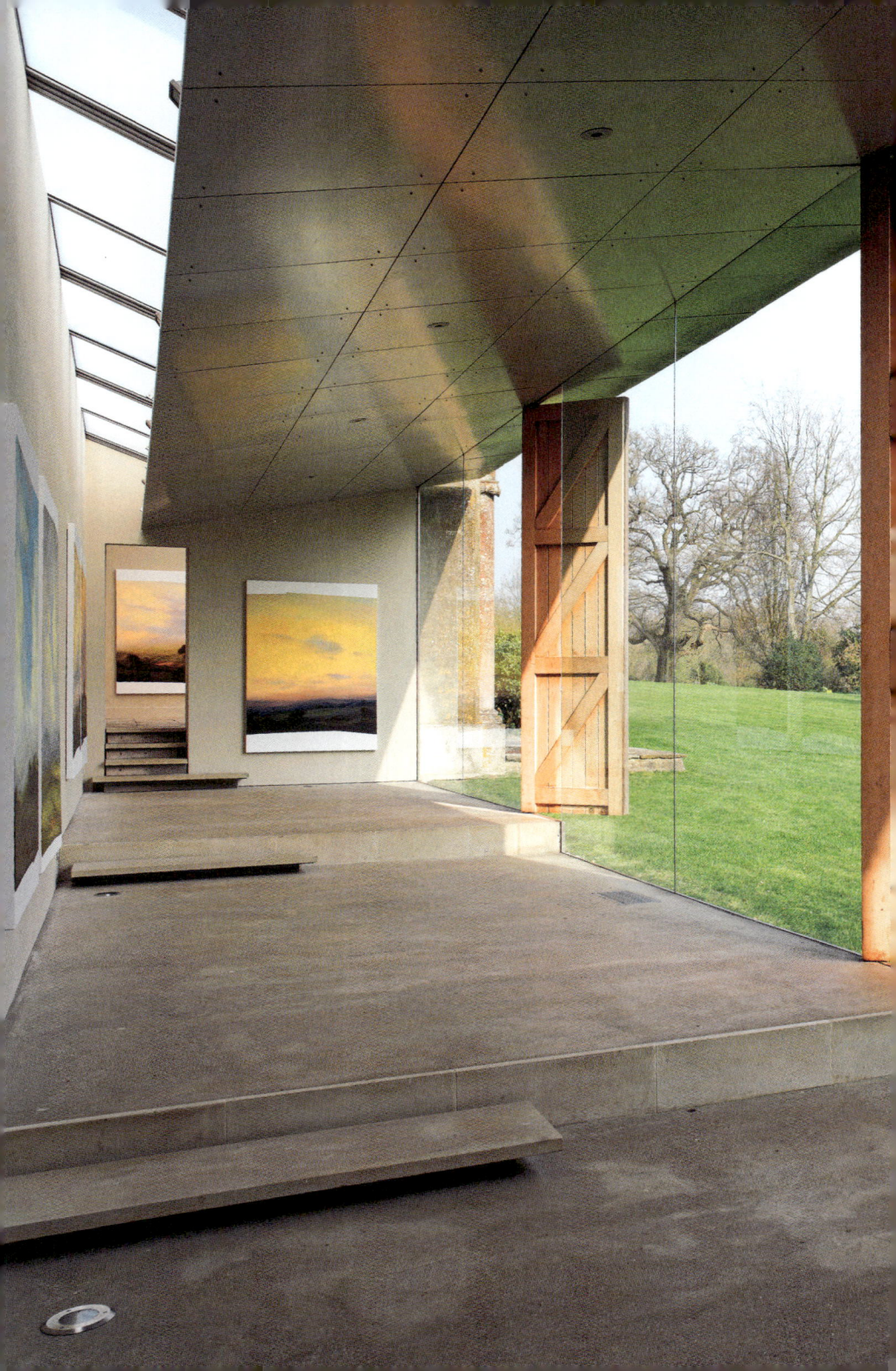

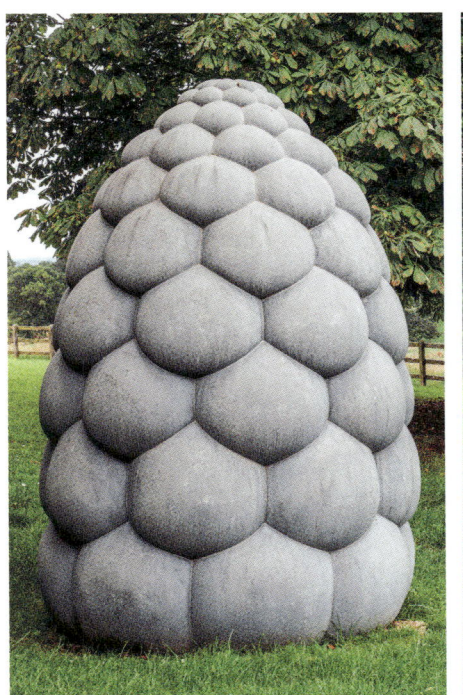
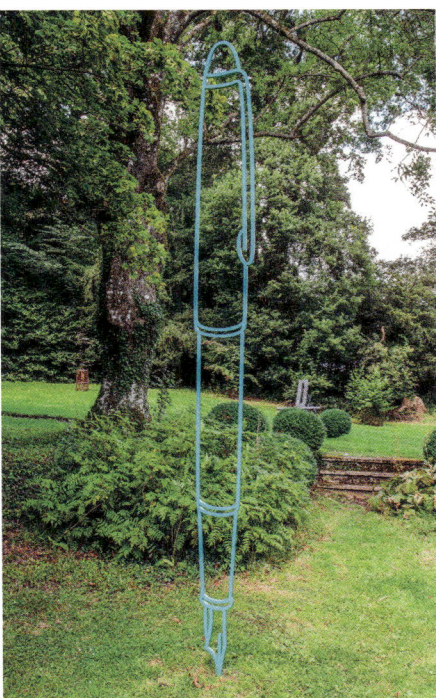
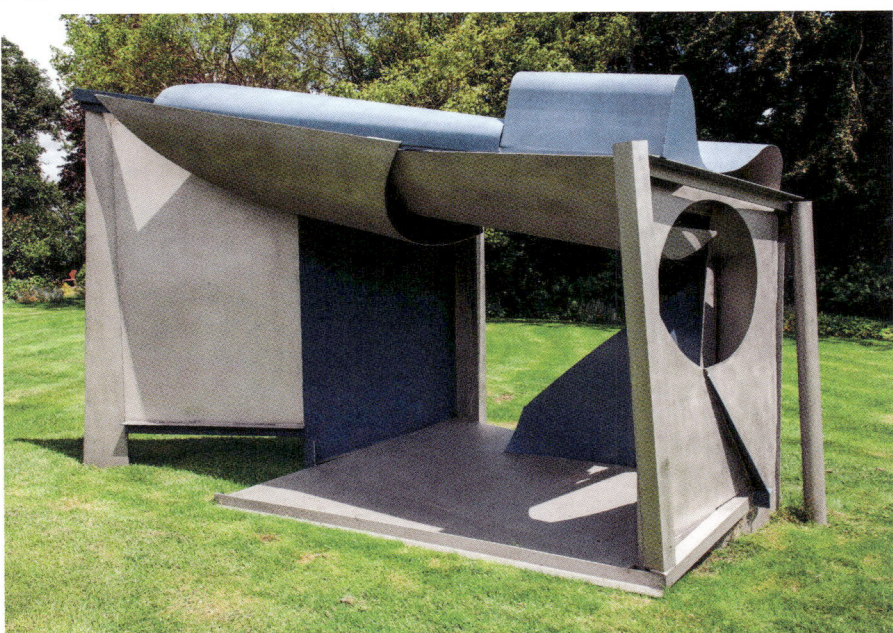

Clockwise from top left: *Fructus*, Peter Randall-Page;
Fountain Pen (turquoise), Michael Craig-Martin; *Palanquin*, Anthony Caro

BARBARA HEPWORTH MUSEUM

Sculptor's spellbinding seaside residence

The house where artist Barbara Hepworth lived, worked and died still feels so rich with her presence, you half expect to encounter her spirit in the studio, chiselling away at a lump of stone. Opened to the public in 1976, in accordance with her wishes, the artist's hilltop abode remains much as she left it, her finished bronzes and furniture still perfectly in place, while her tools, overalls and part-worked pieces patiently await her return. On quiet days, visits to this secluded spot feel rather illicit, but it's rare that a museum offers such a vivid insight into an artist's life. Hepworth's monumental *Two Forms (Divided Circle)*, a late work created following her cancer diagnosis, and *Infant*, a tender work depicting her eldest son Paul as a baby, are just two of the 30-plus sculptures scattered around the atmospheric house and garden, with many more to discover at the nearby Tate (p.128).

Barnoon Hill, St Ives, TR26 1AD
tate.org.uk/visit/tate-st-ives/barbara-hepworth-muse-um-and-sculpture-garden

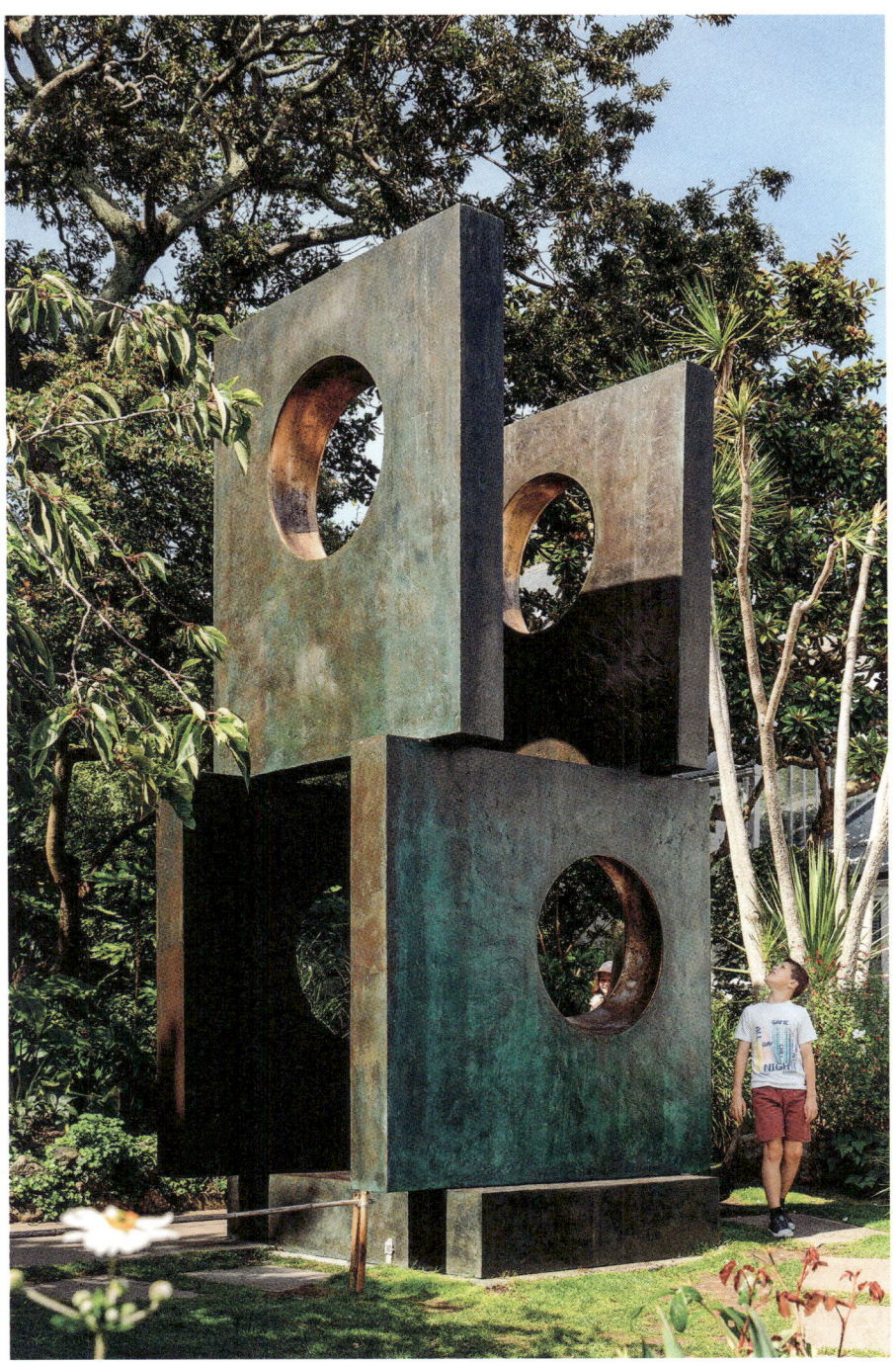

Four-Square (Walk Through), Barbara Hepworth

MESSUMS WEST

Historic barn spotlighting modern sculpture

Messums could exhibit virtually anything beneath its magnificent hammerbeam ceiling and it would never look anything short of spectacular. Happily, the works selected for the gallery's West Country offshoot are reliably impressive themselves, be they Elisabeth Frink's distinctive bronze nudes, Laurence Edwards' ethereal figures or Bridget McCrum's iconic stone birds. Indeed, with over a third of an acre of floor space, the 13th-century tithe barn lends itself particularly well to sculpture, though its recent displays of painting by Rose Hilton and Nicola Wood – as well as an atmospheric soundscape installation by Orlando Gough and Alastair Goolden – have been equally well received. On-site restaurant The Mess is far from your average gallery cafe – its seasonal plates and elite cakes render it a destination in its own right, and its name is a complete misnomer.

Place Farm, Court Street, Tisbury, SP3 6LW

messums.org

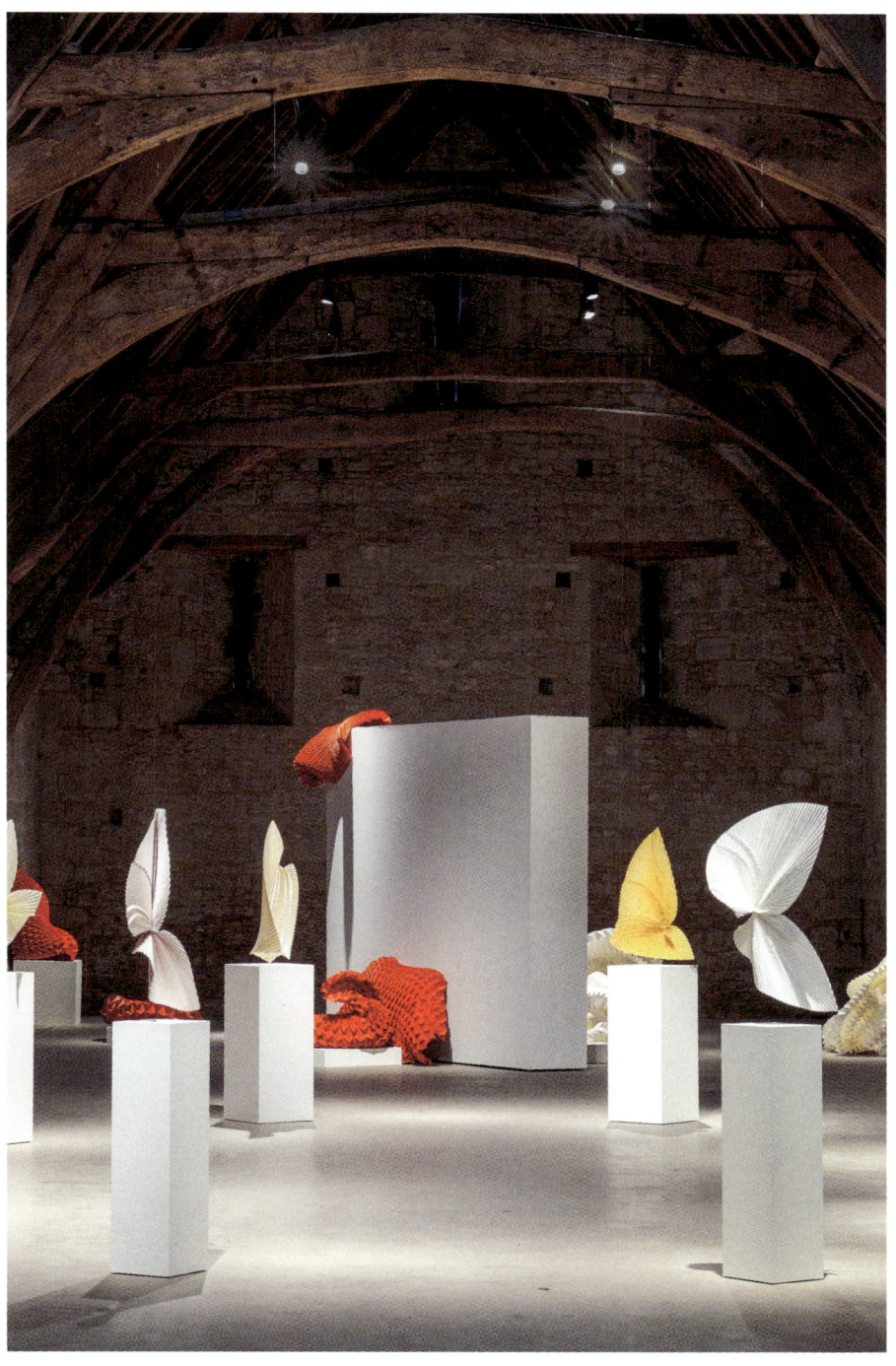

Unfolding, Unfurling, Kaori Kato

TOUT QUARRY
SCULPTURE PARK

Dynamic open-air gallery at former stone works

Thousands flock to St Paul's Cathedral and Buckingham Palace every day of the year but, in spite of its brilliance, the idiosyncratic art attraction that sprang from their site of origin is relatively unknown. Abandoned in 1982, Tout Quarry supplied iconic Portland stone to some of Britain's most famous historical buildings over its 200-year working life before it was revitalised as a sculpture park in 1983, with yearly artists' residencies generating both temporary and permanent work using its remaining limestone. Today, more than 60 sculptures are scattered among the quarry's myriad paths and mini valleys, including many of the original site-specific pieces. Octopuses, dinosaurs, mythical dogs and fireplaces are among the most notable sculptures you'll (quite literally) stumble across as you traverse the craggy terrain, alongside Antony Gormley's *Still Falling*, depicting an infinitely tumbling figure. Download a map from the Dorset Council website for up-to-the-minute intel on this ever-intriguing, ever-evolving site.

Tradecroft Industrial Estate, Isle of Portland, DT5 2LN

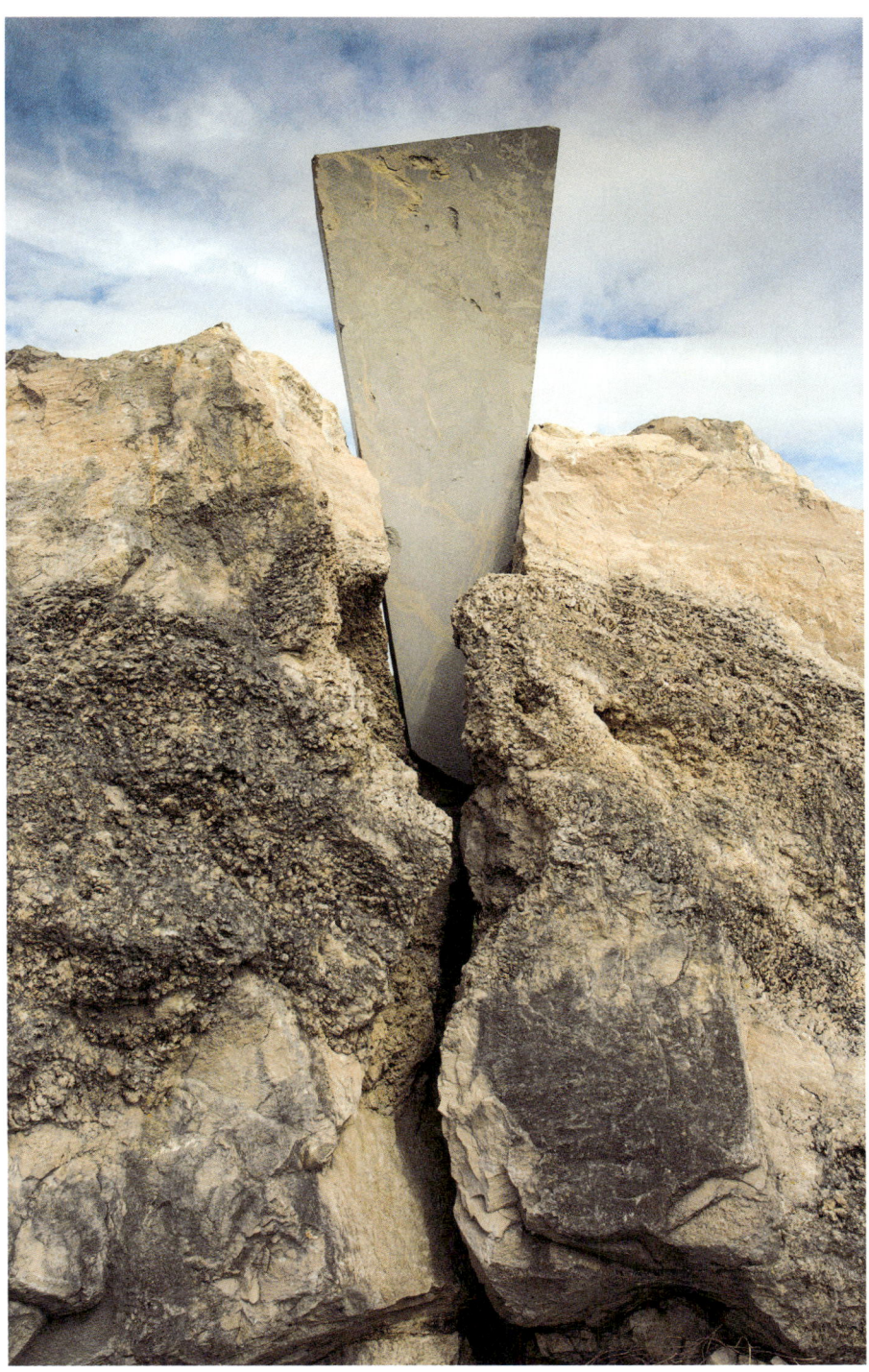

BANKSY'S BRISTOL

Subversive stencils in street artist's hometown

It would be disingenuous to experience Banksy's work any other place than in real life – ideally in its intended habitat. The elusive artist is thought to have left Bristol in around 2000, but his murals pop up on the city's walls to this day, joining works dating back to the 1990s. Begin your tour in Stokes Croft with *The Mild Mild West*, an early mural created in response to police raids on warehouse raves, working south via *Rose on a Mousetrap* and *Well Hung Lover* (said to be the UK's first legal graffiti), before proceeding to Spike Island in pursuit of *Girl with a Pierced Eardrum* (a humorous take on Vermeer's *Girl with a Pearl Earring*). Don't forget *The Grim Reaper* and *Paint-Pot Angel*, on display at M Shed and Bristol Museum and Art Gallery, respectively, or his most recent offering, *Valentine's Day*, in which a girl catapults an explosion of red flowers onto a wall with her slingshot, in the city's Easton neighbourhood.

Various locations
visitbristol.co.uk/things-to-do/street-art/banksy

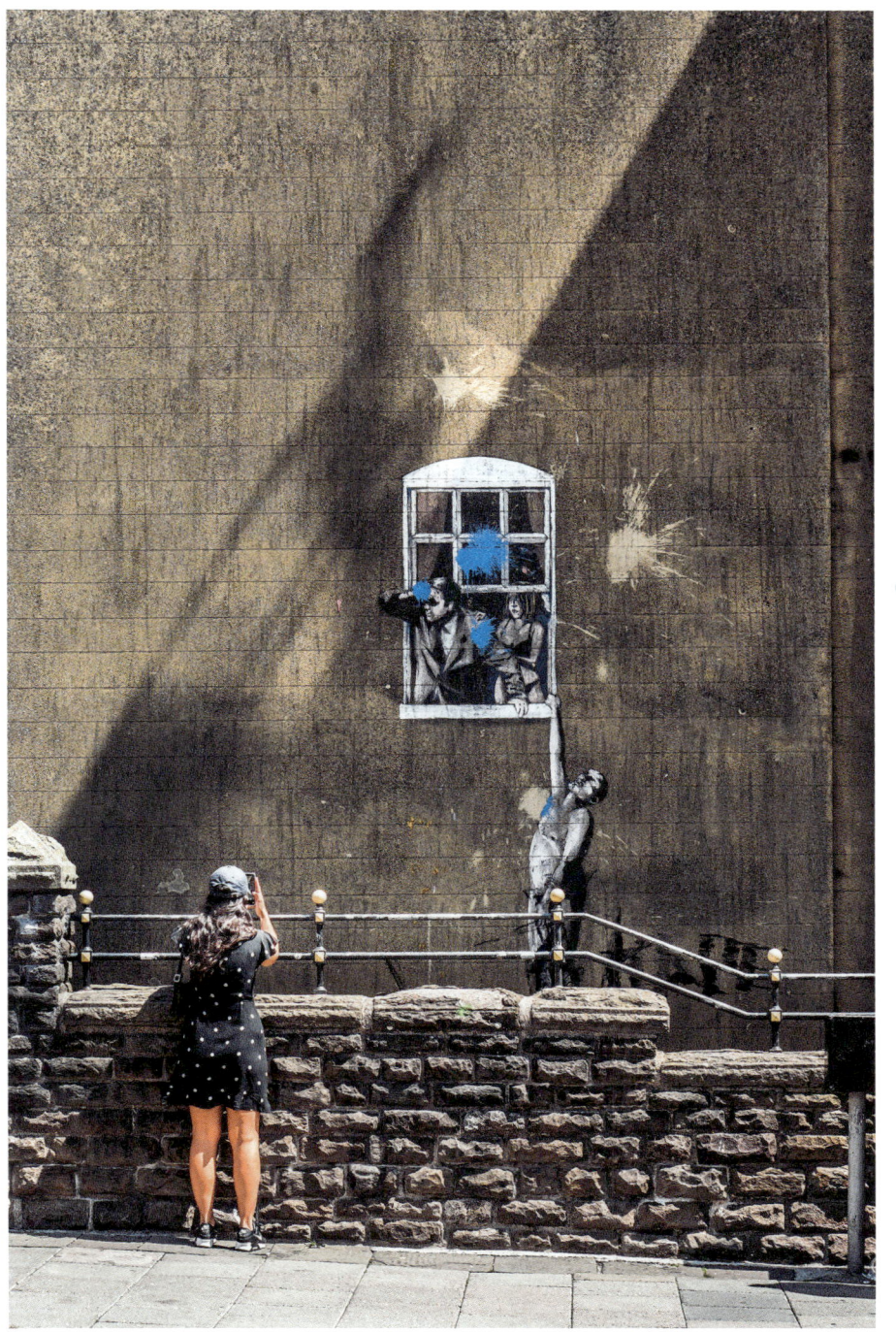

Well Hung Lover, Banksy

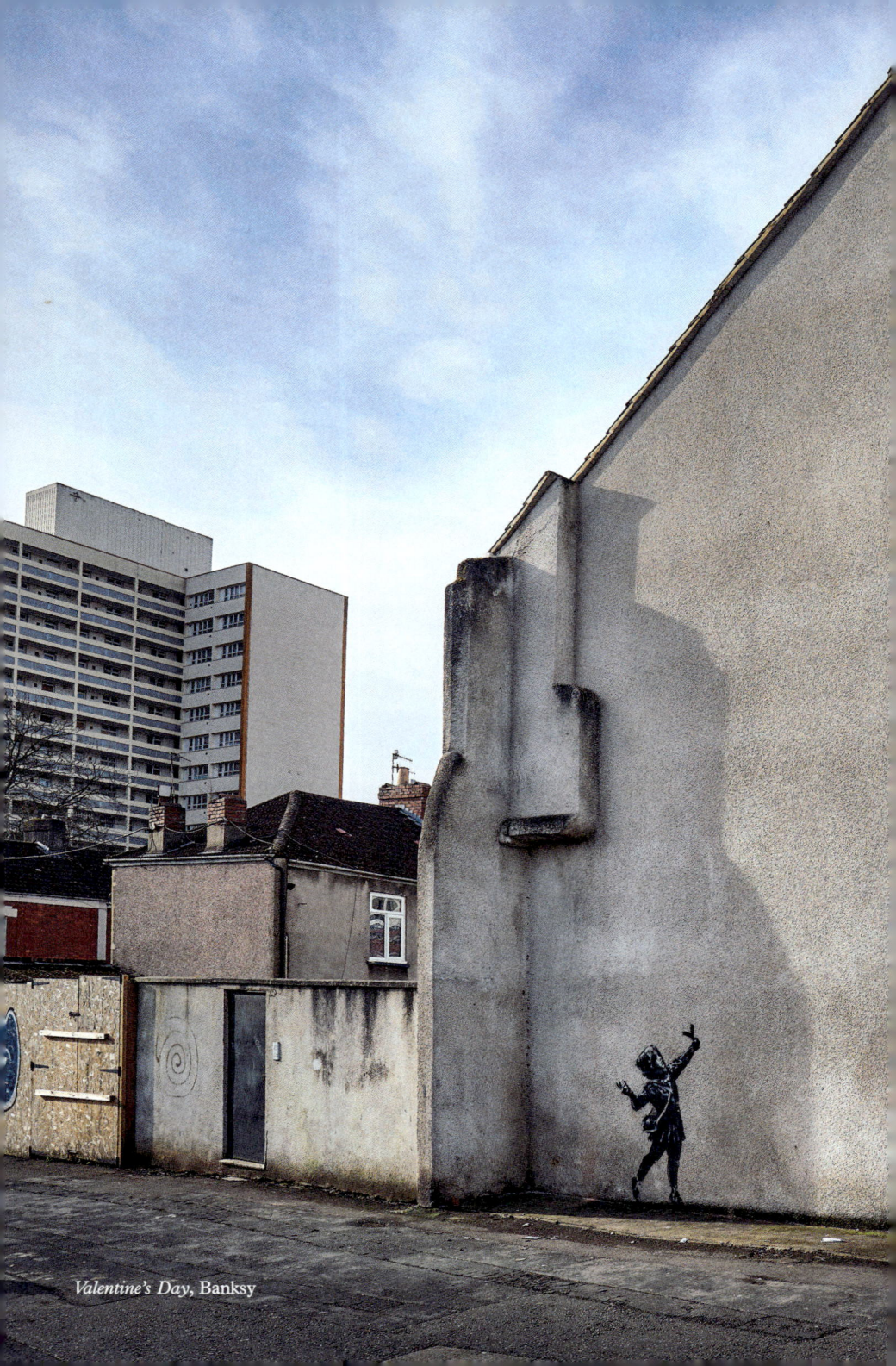

Valentine's Day, Banksy

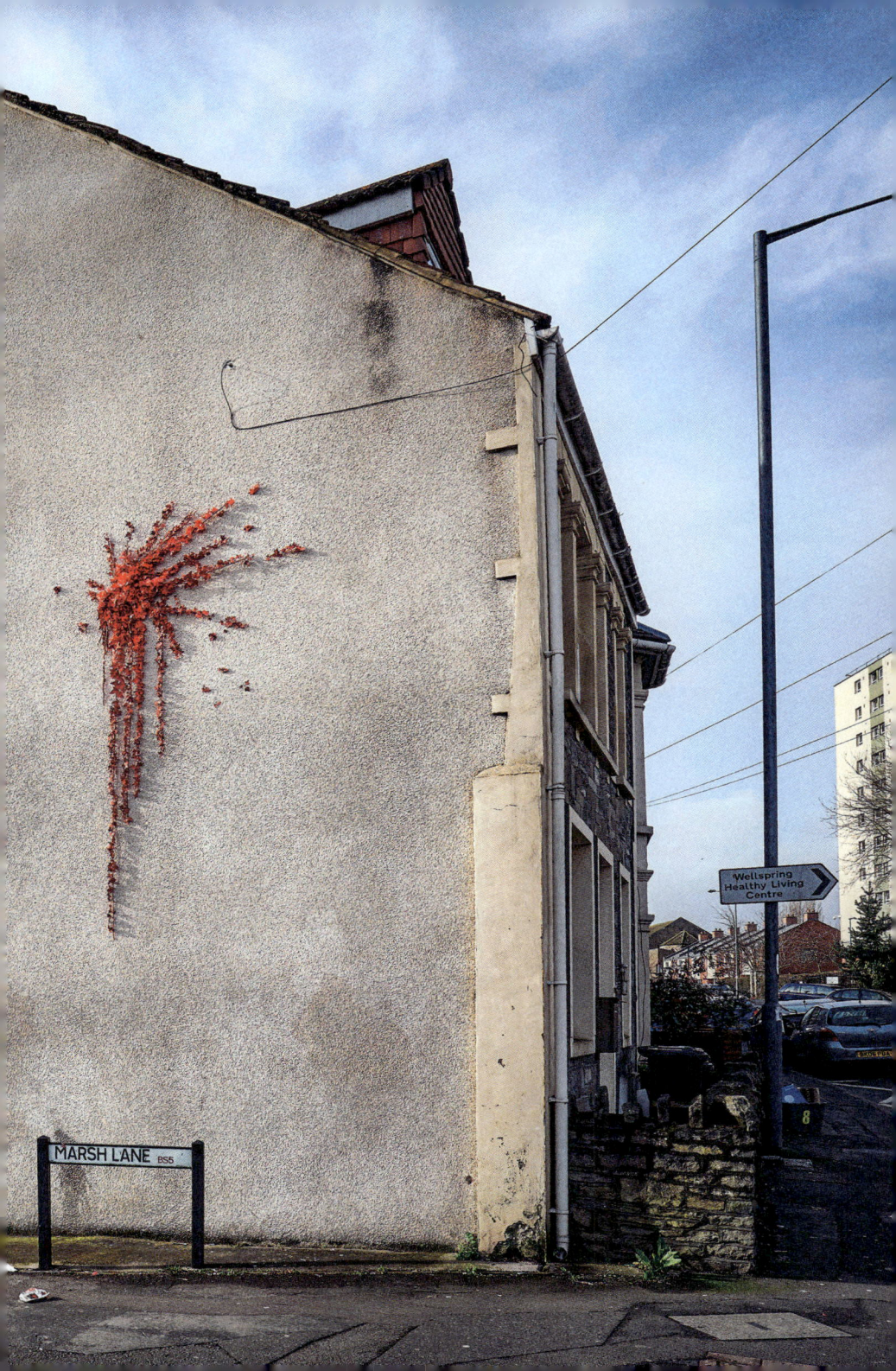

ARNOLFINI

Contemporary gallery with community spirit

A demand that you 'ENJOY YOURSELF' plastered in huge letters on the wall of its entrance hall sets the tone for this lively gallery. The establishing principle of co-founder Jeremy Rees, who launched the original space with collaborators Annabel Lawson and John Orsborn above a Clifton bookshop in 1961, this insistent sentiment seems to reverberate through everything that happens in the now much bigger Bush House premises (occupying the bottom four floors of an old iron foundry warehouse). Chantal Joffe, Paula Rego, Paul McCartney and Louise Bourgeois are among the glittering line-up of artists who've exhibited over the last half-century, though exhibitions are just the tip of the iceberg at the Arnolfini, which also offers an effervescent programme of performance, music, talks and screenings. Head down in the summer months, when the gallery's vibey cafe–bar spills out onto a picturesque deck overlooking Bristol Harbour, bringing Rees' command to life.

16 Narrow Quay, Bristol, BS1 4QA
arnolfini.org.uk

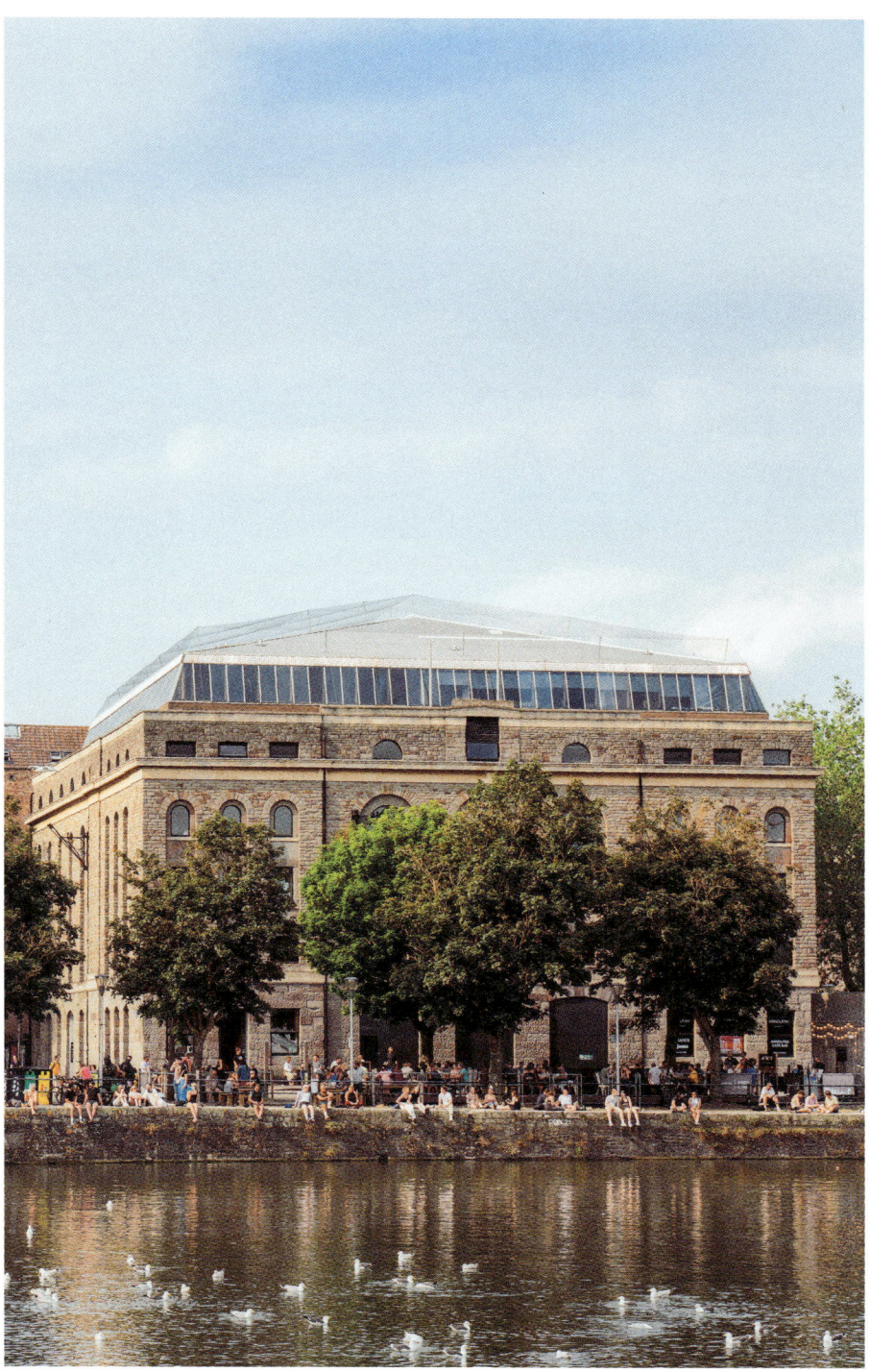

THE HOLBURNE MUSEUM

Grand Georgian treasure trove

At the end of one of Europe's most impressive Georgian streets lies one of the UK's most inspiring museums, itself home to one of the finest displays of 18th-century British portraiture. Originally built as a hotel, this magnificent Grade I-listed building has housed the collection of Sir William Holburne since 1882, when his sister Mary bequeathed more than 4,000 pieces of fine and decorative art to the people of Bath. The hoard has since more than doubled in size, boasting works by Gainsborough, Reynolds, Constable and Stubbs, along with numerous pieces by local painter Thomas Barker. In 2011, a radical three-storey extension almost doubled the interior space, creating a tranquil garden cafe along with additional learning and exhibition areas. Alongside its permanent galleries, the Holburne hosts a diverse programme of fluctuating exhibitions, while its starring role as Lady Danbury's house make it a mecca for *Bridgerton* fans.

Great Pulteney Street, Bathwick, Bath, BA2 4DB
holburne.org

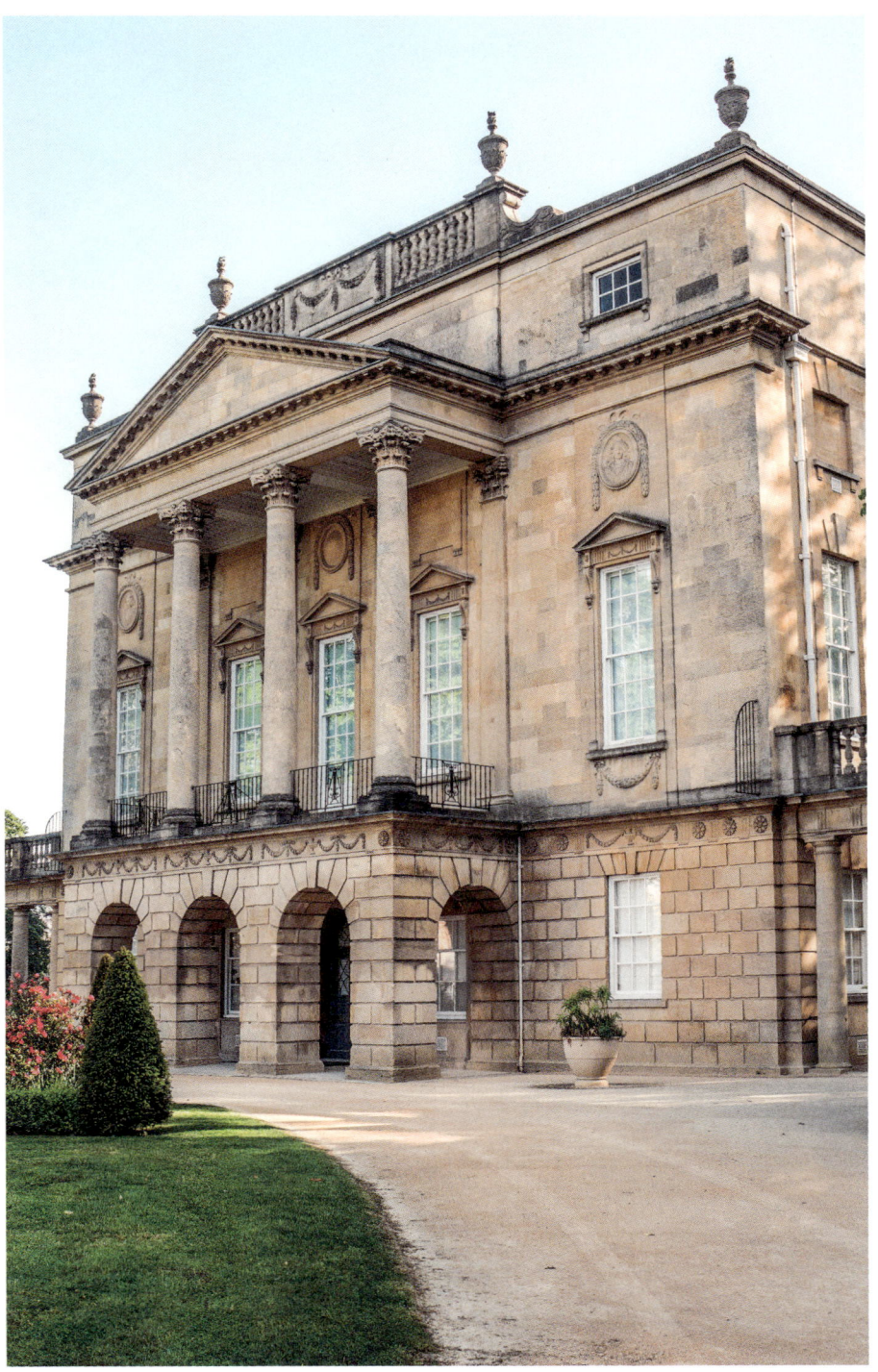

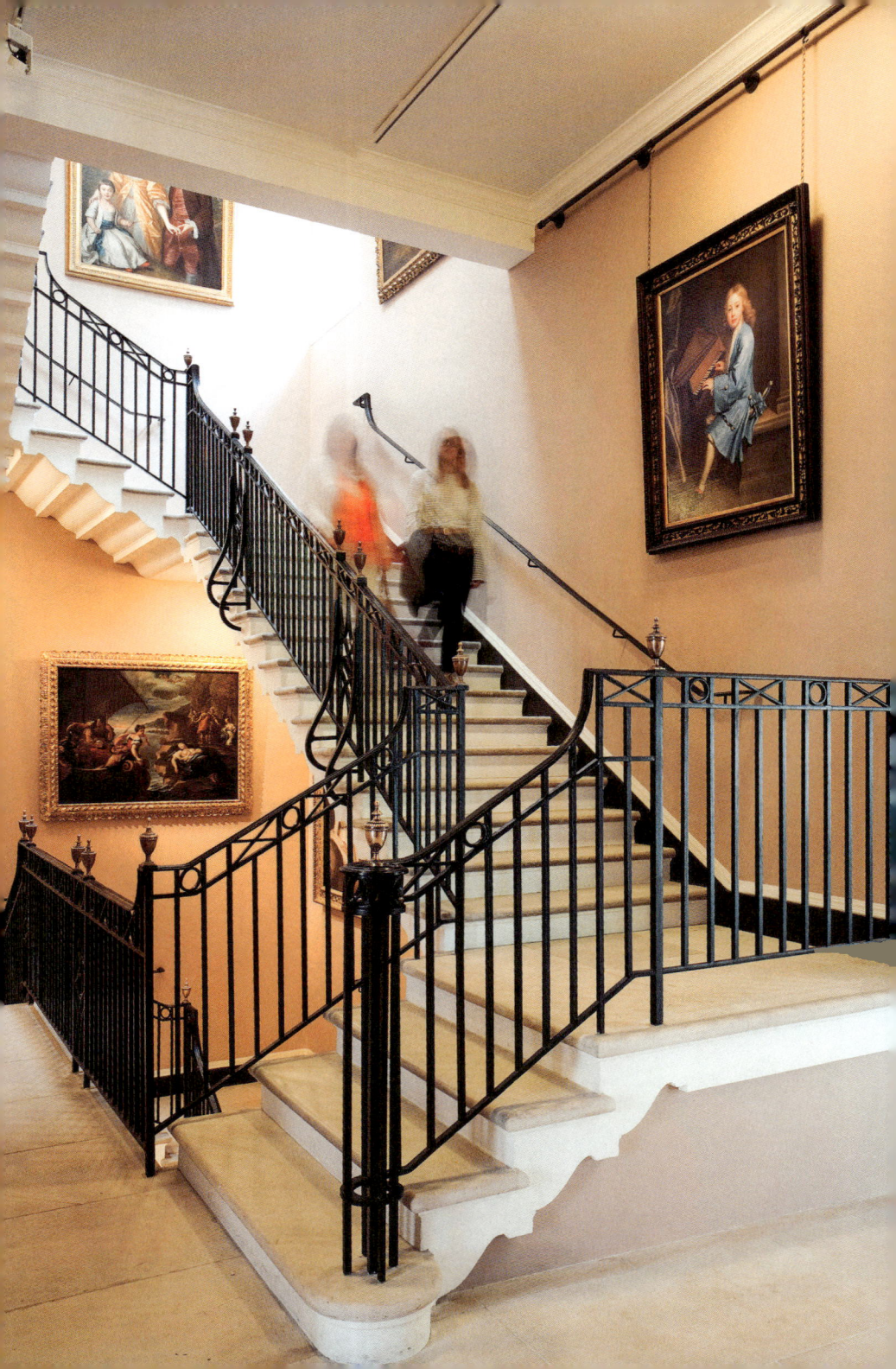

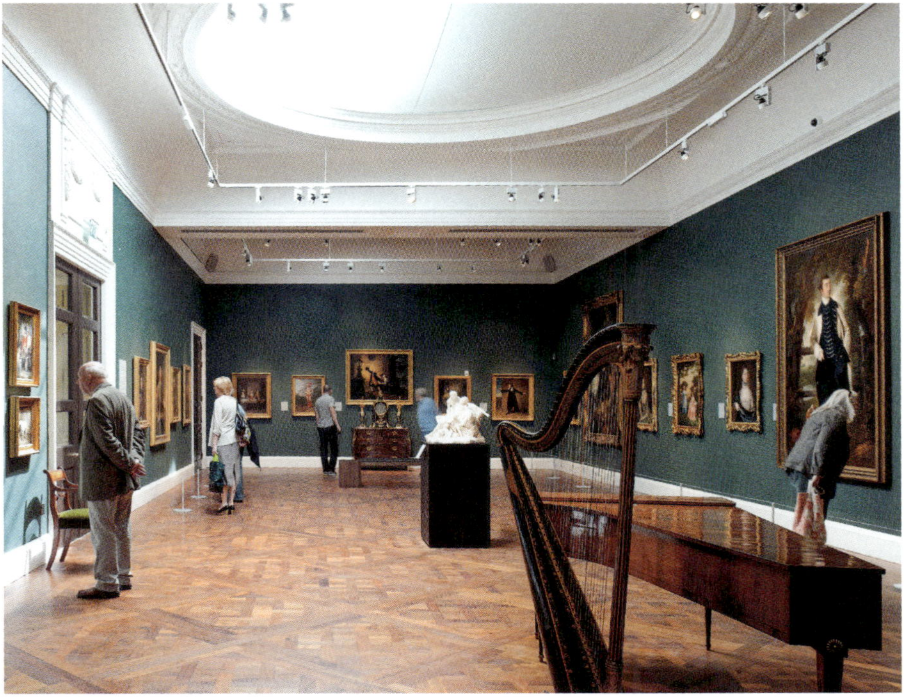

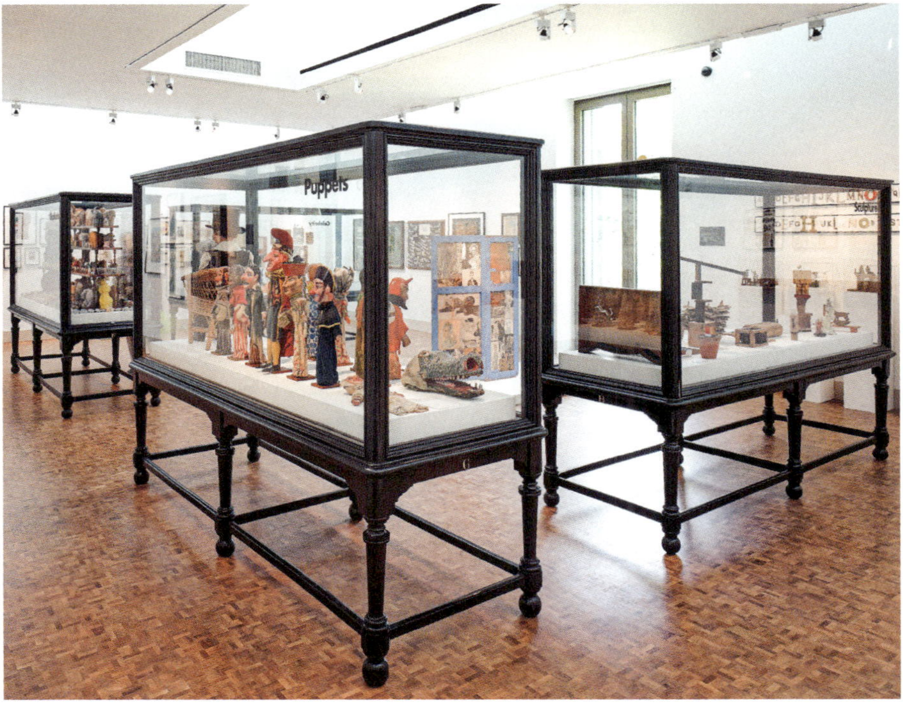
Puppets

TATE ST IVES

Art giant's seaside chapter

A tiny Cornish fishing town might seem like an odd choice of location for Tate's fourth national outpost, but St Ives' artistic ties run deep. Enticing artists since the late 19th century with its dramatic scenery and ever-changing light, the town has witnessed significant artistic developments at the hands, brushes and chisels of the prominent St Ives School, and remains a vital centre for modern and abstract British art. Opened in 1993 on the site of a former gasworks, Tate St Ives is a striking showcase for key works by Barbara Hepworth, Marlow Moss, Partou Zia and Alfred Wallis with its cliff-sunken galleries and breathtaking views. As with its larger urban siblings, the Tate supplements its permanent collection with a rich programme of changing exhibitions and activities for all ages. The tantalising top-floor restaurant, with its seasonal, local menu and spectacular ocean-view terrace, is not to be missed.

Porthmeor Beach, St Ives, TR26 1TG
tate.org.uk/visit/tate-st-ives

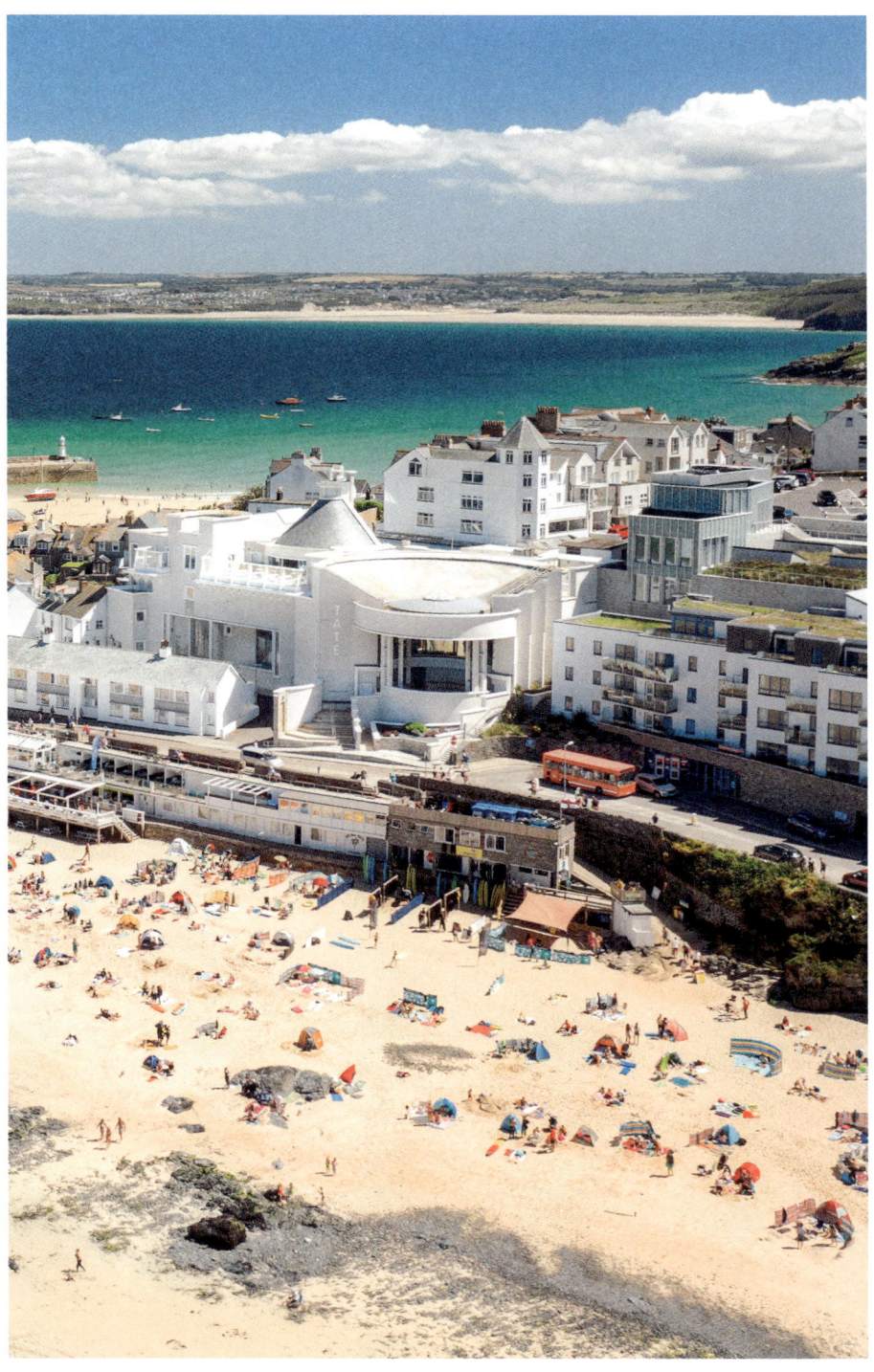

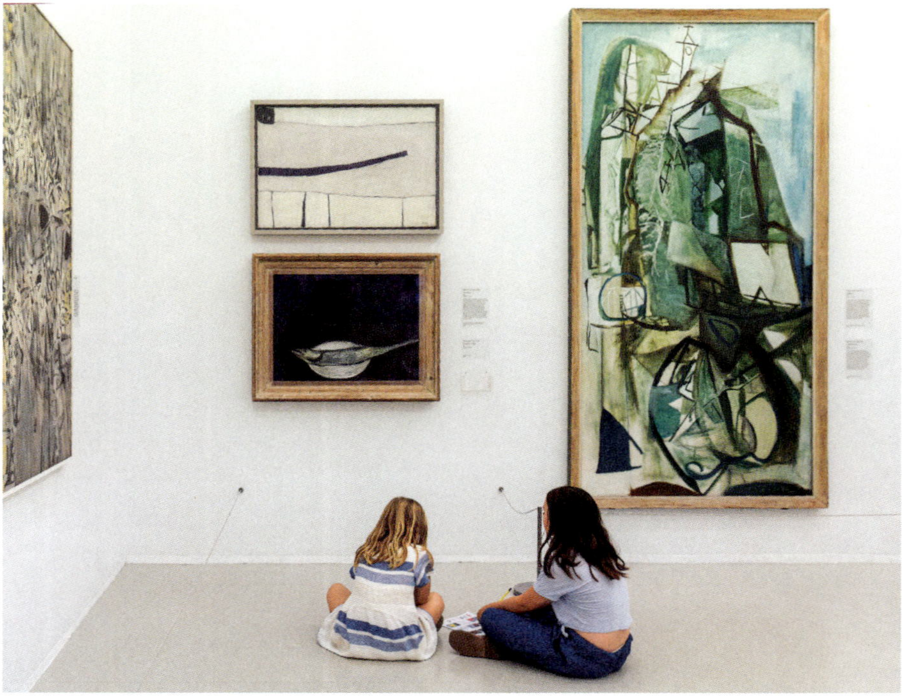

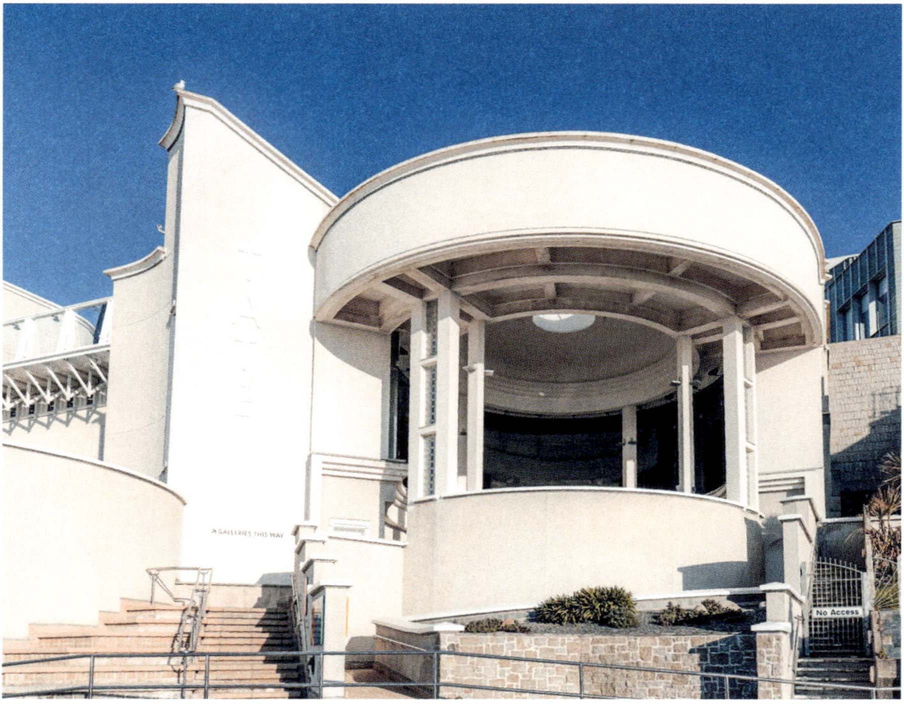
GALLERIES THIS WAY
No Access

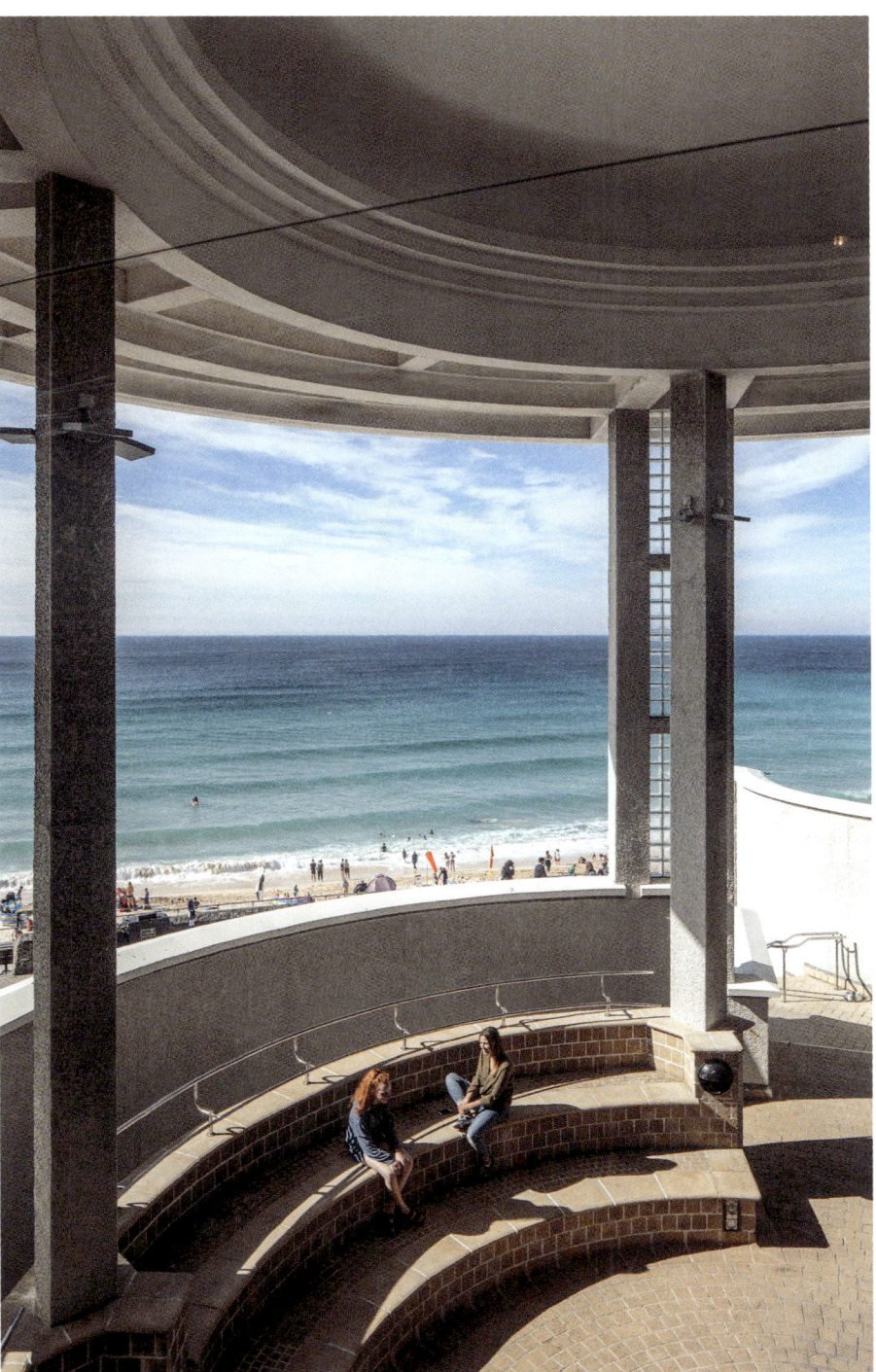

IKON

Birmingham bastion of art

Ikon by name, icon by nature, this central Birmingham gallery has provided the city with a cultural hub for more than six decades – despite only having a permanent home for three of them. Originally conceived as a programme of touring shows, Ikon retains much of its avant-garde spirit, favouring an eclectic and internationalist programme of temporary exhibitions from emerging and established artists. Olafur Eliasson, Julian Opie, Marcel Dzama and On Kawara are just some of the big names who've taken over the gallery since it opened in its current home – a commanding neo-Gothic former boarding school – in 1998, while especially 'ikonic' exhibitions have included dystopian architectural survey *Horror in the Modernist Block* and Krištof Kintera's surreal environmental study *THE END OF FUN!* Make time for a leisurely brunch stop at the in-house Yorks Cafe, where oozy Arabian buttered eggs and spiced Persian shakshuka await hungry art fans.

1 Oozells Square, Brindleyplace, Birmingham, B1 2HS
ikon-gallery.org

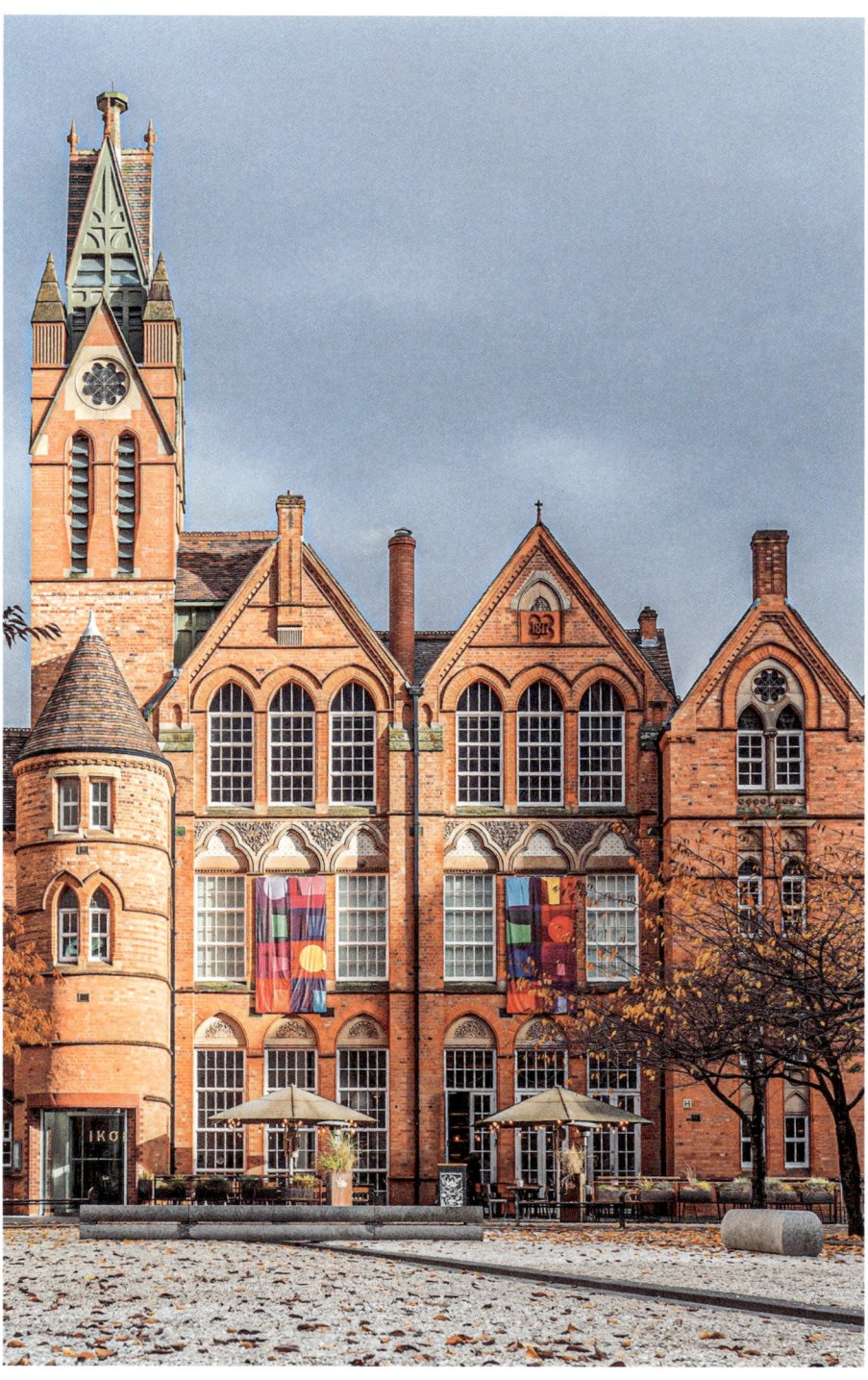

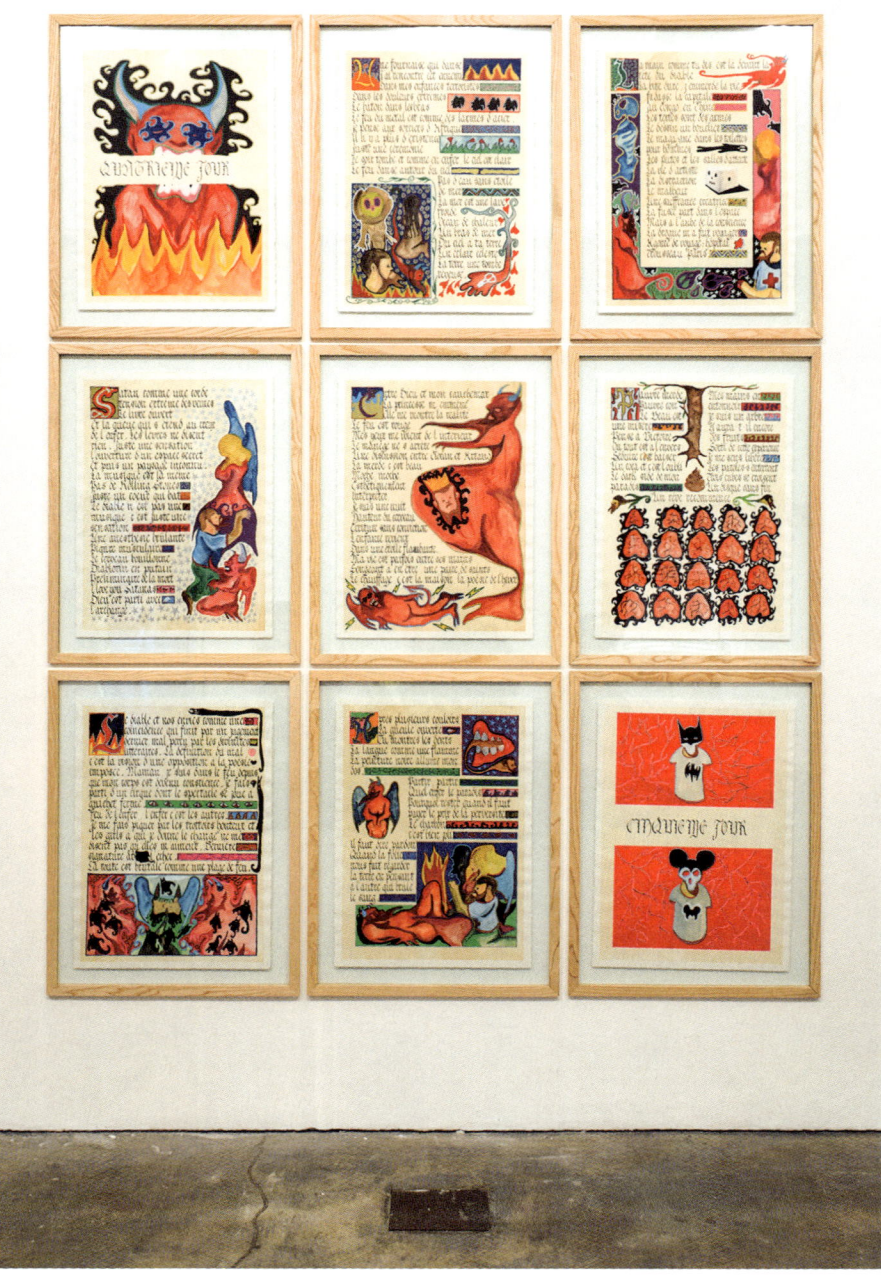

Above: *Seven Days Hotel*, Fabien Verschaere
Opposite above: *Strangelets*, Luke Routledge
Opposite below: *Structure de correction, table de débat*, Niek van de Steeg

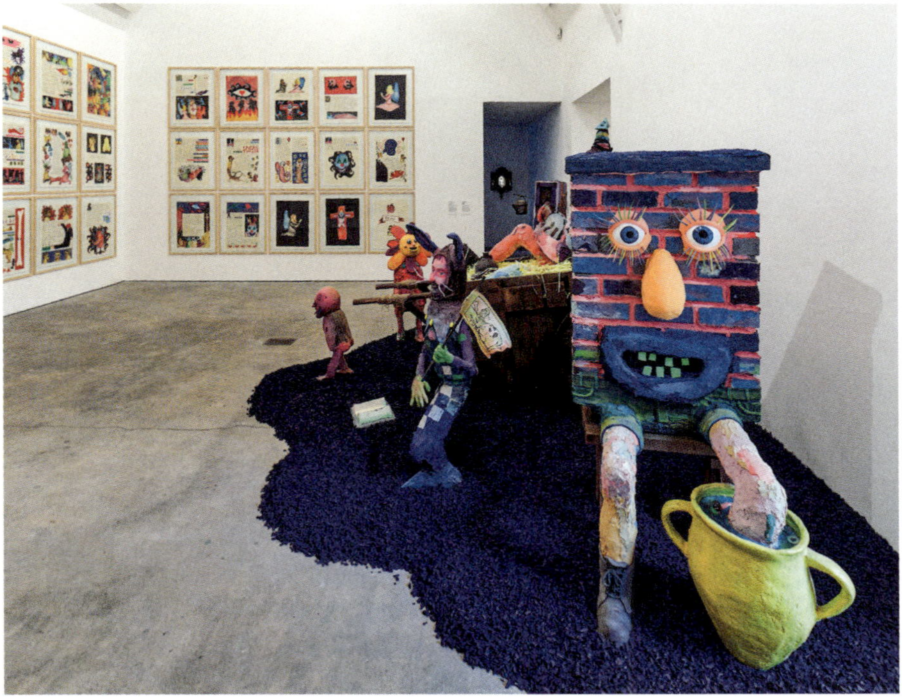

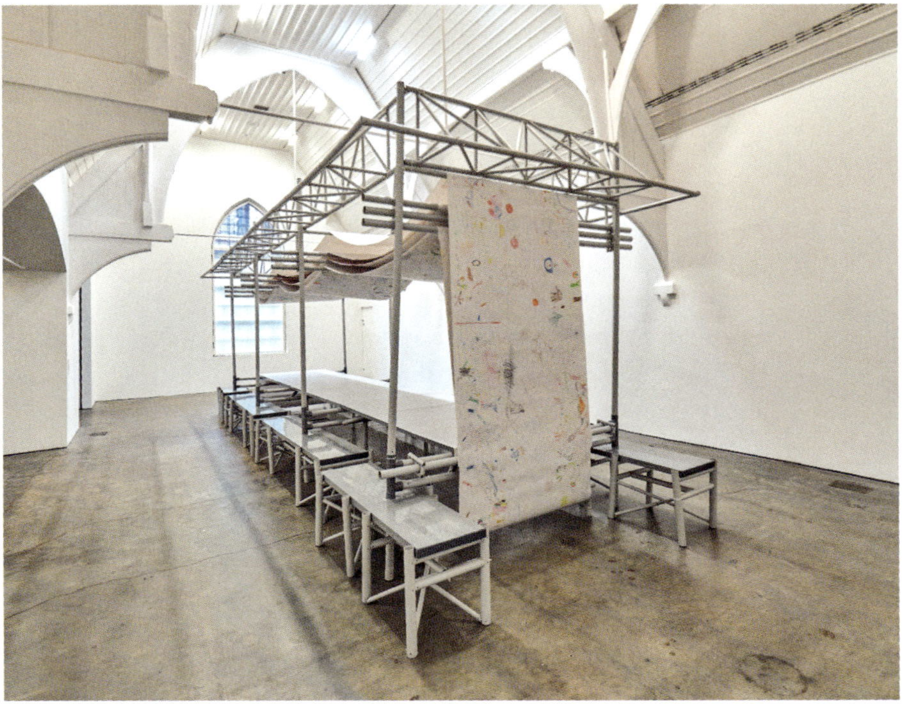

COMPTON VERNEY

Eclectic artworks scattered across historic estate

A life-size horse and cart waits patiently, marrow-laden, on the lawn. Elsewhere, a huge spider stands poised, as if ready to spin a gargantuan web, while a quartet of sphinxes looks on. It might sound like a roll call for the world's most eccentric zoo, but these fantastic beasts are actually part of the alfresco sculpture collection at Compton Verney, a Warwickshire mansion-turned-gallery whose countless treasures spill enticingly into its grounds, designed by Capability Brown. Annual outdoor installations, such as Morag Myerscough's technicolour *The Village*, and a chance to get hands-on with power tools courtesy of constructive play wizards Woodland Tribe make this gallery a family favourite – and might deceive you into thinking you needn't venture indoors, but there's plenty more to explore beyond the Georgian facade. Don't miss the collection that inspired London transport textile designer Enid Marx, the UK's largest collection of British folk art and the gallery's enigmatic – and recently acquired – painting, *Two Women Wearing Cosmetic Patches*.

Compton Verney, CV35 9HZ
comptonverney.org.uk

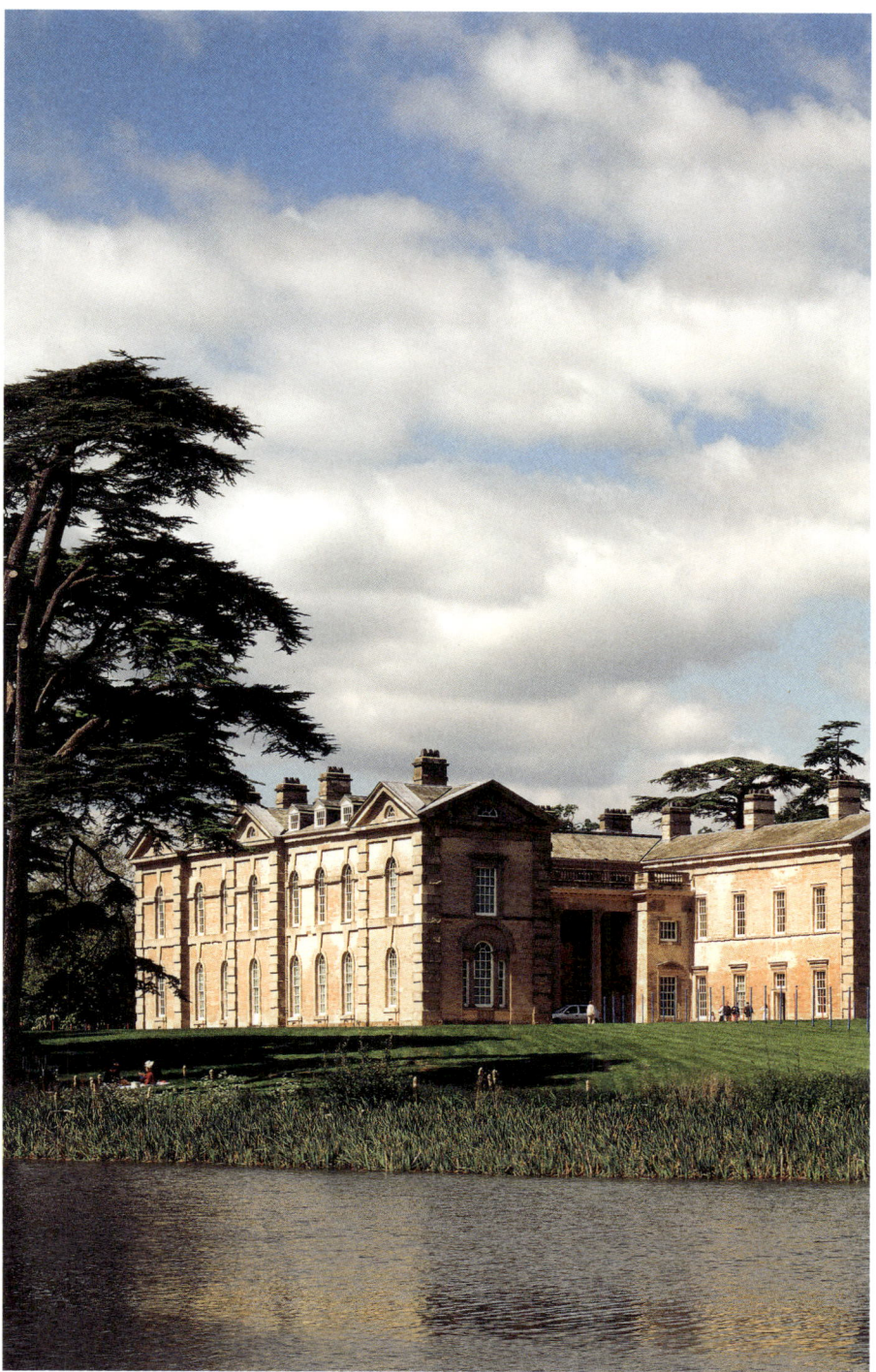

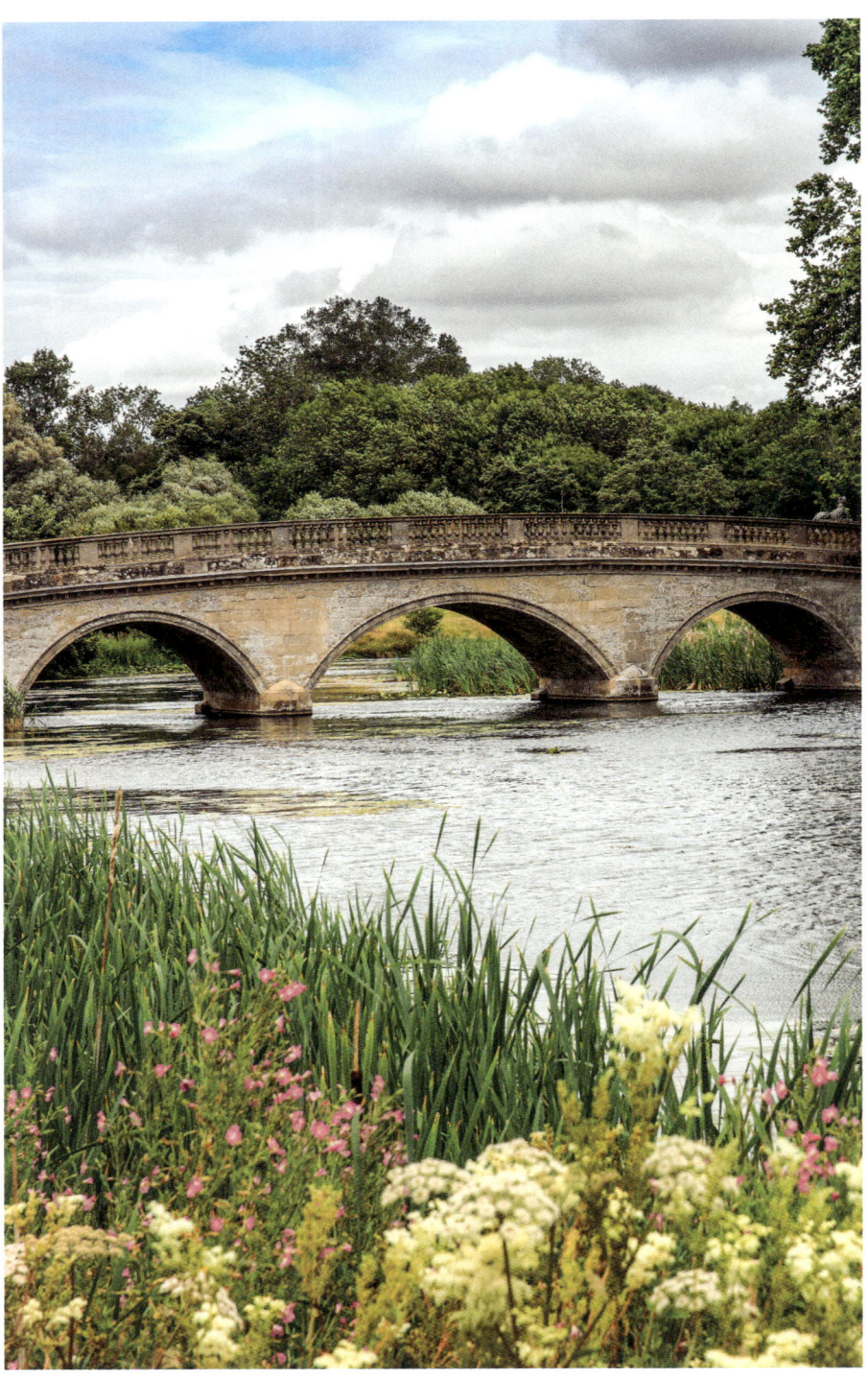

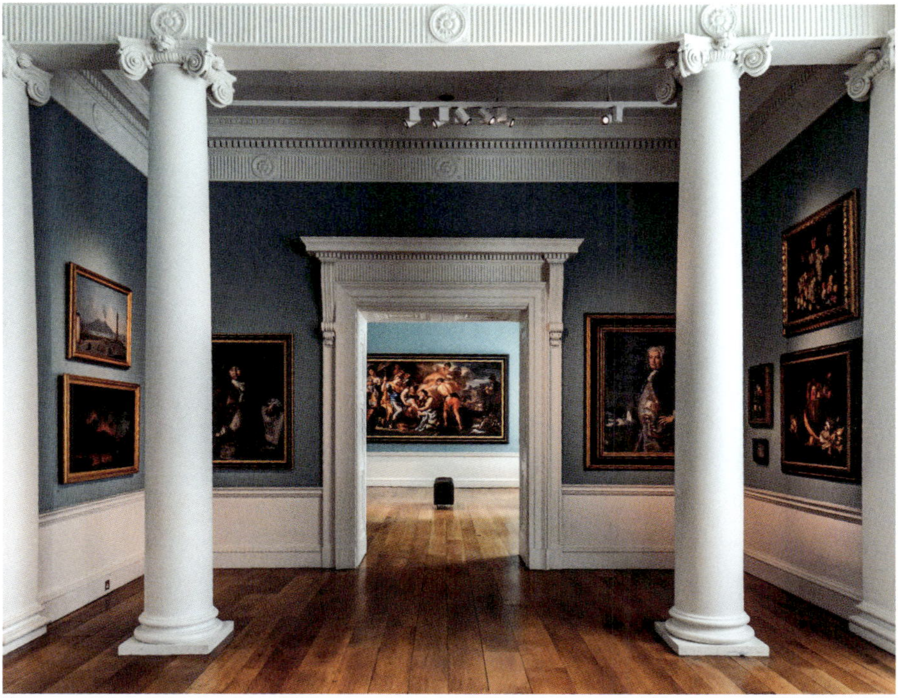

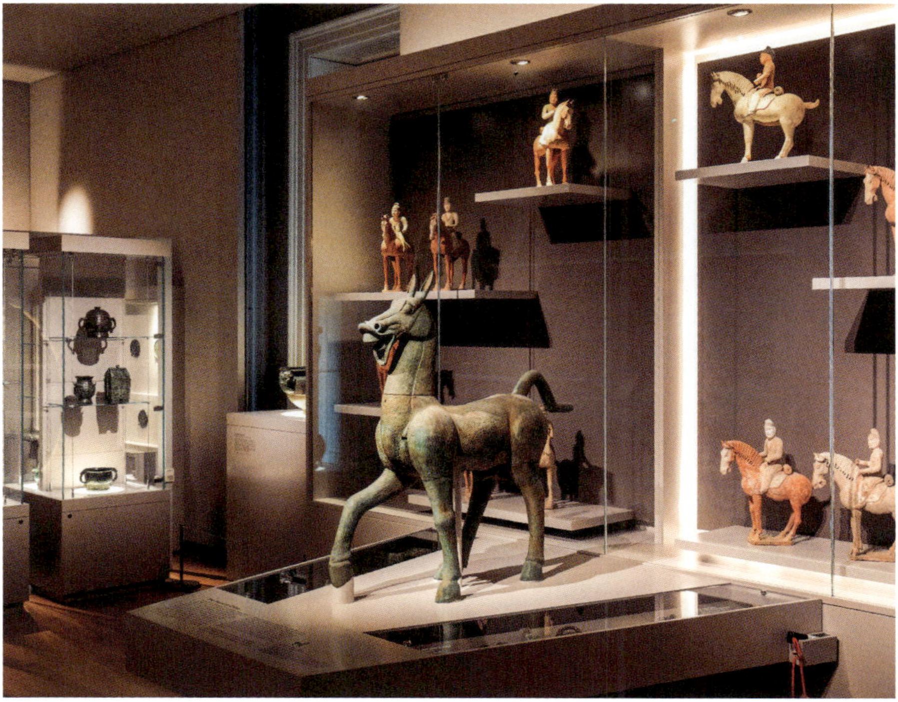

NOTTINGHAM CONTEMPORARY

Architectural landmark with ambitious programme

It might be contemporary by name, but this striking gallery pulses with history, occupying a site that at various times has housed a Saxon fort, a medieval town hall and the beating heart of the Victorian hosiery industry. Oddly pretty in lace-patterned concrete (a reference to the aforementioned industry, after which the city's Lace Market neighbourhood was named), this RIBA award-winning, Tardis-like gallery recalls artists' studios in 1960s New York while offering a suitably theatrical backdrop to its diverse international programme. Unafraid to take risks, by its own admission, the centre has hosted everything from a celebration of the work of legendary jazz musician and Afro-Futurist Sun Ra to a children's playground dreamt up by Italian-Brazilian architect Lina Bo Bardi, via a major survey of cave art. Swing by the gift shop for design-led treats and save the date for its popular print and craft fairs.

Weekday Cross, Nottingham, NG1 2GB

nottinghamcontemporary.org

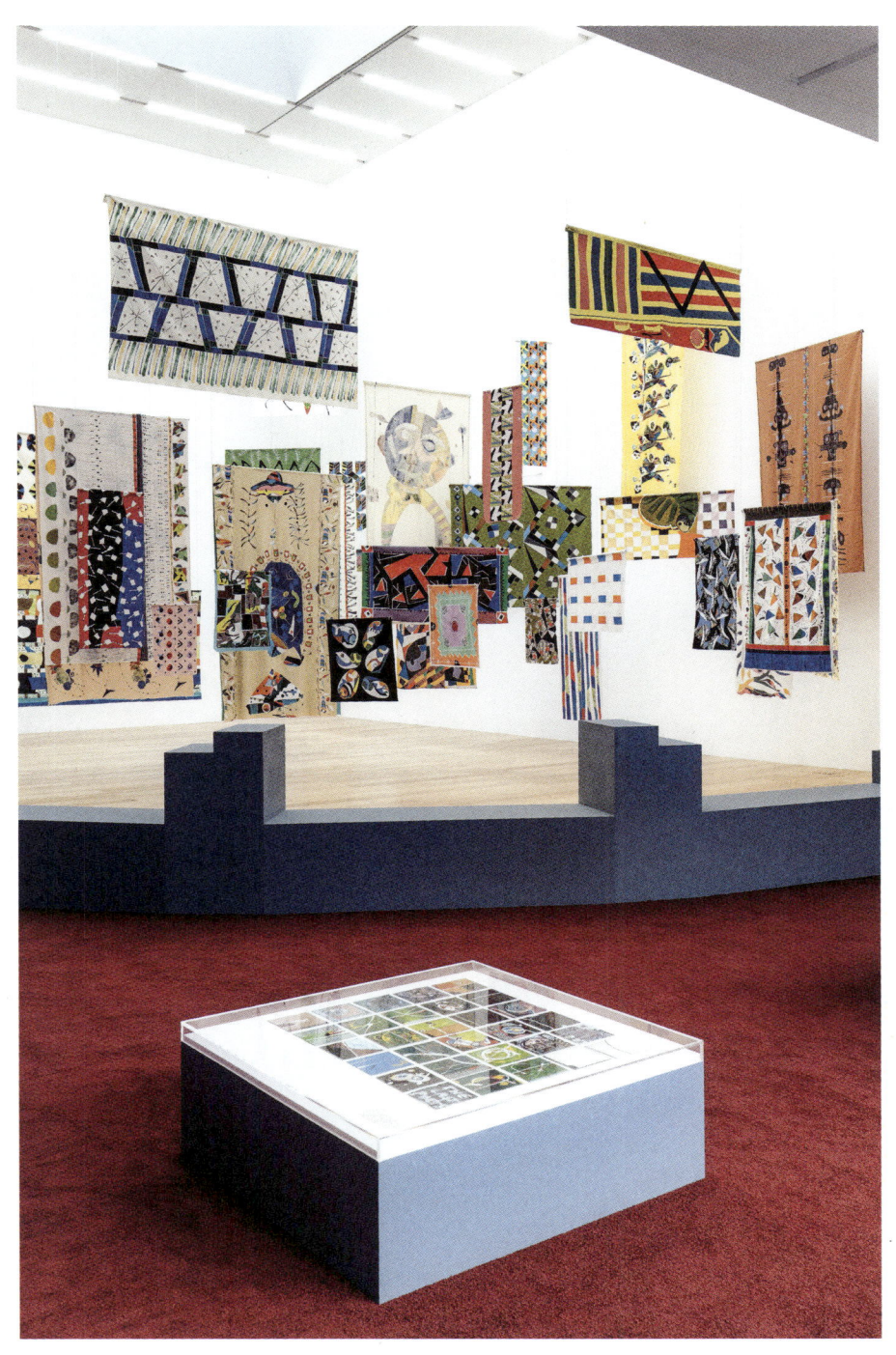

Two Steps at a Time, Hamid Zénati

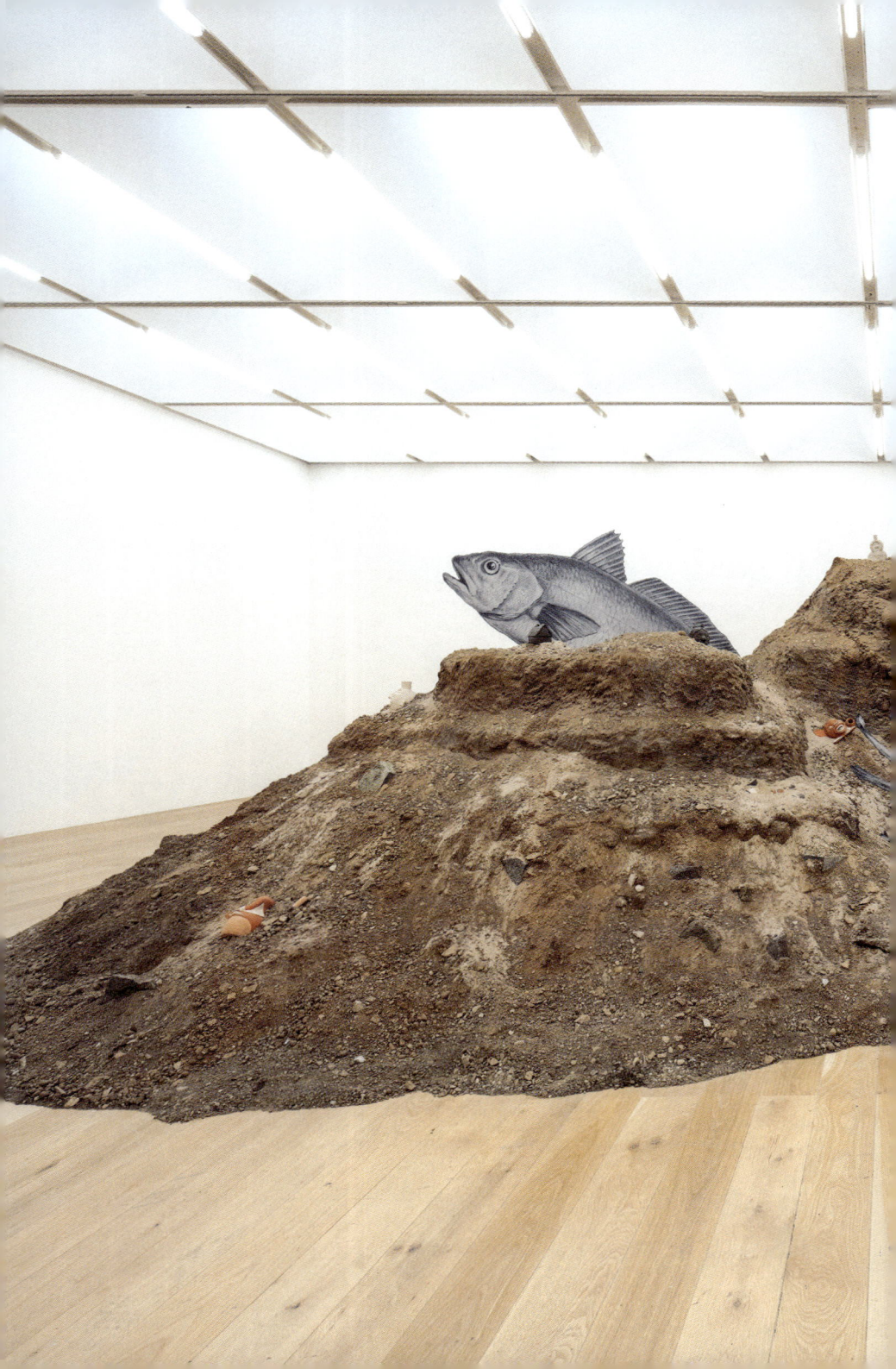

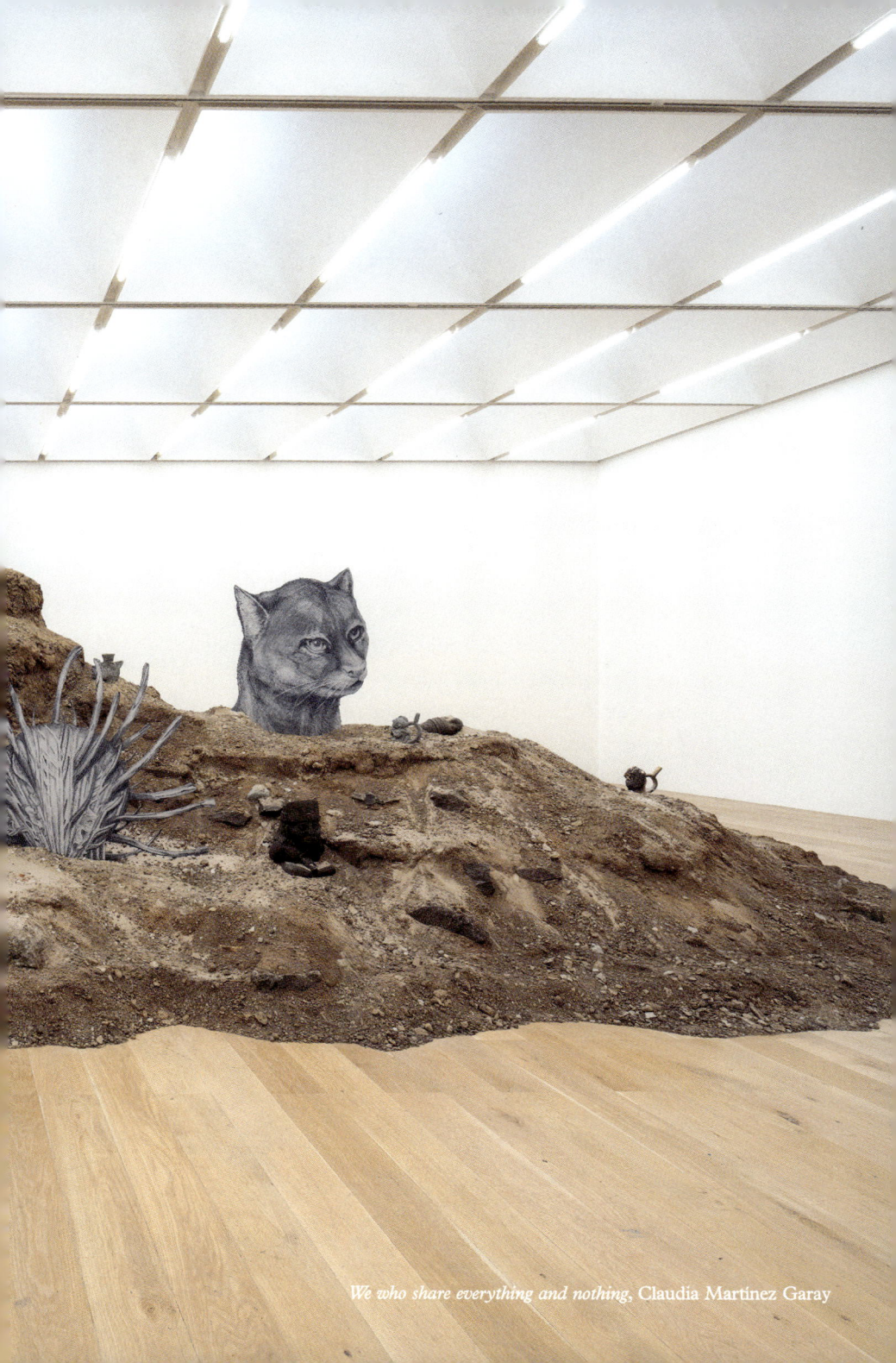

We who share everything and nothing, Claudia Martinez Garay

NATIONAL MUSEUM CARDIFF

Glittering art hoard within Welsh history giant

Bypass this national treasure's majestic natural history galleries, resisting the lure of the resident dinosaurs, woolly mammoths and open-mouthed basking shark, and you're in for a seriously impressive art experience. Hidden away on the museum's first floor, its 15 capacious art galleries are home to one of Europe's most prized collections, representing half a millennium of staggering human creativity. Works by Old Masters such as Cima da Conegliano and Jan van de Cappelle hang alongside examples by Wales' most notable artists – from Kyffin Williams' landscapes to Augustus John's portrait of Dylan Thomas. Perhaps most pertinent is the museum's jaw-dropping hoard of Impressionist and post-Impressionist art, featuring works from Monet's *Water Lilies* series, Renoir's life-sized *La Parisienne* and *Rain – Auvers*, one of the last ever paintings by Van Gogh.

Cathays Park, Cardiff, CF10 3NP
museum.wales/cardiff

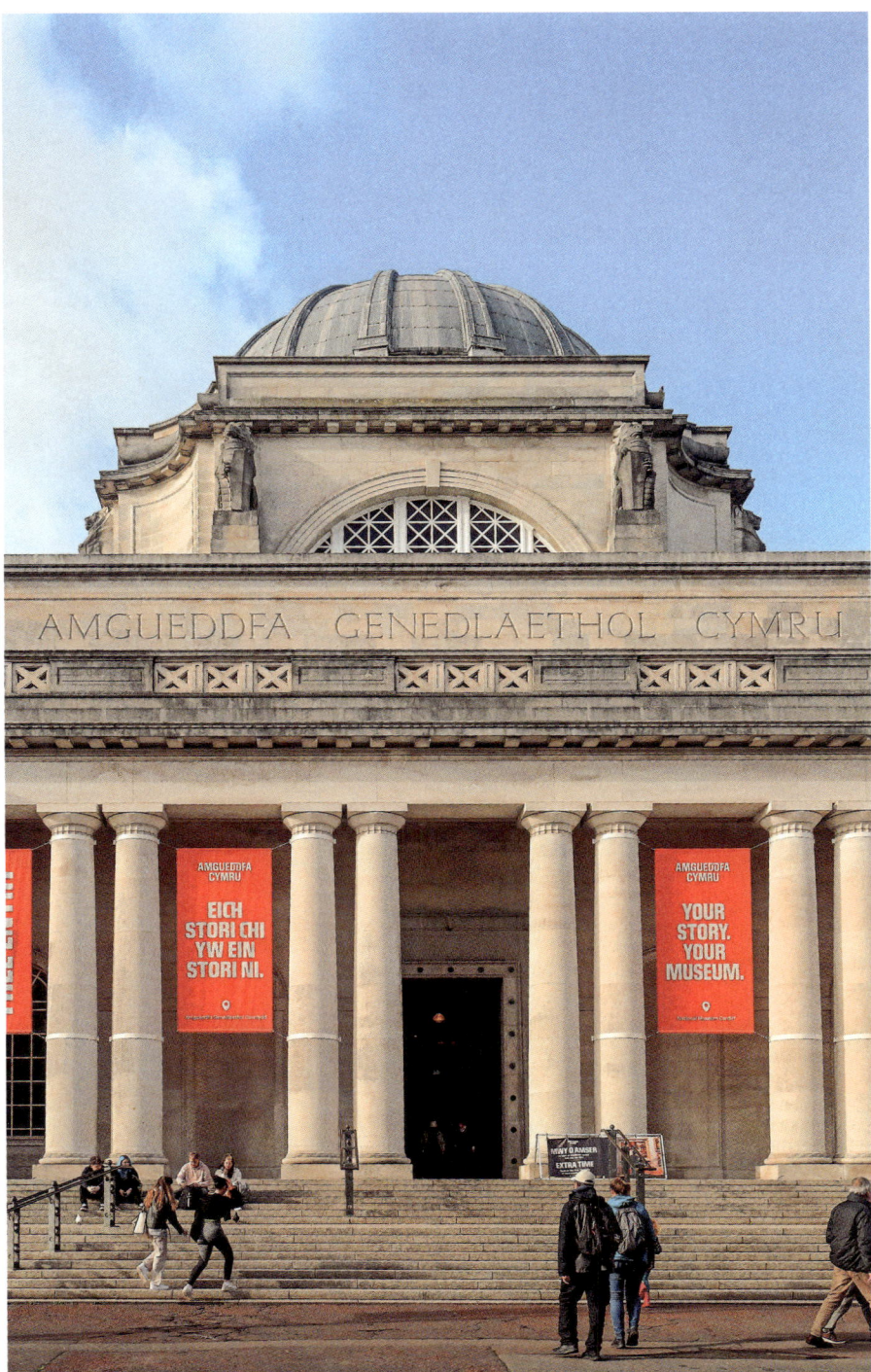

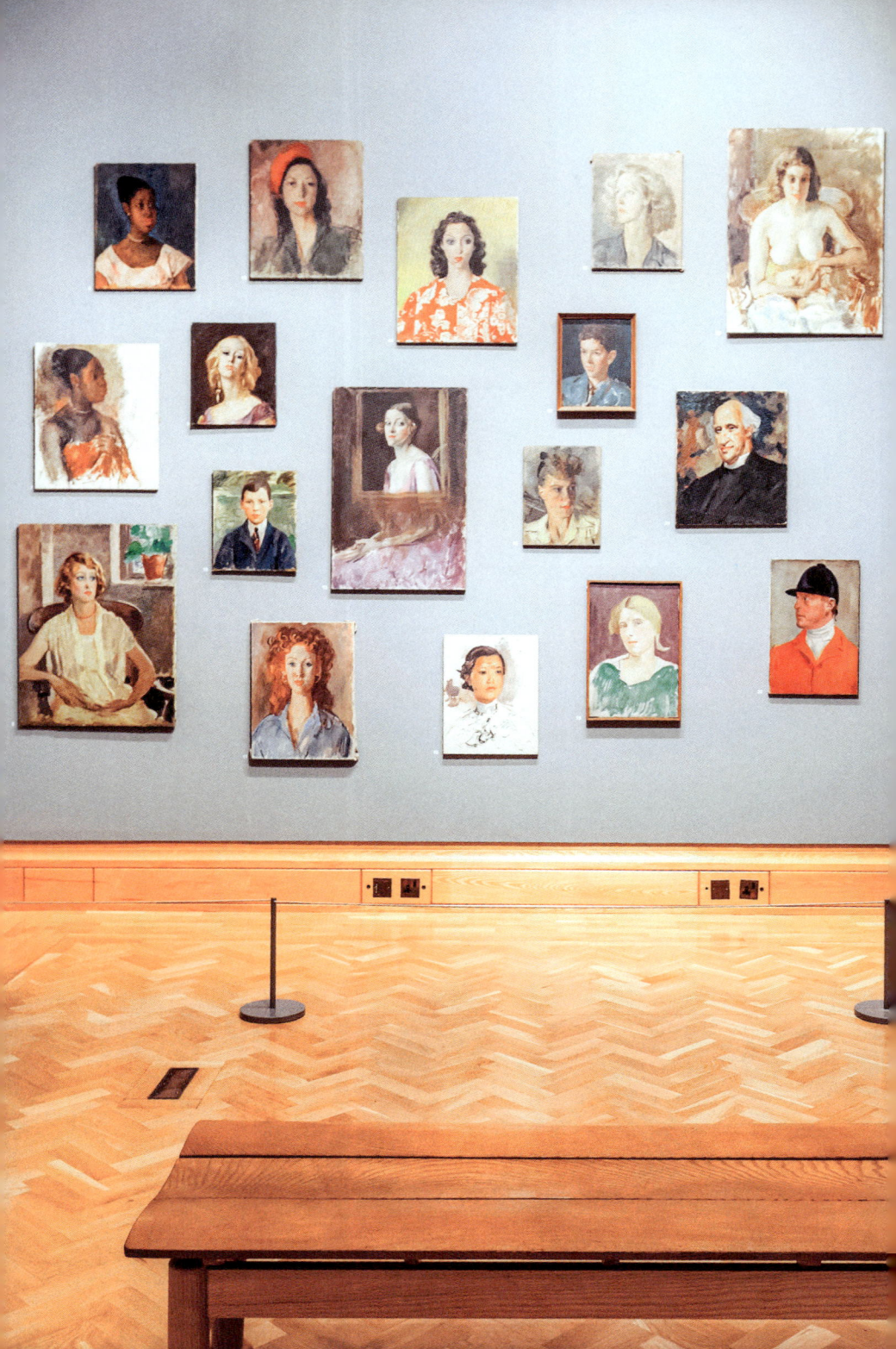

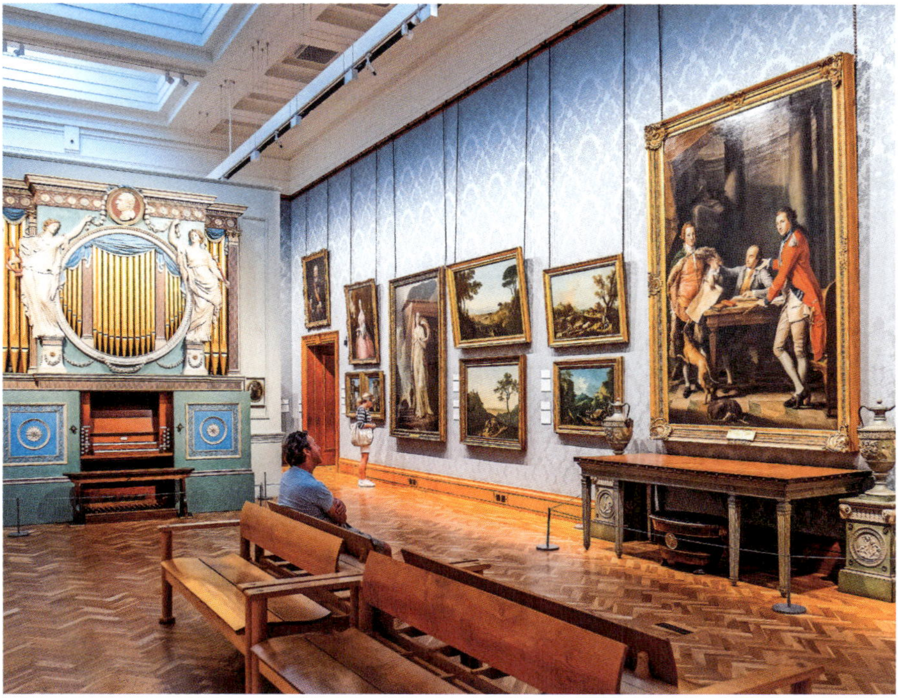

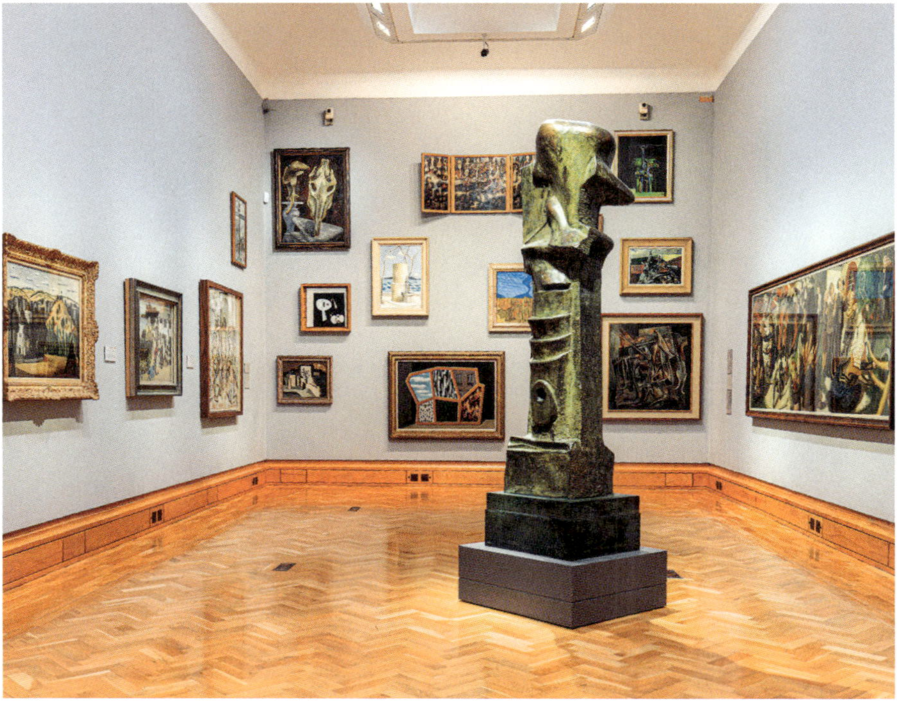

MOSTYN

Pioneering cultural hub

Beyond its Edwardian brick facade, everything about Wales' largest contemporary gallery feels progressive. Founded in 1901 by Lady Augusta Mostyn to showcase the work of the Gwynedd Ladies' Art Society members – all of whom had been spurned by other local art societies based on their gender – Mostyn became the world's first gallery to exclusively exhibit work by women artists. Today, the gallery champions art by all, but continues to amplify the voices of underrepresented groups and emerging talent, with conceptual work often given particular attention. Noteworthy exhibitions in recent years have included a display of local artist Cerith Wyn Evans' intricate neon sculptures and a series of shows exploring the gallery's past lives as a chemist, a piano showroom and even a rifle club. Seek out the brilliant cafe, whose name reclaims the gallery's lost 'Oriel' prefix, and you categorically cannot miss the Dominic Williams-designed Brutalist staircase.

12 Vaughan Street, Llandudno, LL30 1AB
mostyn.org

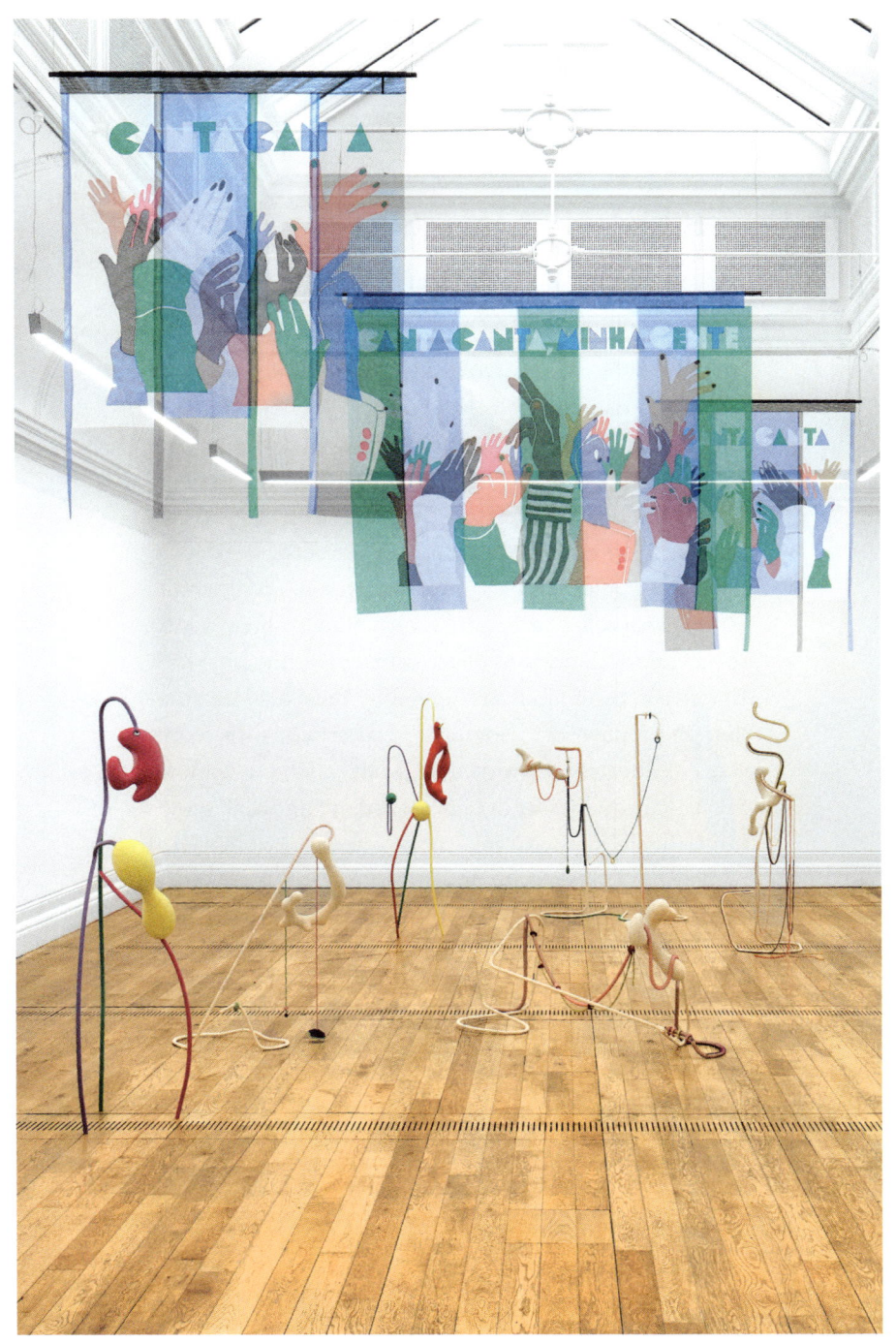

Roda Viva, Vanessa da Silva

ORIEL DAVIES GALLERY

Welsh contemporary art space

It might be a medium-sized gallery in a medium-sized town, slap bang in the middle of Mid Wales, but there's nothing middling about Oriel Davies. Purpose-built in 1967 to a design by pioneering low-energy architect Alex Gordon, using a legacy from legendary Welsh art-collecting sisters Margaret and Gwendoline Davies, the since-extended gallery boasts a dynamic programme of contemporary art exhibitions across three sunny spaces, alongside a zero-waste cafe and quirky gift shop. Its eclectic exhibitions are united by their fearless cura-tion and tendency to spotlight local artists, with recent shows featuring the psychologically charged work of Shani Rhys James and Laura Ford's whimsical sculp-tures. In addition to showcasing work by established names, the gallery is committed to nurturing emerging artists – its Test Bed space proving a crucial stepping stone in the careers of landscape painter Eleri Mills and mixed-media artist Carwyn Evans, among many other fledgling talents.

The Park, Newtown, SY16 2NZ
orieldavies.org

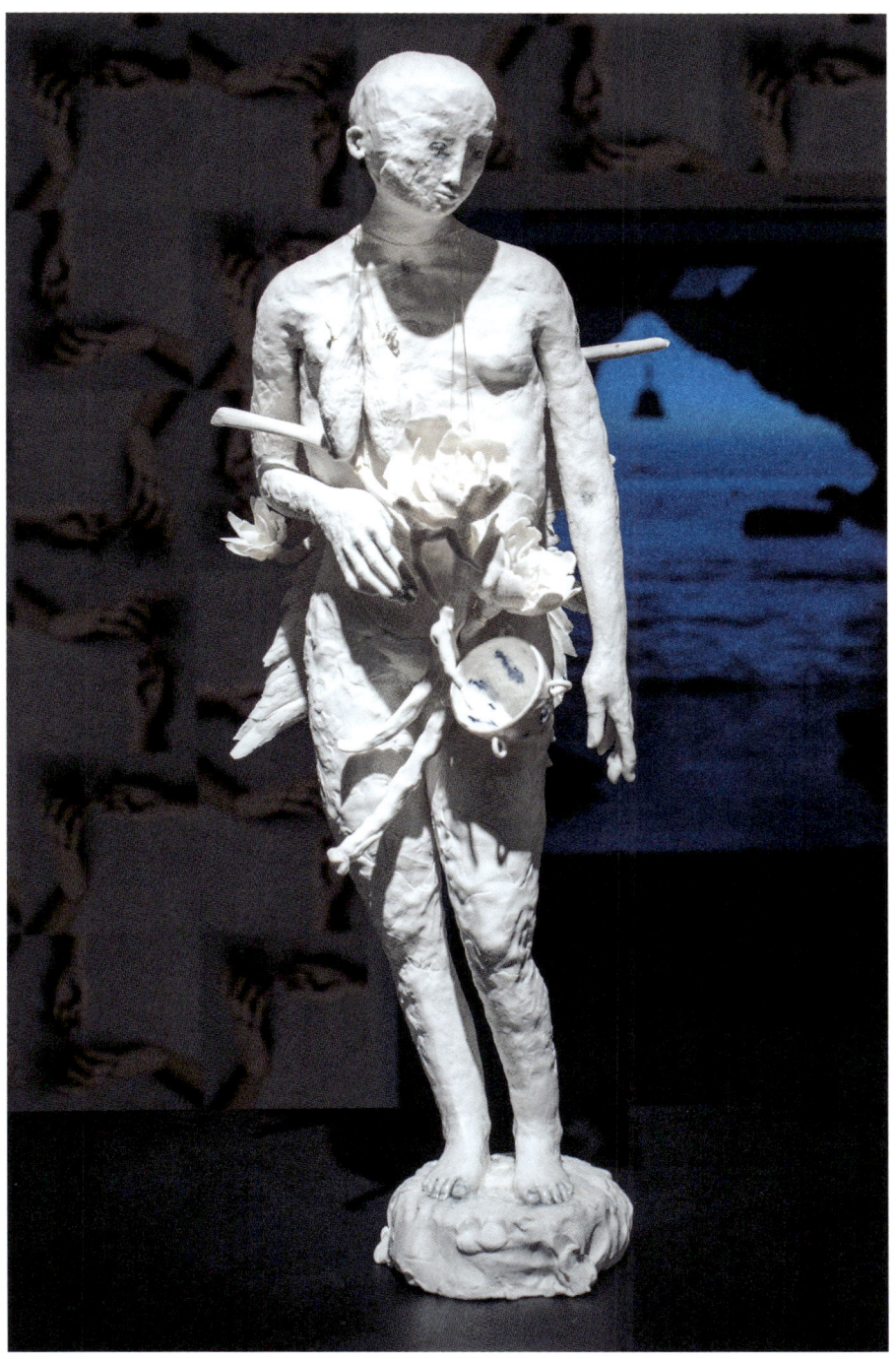

Pilgrim, Claire Curneen

KIELDER FOREST ART & ARCHITECTURE TRAIL

Large-scale works in lakeside location

Confounding mazes, underground burrows and cosy shelters are just some of the ultra-large-scale works you'll encounter on this spectacular outdoor trail, which traces the 27-mile periphery of the UK's largest artificial lake, Kielder Water. While almost impossible to complete on foot in a day, clusters of artworks on the reservoir's south-western and north-western edges allow for shorter – but nonetheless exhilarating – walks, while the full route is perfectly suited for bike rides. Many of the 20-plus works invite an immersive experience, whether you're getting lost in the *Minotaur* maze or meditating on clouds from the *Kielder Skyspace*. Others, such as *Shadow* – which uses Whinstone, earth and sandstone to echo the textures of the surrounding beech trees – offer a purely scenic (but no less moving) encounter. The website offers downloadable trail maps, or you can simply begin at one of the two visitor centres and see where the water takes you.

Kielder, Hexham, NE48 1ER
visitkielder.com

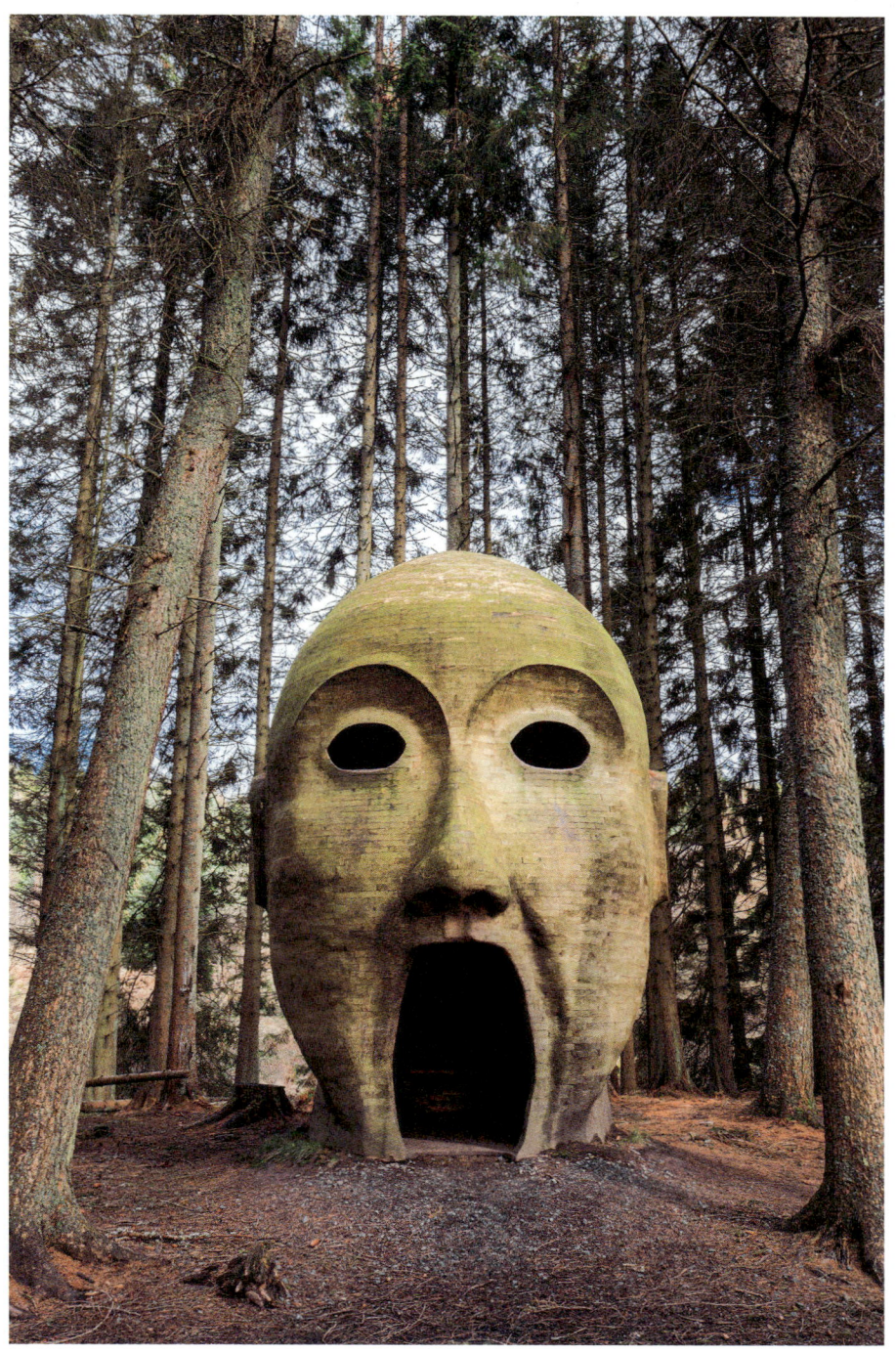

Silvas Capitalis, SIMPARCH

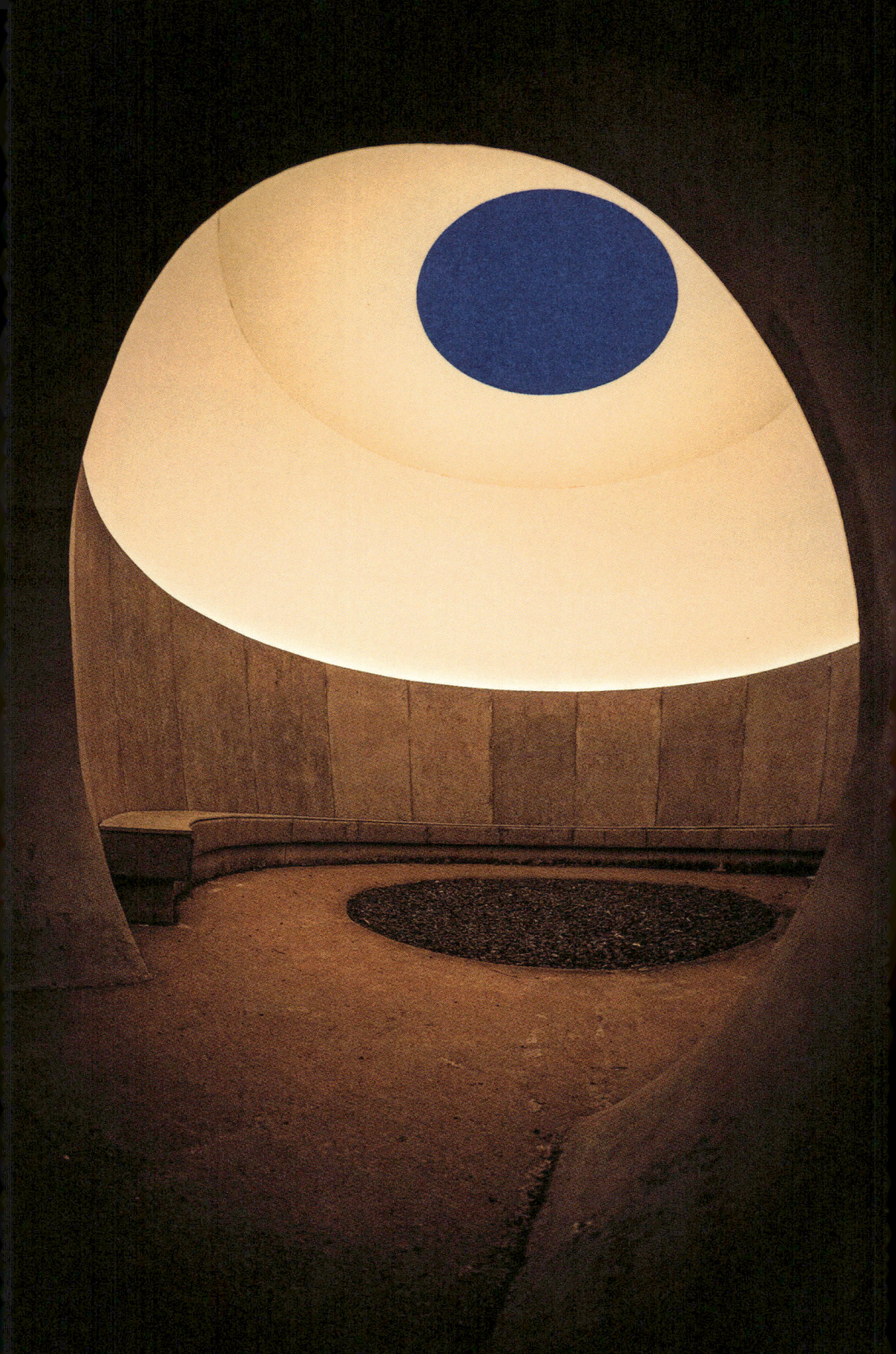

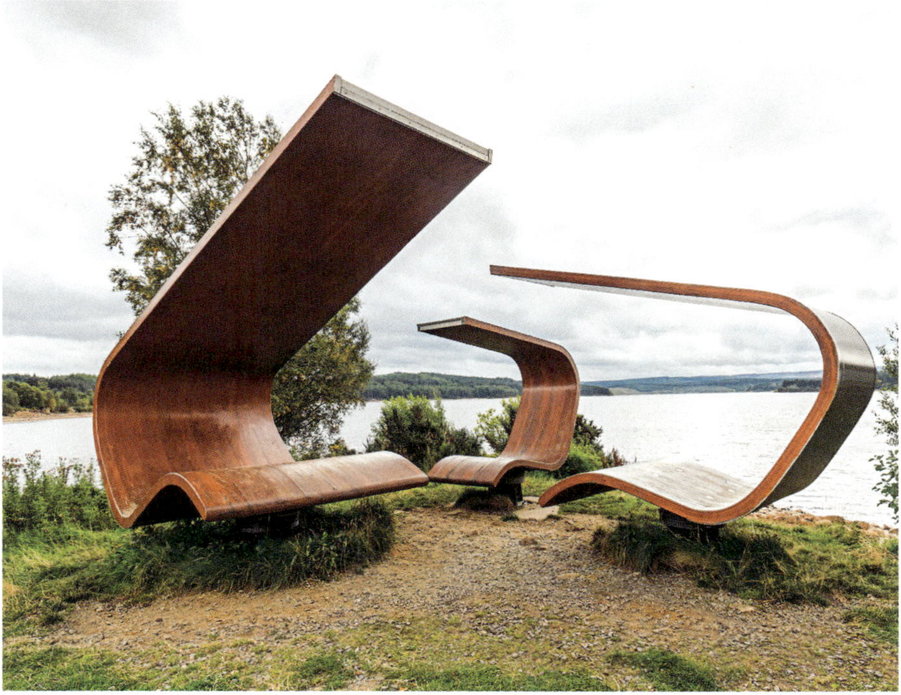

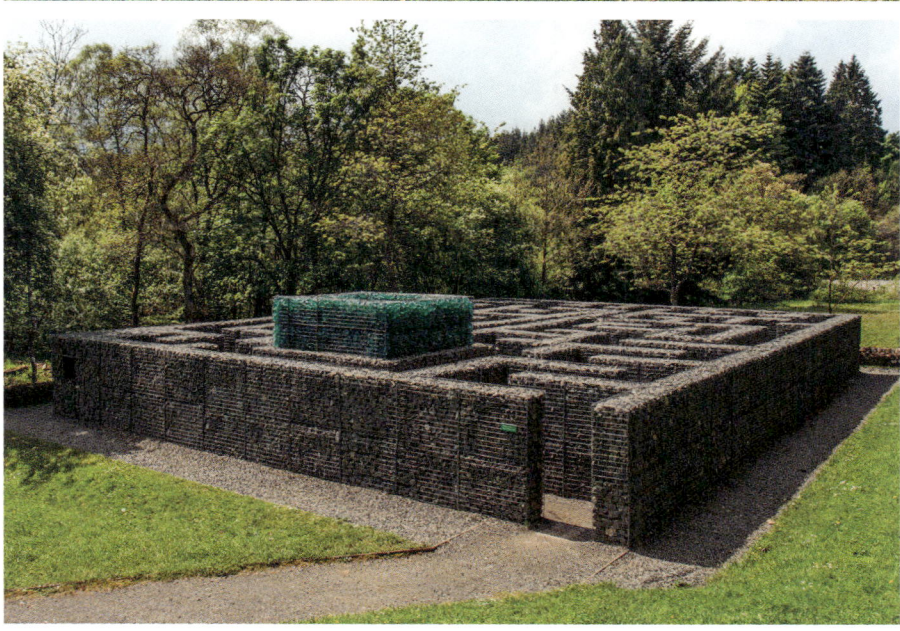

Opposite: *Kielder Skyspace*, James Turrell
Above: *Janus Chairs*, Ryder Architecture
Below: *Minotaur*, Nick Coombe & Shona Kitchen

ANGEL OF THE NORTH

Celestial colossus on edge of A1

Is it a bird? Is it a plane? Antony Gormley's famed motorway messenger might appear more industrial than celestial, with its rusted steel body and wingspan, which is bigger than a Boeing 757's. It's most often glimpsed in a flash from fast-moving vehicles – but stop the car, climb the hill and stand in the shadow of the so-called Gateshead Flasher's outstretched appendages, and you might experience something approaching the sublime. Like many of Gormley's works, the angel is modelled on the artist's body and takes a characteristically featureless form, refuting any religious affiliation while encouraging spectators to attach their own identity and meaning. Said to be the largest angel sculpture on the planet – as well as the first significant example of gigantism in British sculpture – the 200-tonne titan speaks to Gateshead's past and future. It honours the sacrifice of the miners who worked beneath the site for two centuries and provides an otherworldly focus for viewers' hopes and dreams – and was an unwitting catalyst for the area's cultural regeneration.

Durham Road, Low Eighton, Gateshead, NE9 7TY

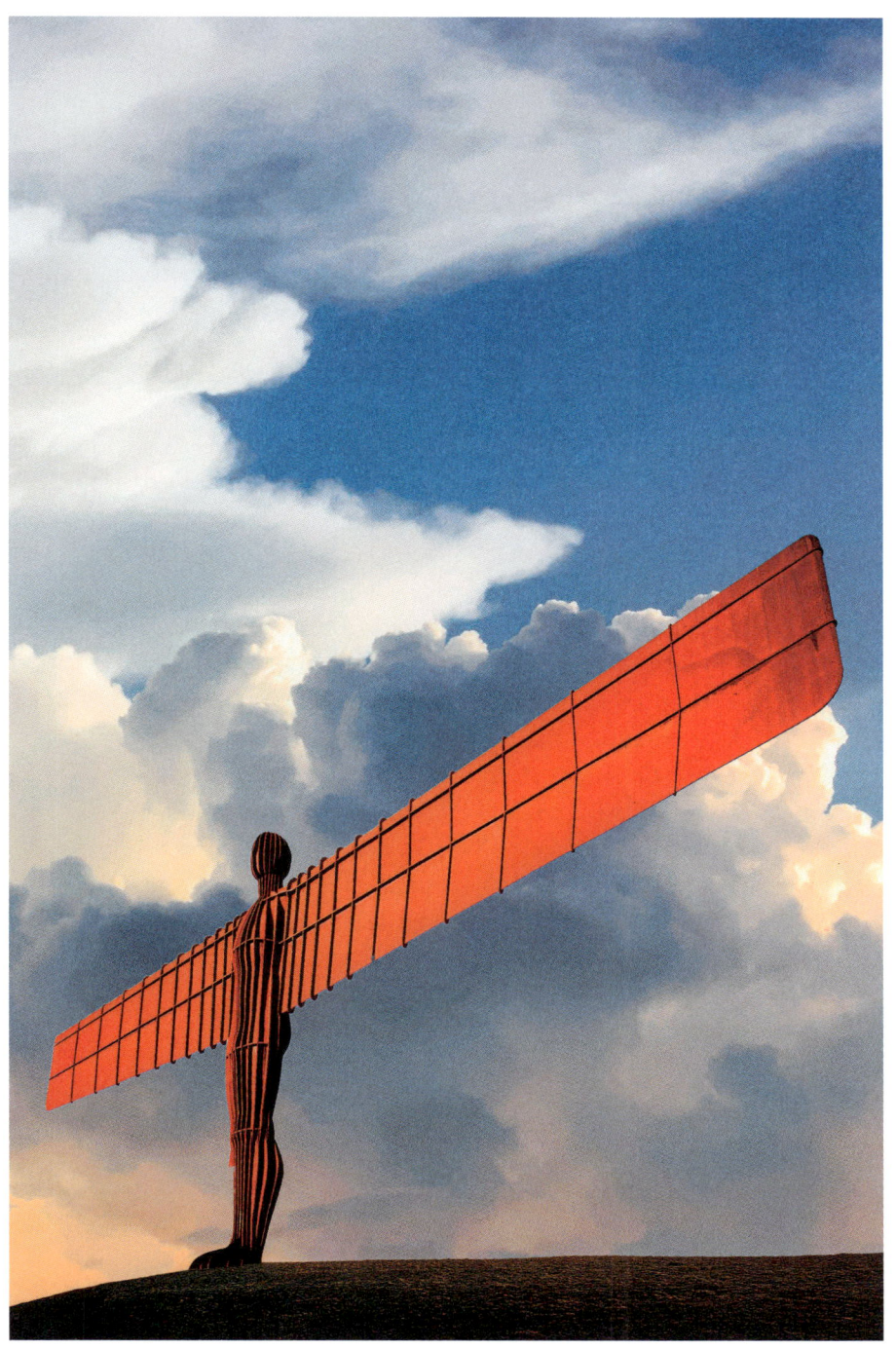

Angel of the North, Antony Gormley

GRIZEDALE FOREST

Bewitching sculpture trail

The Lake District isn't short of photogenic scenery, but the ten square miles that make up Grizedale Forest are positively spellbinding, with tranquil lakes, soaring fells and striking sculptures all tussling for attention. An art lover's paradise since 1977, Grizedale has hosted several hundred sculptures over the decades, with many earlier works having since disappeared into the forest vegetation. Today, around 50 sculptures can be glimpsed across eight distinctive trails spanning family-friendly strolls, drawn-out treks and strenuous hill climbs. For the former, take the Ridding Wood Trail, where Greyworld's *Clockwork Forest* will delight little ones with its wind-up musical trees. Or, if time is on your side, follow the Silurian Way path past Robert Koenig's pensive figures, Richard Harris's robust *Dry Stone Passage* and Gregory Scott-Gurner's incongruously suburban *Please Close the Gate (Picket Fence)*. Pick up a trail guide before you set off or prepare to get *very* lost.

Grizedale Forest, Hawkshead, LA22 0QJ
grizedalesculpture.org

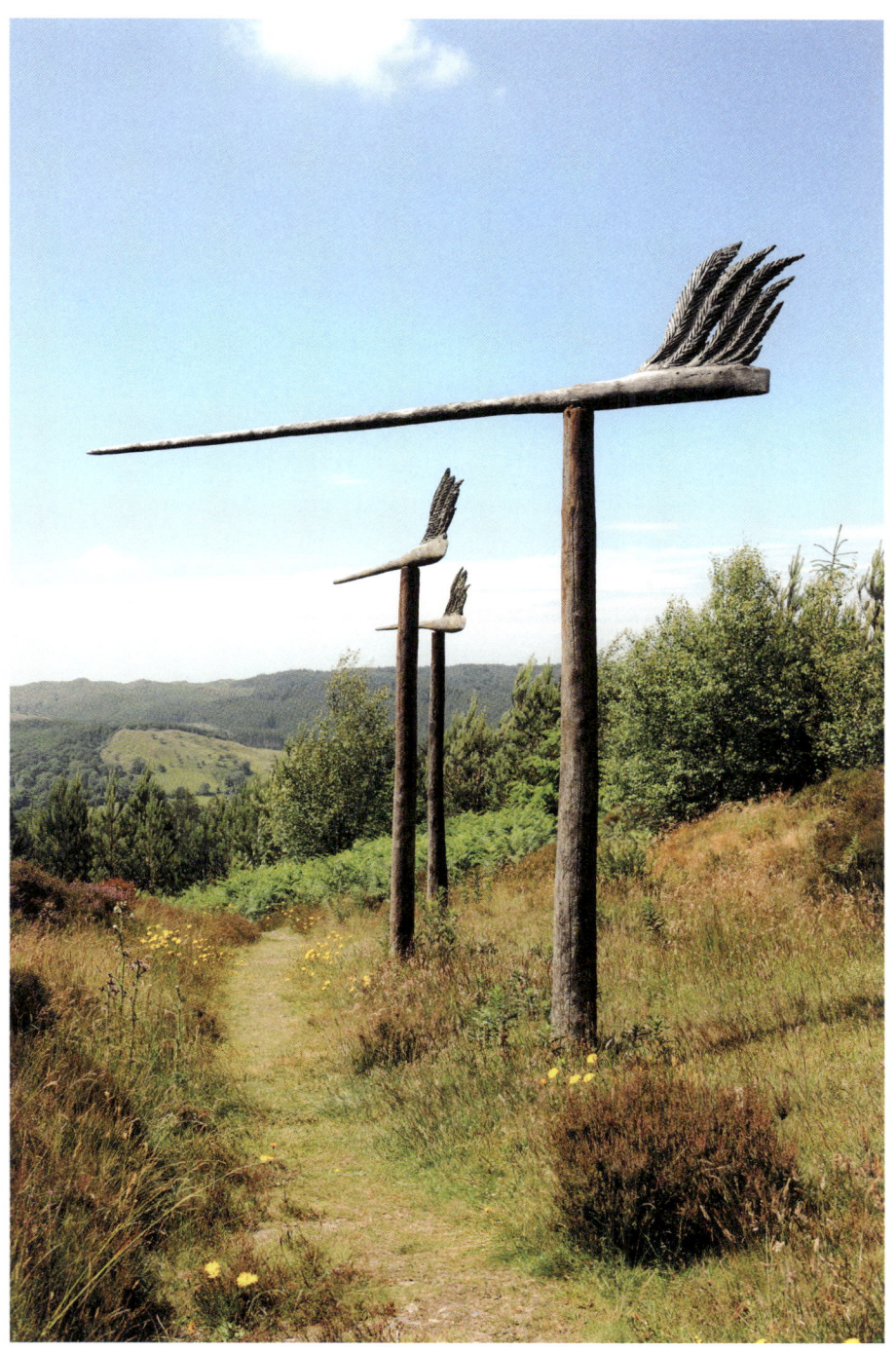

Wind Thrust, Jony Easterby

WHITWORTH ART GALLERY

Rotating exhibits in serene surroundings

Whether you like your art from the 21st century or prefer it with a healthy dose of history, wish to admire it within four walls or would rather enjoy it alfresco, there's something for everyone at this glorious gallery – the first in England to open inside a public park. While no artworks are on permanent display, the Whitworth's hoard is made up of an astonishing 60,000 works, with highpoints including Jacob Epstein's voluptuous *Genesis* and William Blake's dramatic *The Ancient of Days*, along with the largest collection of Outsider Art in a UK public gallery. The park-side location is significant not only for the verdant views afforded by its colossal windows – in particular from the superb cafe, serving hot sandwiches that are works of art in their own right – but for its ability to host a tranquil art garden, whose contemplative works include Nate Lowman's bronze (and thus undying) snowman, and a hoax commemorative plaque by Cornelia Parker.

Oxford Road, Manchester, M15 6ER
whitworth.manchester.ac.uk

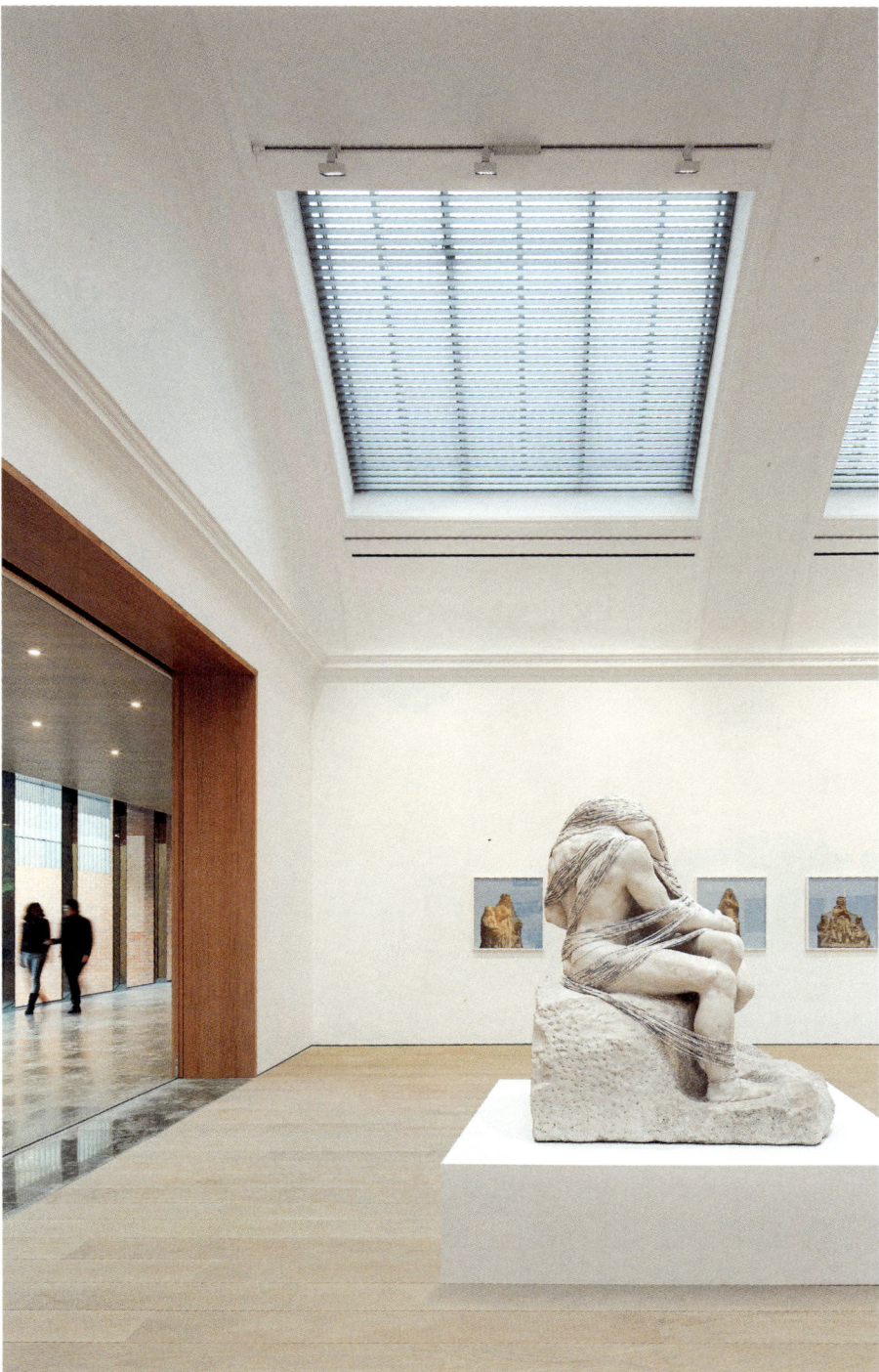

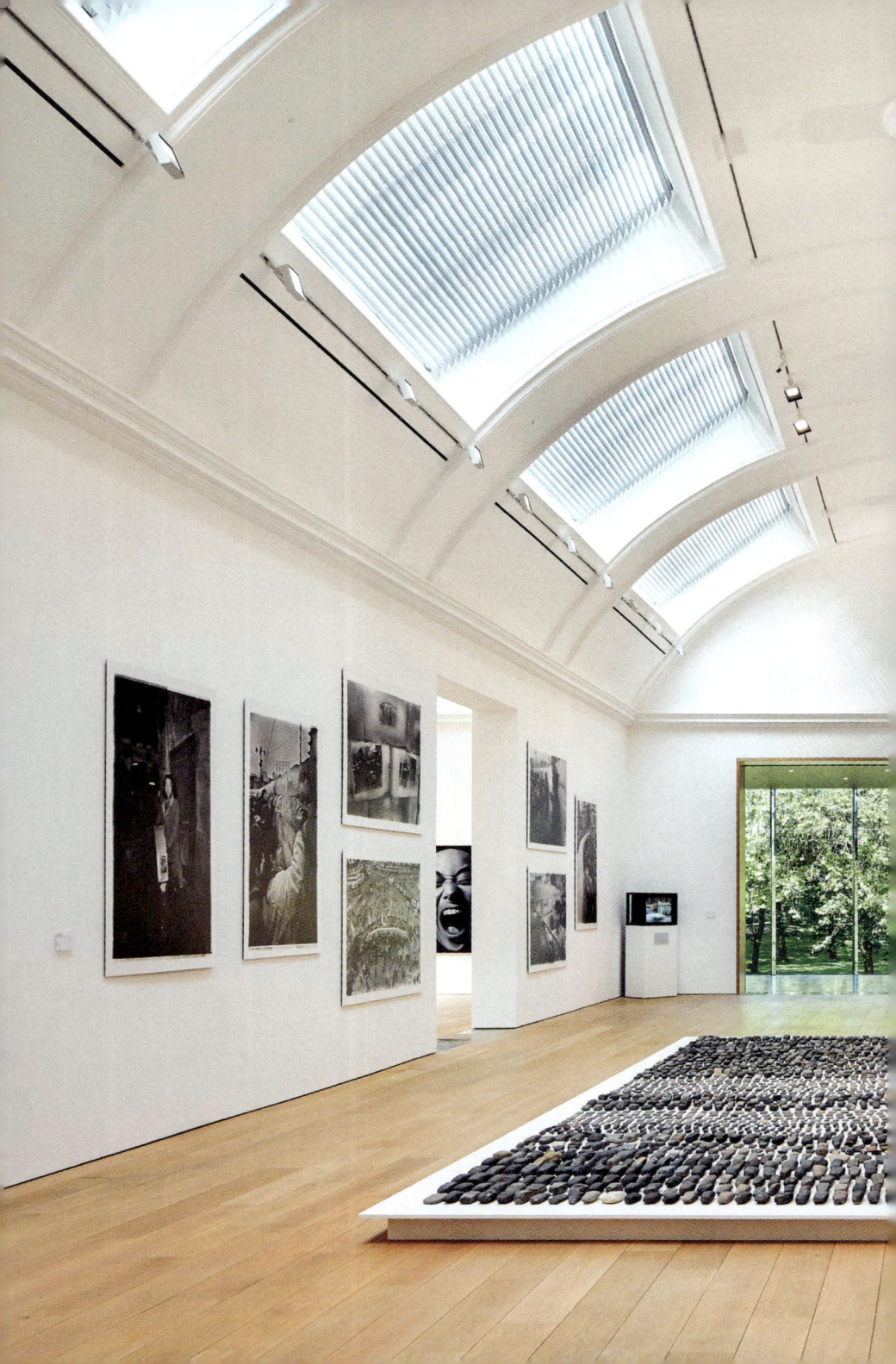

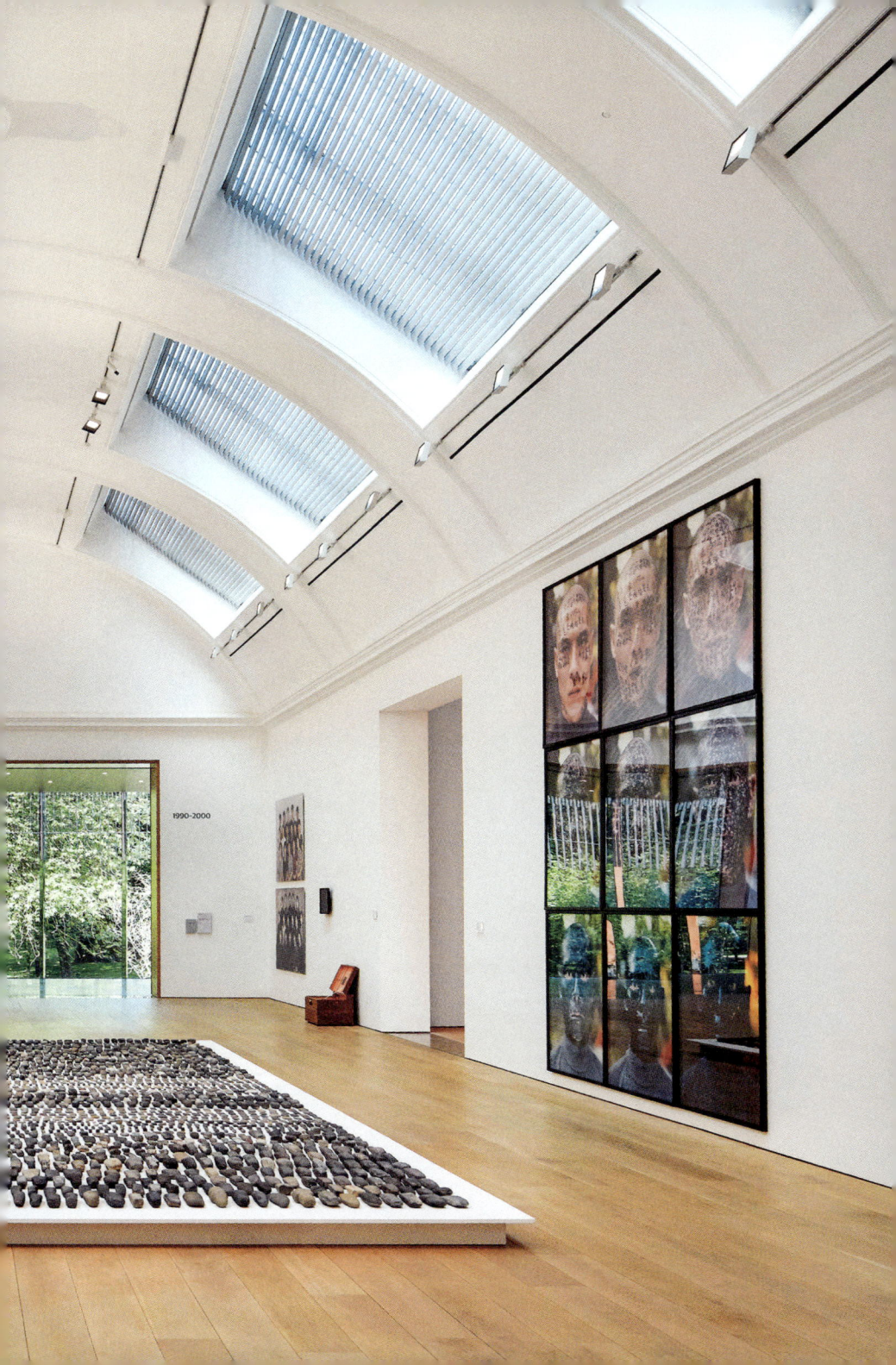

1990–2000

BALTIC CENTRE FOR CONTEMPORARY ART

Bold contemporary art in ex-flour mill

There's always something fresh to sink your teeth into at this intrepid Tyneside gallery, whose dynamic programme of groundbreaking shows – established by a colossal Anish Kapoor artwork that preceded the installation of the gallery's floors – negates any need for a permanent collection. A key component in Gateshead's early-2000s post-industrial riverside regeneration, this imposing former flour mill buzzes with innovation, from its design-led ground-floor gift shop to its celebrated sixth-floor restaurant. Sandwiched in between, the four vast galleries have showcased everything from Antony Gormley's ethereal, 287-figure *Domain Field* to Ed and Nancy Kienholz's seedy *The Hoerengracht* – a walk-in recreation of Amsterdam's notorious red-light district. Once you've soaked up the latest exhibitions, take the glass lift to the fifth floor viewing box for matchless views over the Tyne, then exit via the seemingly never-ending spiral staircase – courtesy of artist Mark Wallinger's shrewdly placed mirrors.

South Shore Road, Gateshead, NE8 3BA
baltic.art

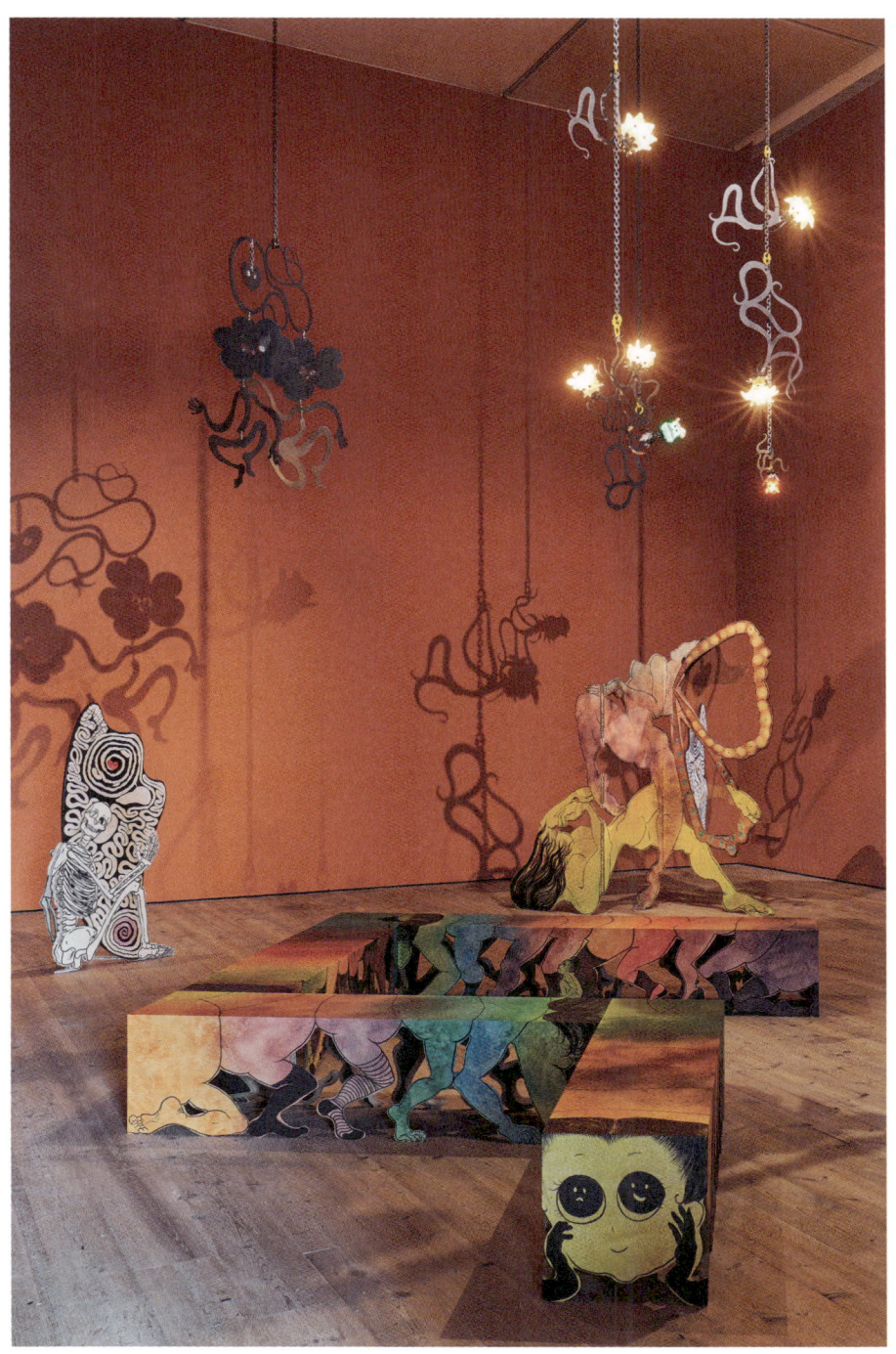

A Joyful Parasite, Saelia Aparicio

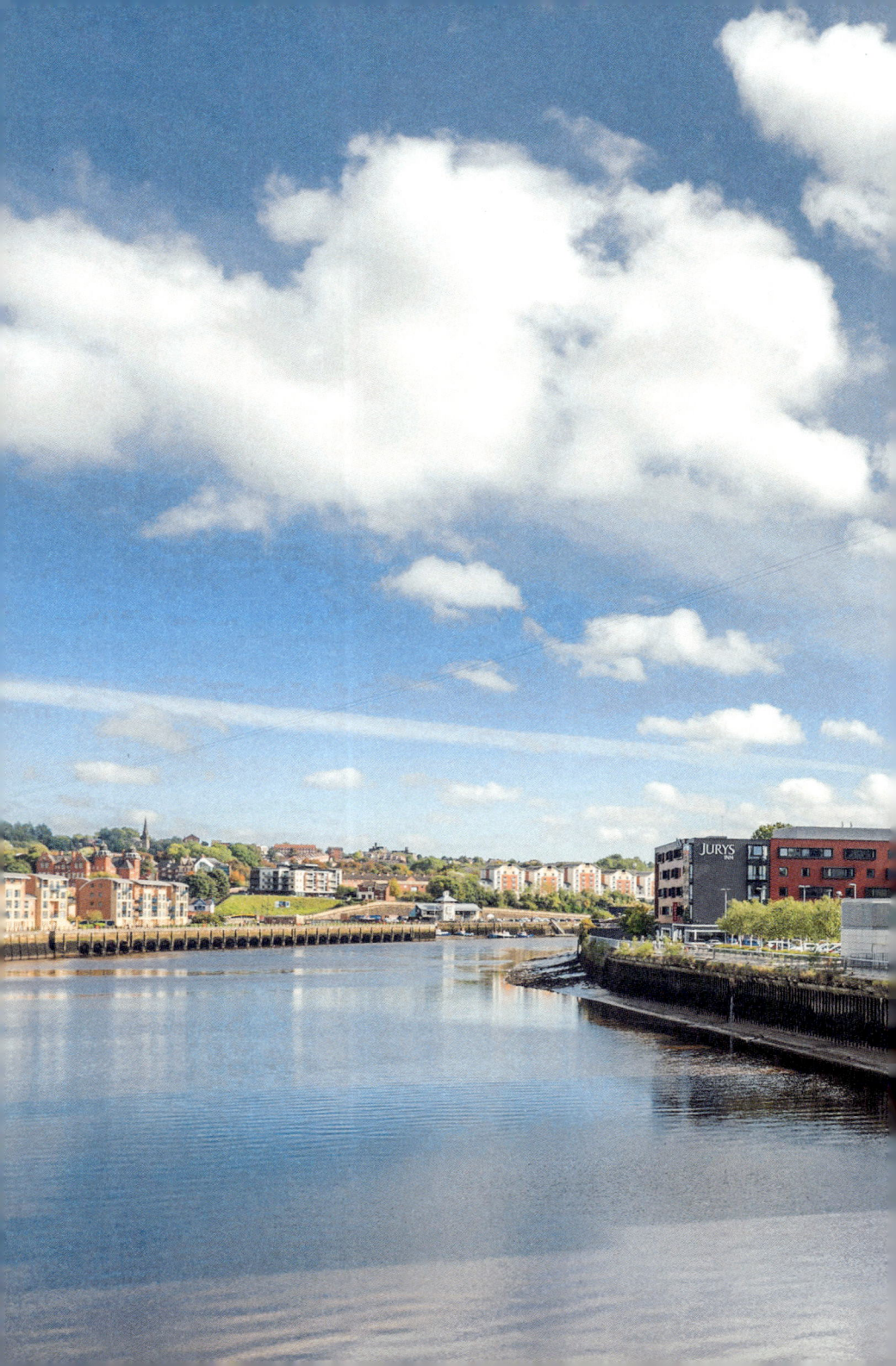

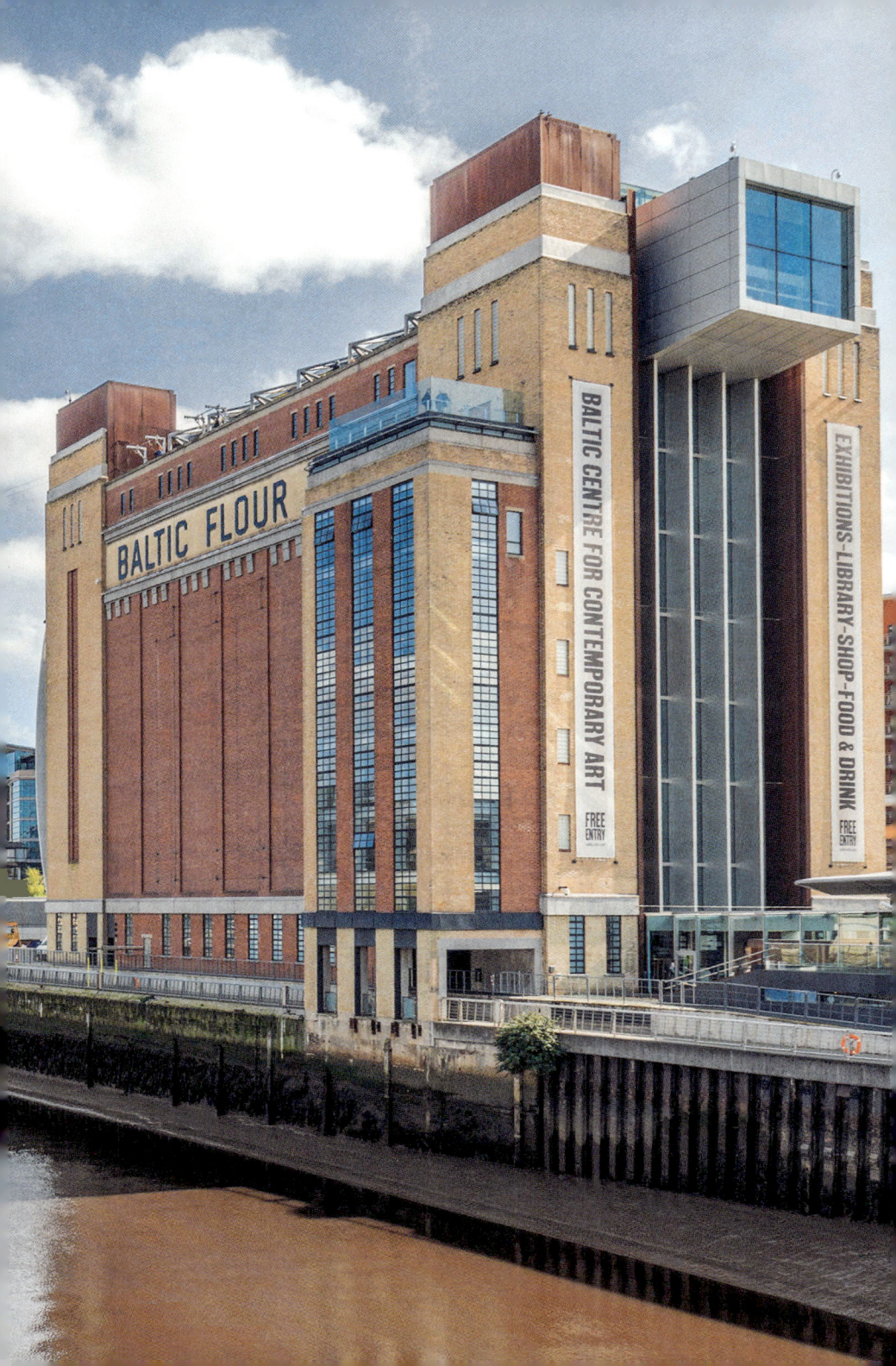

SALTS MILL

Hockney mecca in former factory

Any David Hockney fan worth their salt should make
the pilgrimage to this palatial former textile mill, home
to the world's largest permanent collection of the
Bradford-born artist's works.' Once the roaring epi-
centre of the Victorian model village of Saltaire (now
a UNESCO-listed site), this sensitively converted arts
centre affords a fittingly theatrical stage for the artist's
diverse back catalogue with its expansive galleries and
vaulted brick ceilings. Behold *The Arrival of Spring* –
a 49-piece chronicle of the changing seasons captured
via iPad – in its own dedicated space, before inspect-
ing the huge permanent collection in the grand 1853
gallery, whose designation marks the year that founder
and namesake Titus Salt opened the mill. Devour something sweet at Cafe in to the Opera beside Hockney's
Punchinello mural, or something a little heartier from the
upscale Salts Diner, where specially commissioned mill
paintings hang. Finish with a mooch around the inspiring gift shop, or Saltaire's eclectic indie boutiques.

Victoria Road, Saltaire, BD18 3HU
saltsmill.org.uk

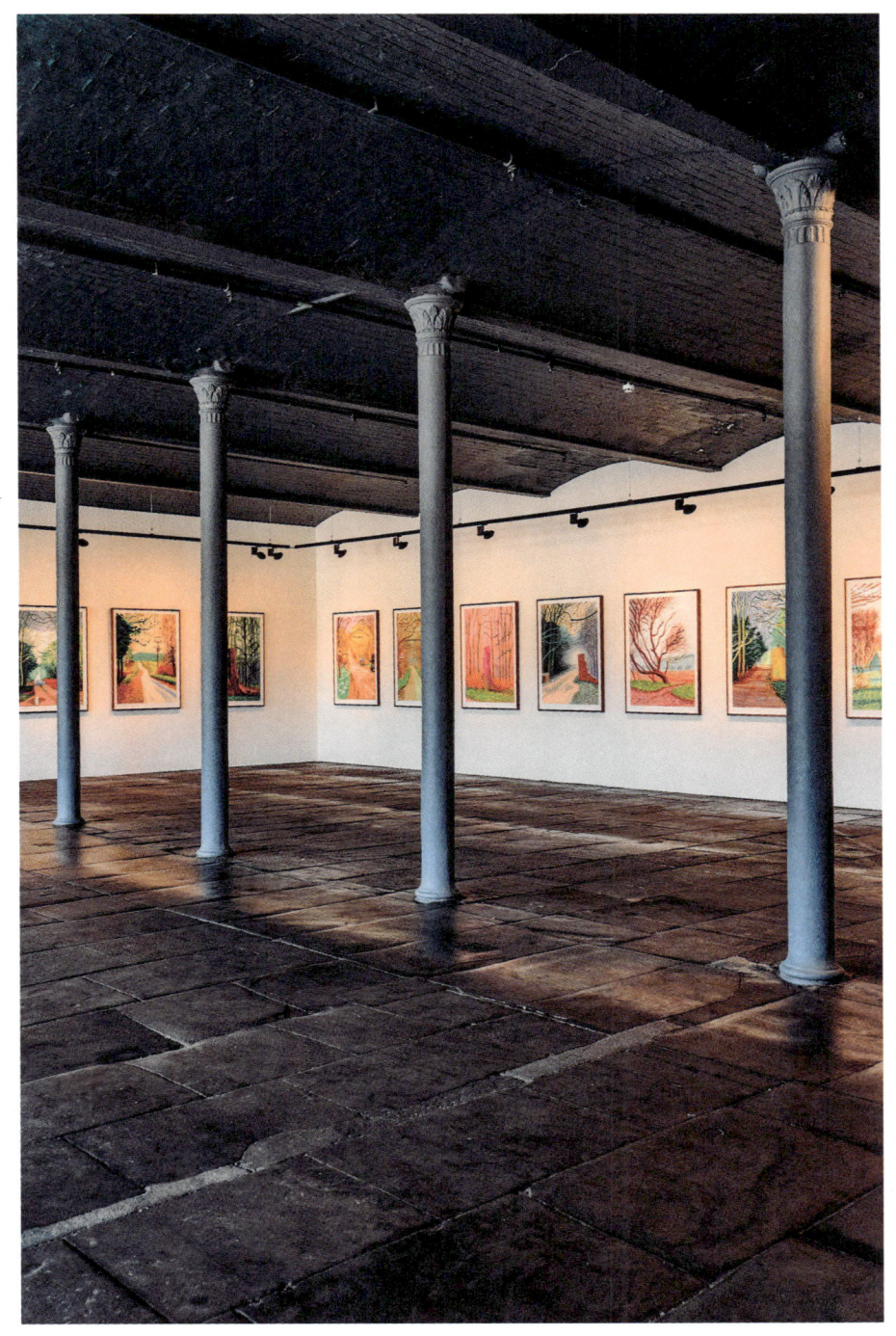

The Arrival of Spring, David Hockney

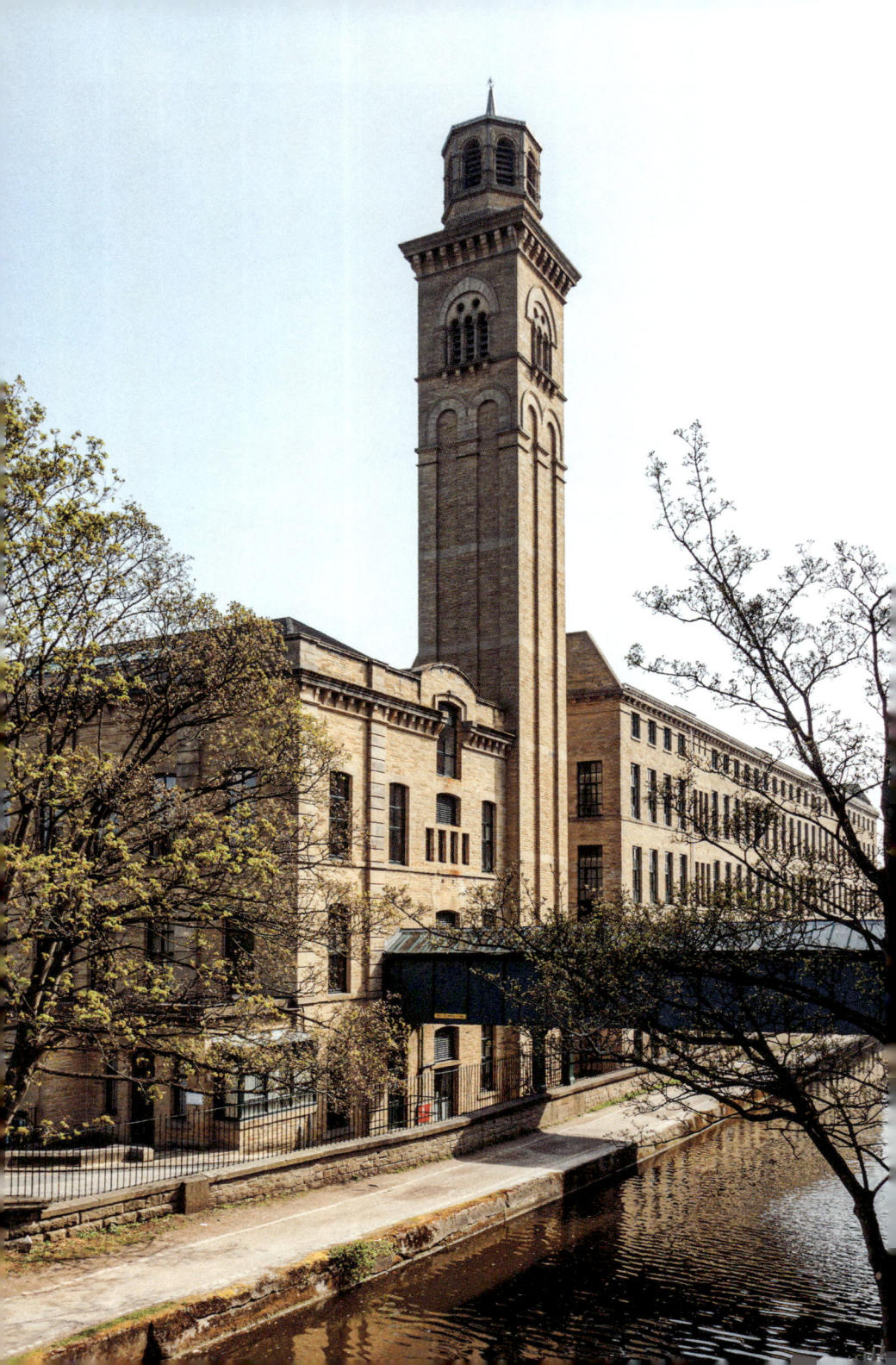

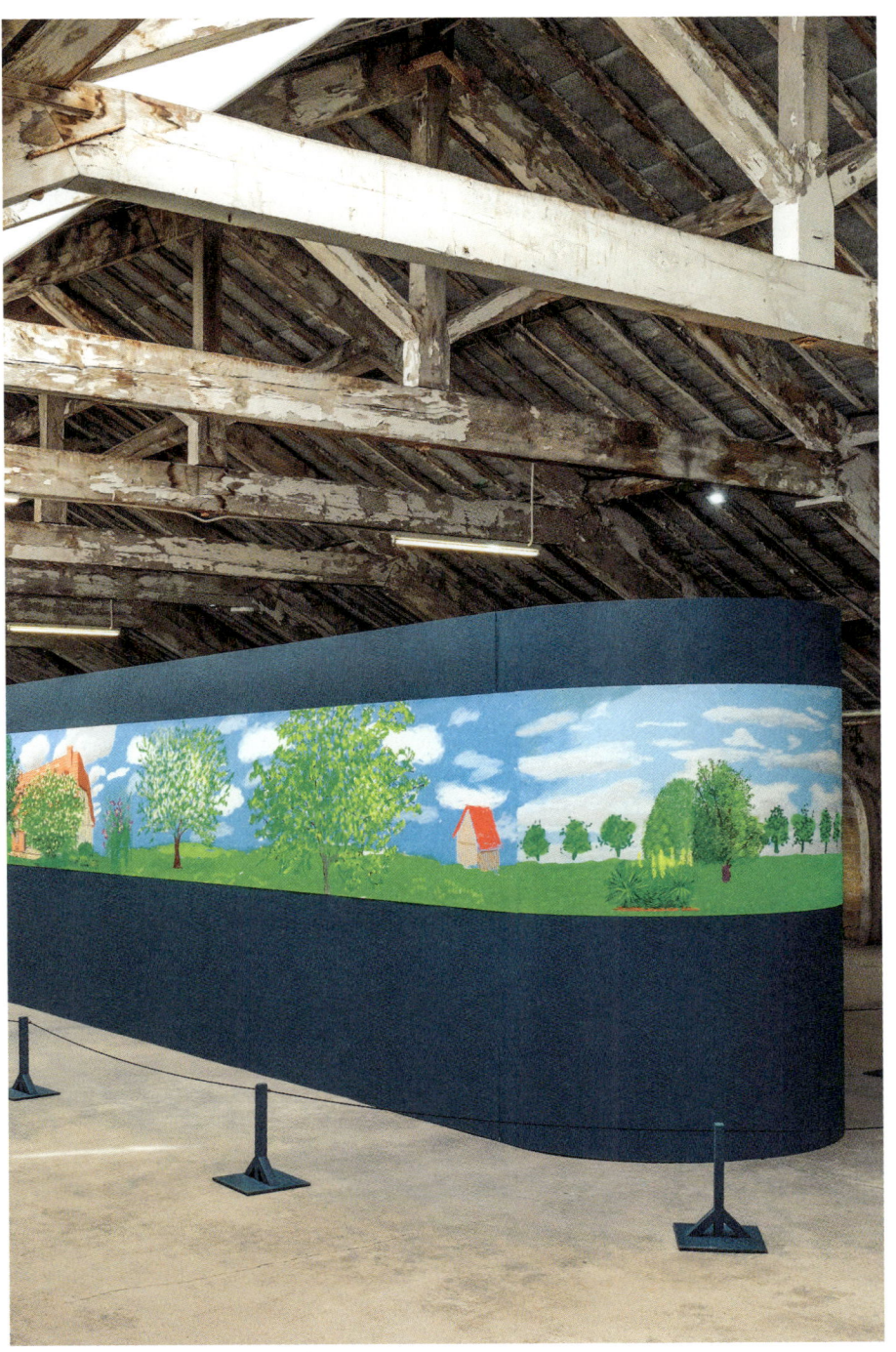

A Year in Normandie, David Hockney

THE LOWRY

Iconic industrial landscapes

It might not quite be the Guggenheim – as implied by Manchester MP Sir Gerald Kaufman on its opening in 2000 – but this steel-clad fortress is a must for fans of its namesake artist, who spent almost half his life in the area. Part of the redevelopment of the derelict Salford docks (itself a favourite subject of Lowry's), this striking wedge-shaped arts centre functions both as a theatre and a gallery, with the latter's permanent *Modern Life: The L.S. Lowry Collection* housing more than 400 works. *Coming from the Mill, Going to the Match, Mill Scene* and *Market Scene, Northern Town* are just a few of the iconic, matchstick-person-filled industrial landscapes you'll find, displayed alongside charismatic portraits such as *Head Of A Man (With Red Eyes)* and *Portrait of Ann*. Refuel post-peruse at the vibrant bar and kitchen before purchasing your favourite print from the well-stocked gift shop.

Pier 8, The Quays, Salford, M50 3AZ
thelowry.com

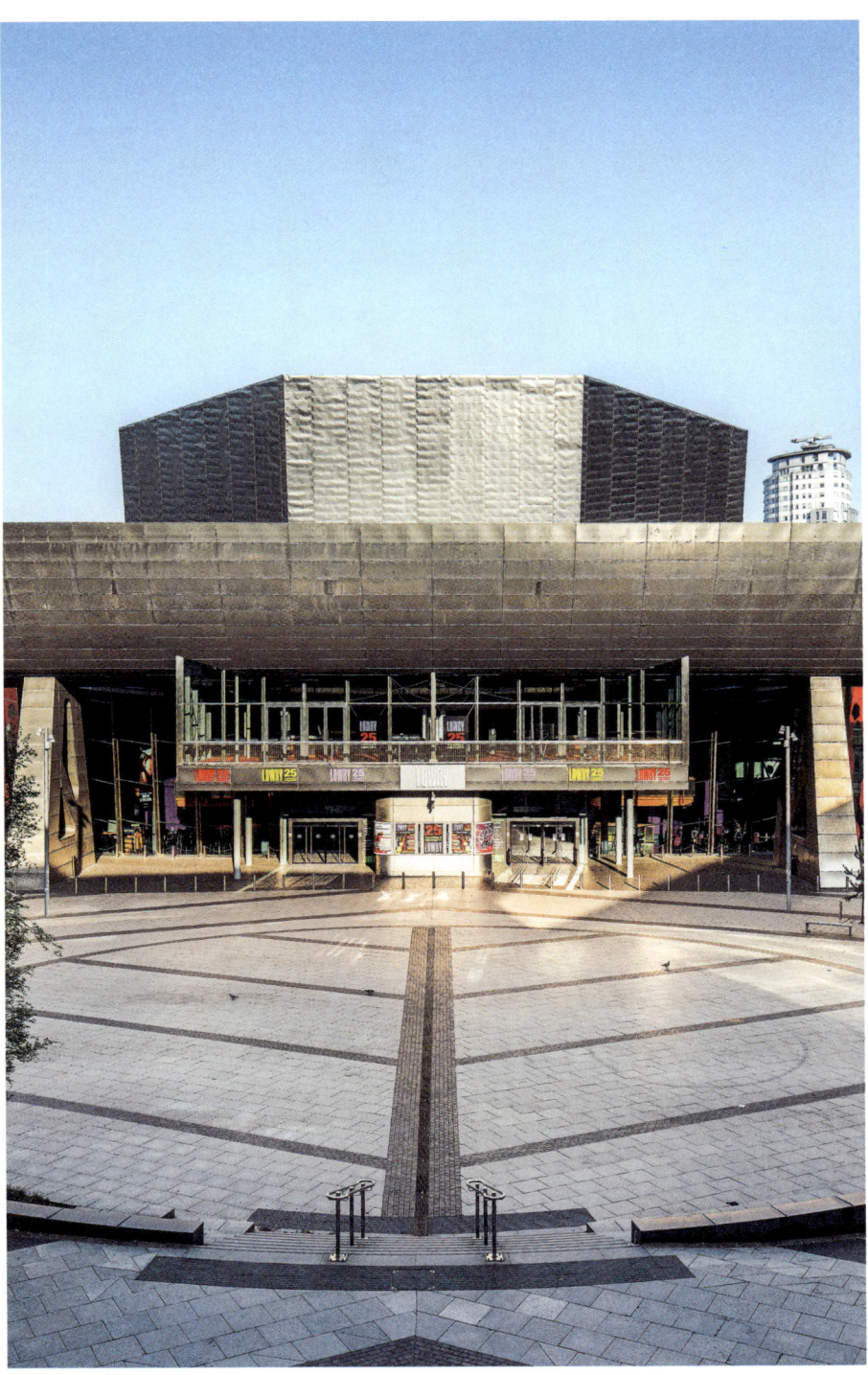

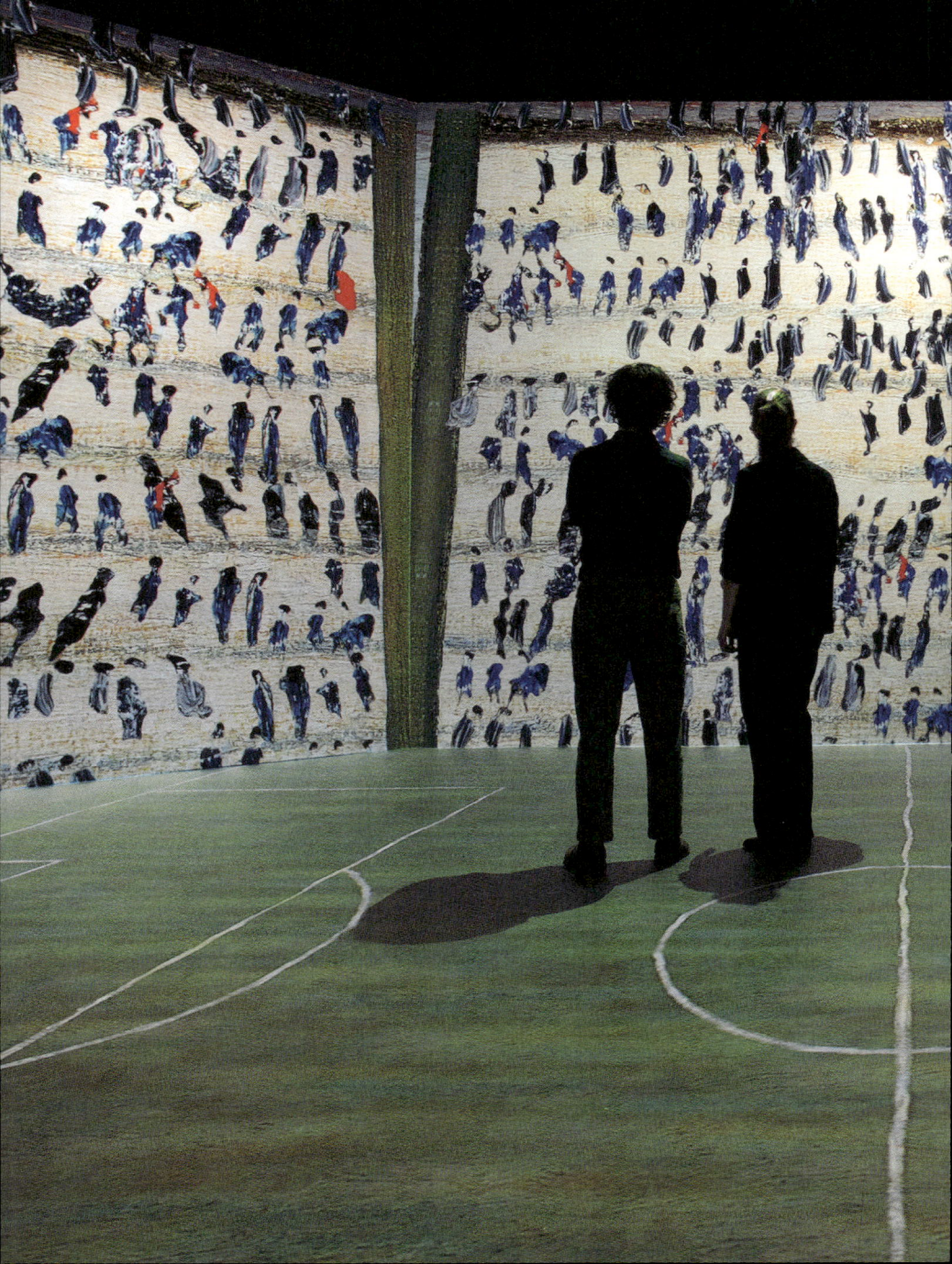

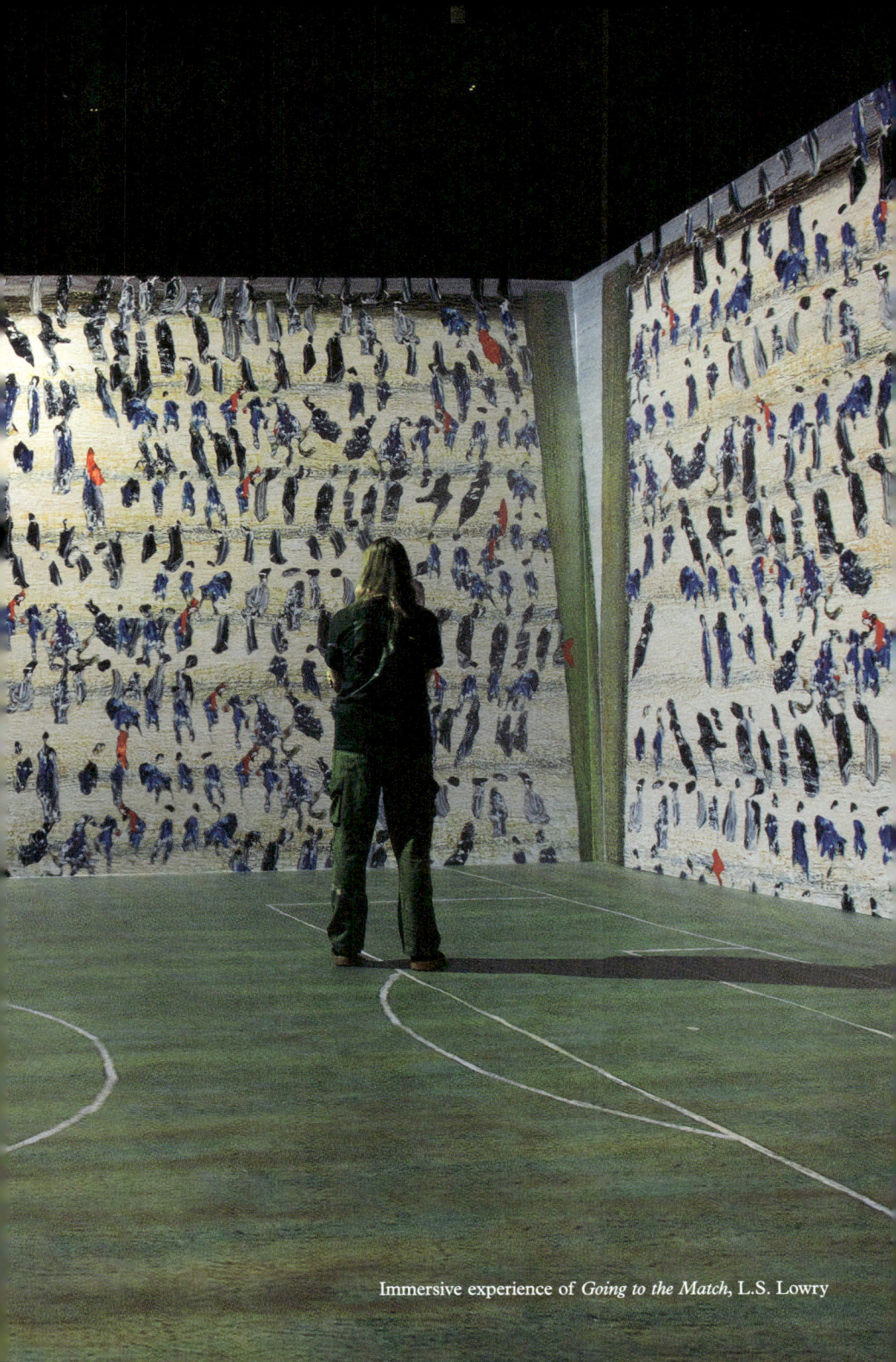

Immersive experience of *Going to the Match*, L.S. Lowry

YORKSHIRE SCULPTURE PARK

Europe's largest outdoor gallery

Like an ever-evolving sculptural safari, YSP invites art fans to take a walk on the wild side, roaming freely through 500 acres of glorious parkland in pursuit of up to 100 inspiring contemporary works. Wowing sculpture vultures and nature lovers since 1977, YSP's breathtaking grounds are home to six indoor galleries and two award-winning visitor centres, but it's the park's open-air exhibits where the magic really happens. Along with permanent fixtures such as Yorkshire natives Damien Hirst's towering *The Virgin Mother* and the entirety of Barbara Hepworth's totemic *The Family of Man*, YSP's sprawling grounds host a rolling programme of outdoor sculpture. Historic shows featured Anthony Caro's monumental metalwork, disabled artist Jason Wilsher-Mills' giant inflatables and Roger Hiorns' interactive foam works. The space can be bewildering – particularly with tots in tow – so download the map in advance and swing by the information desk for engaging children's activities to complete on-the-go.

West Bretton, Wakefield, WF4 4LG

ysp.org.uk

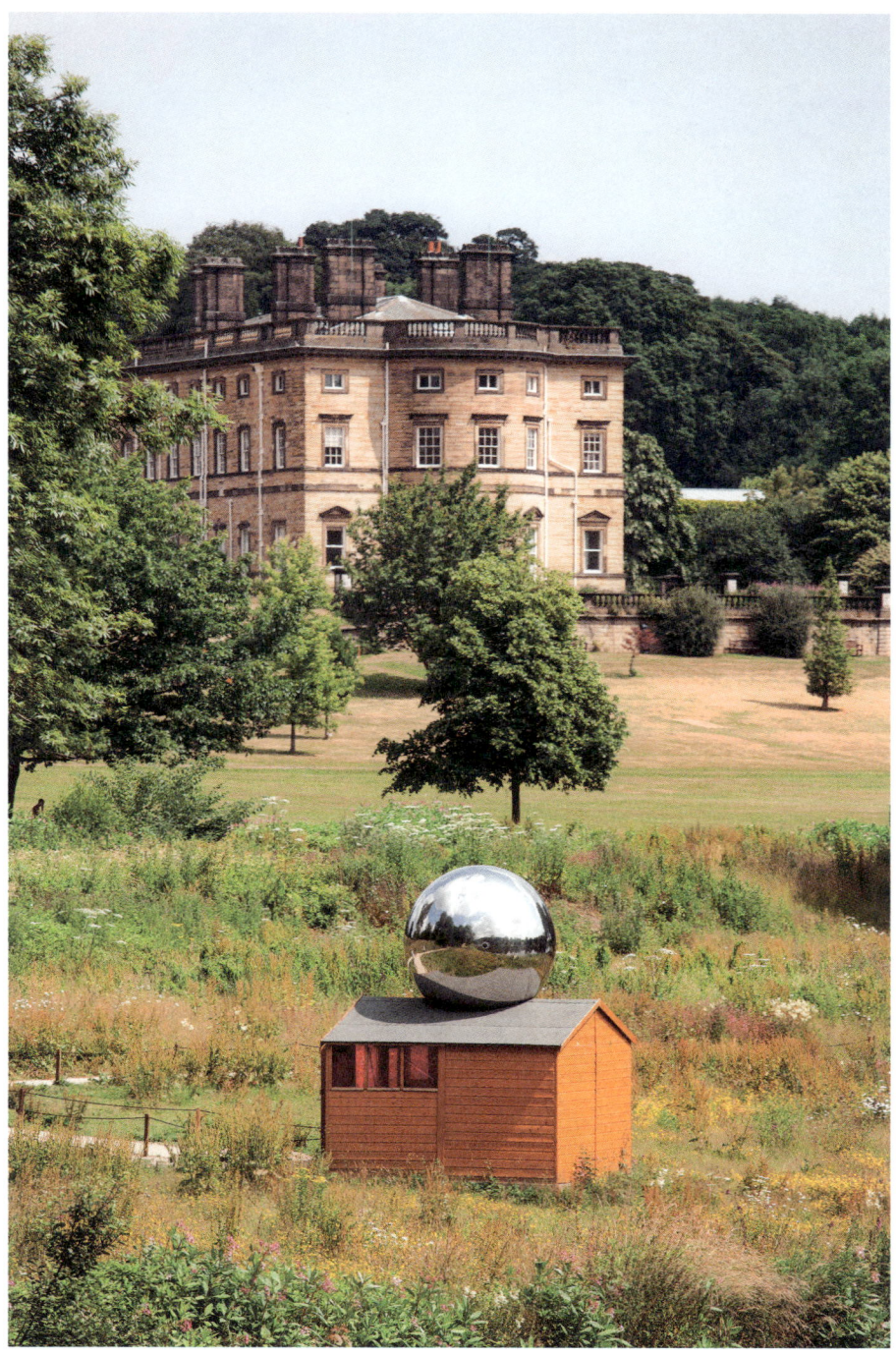

Spiegelei, Jem Finer

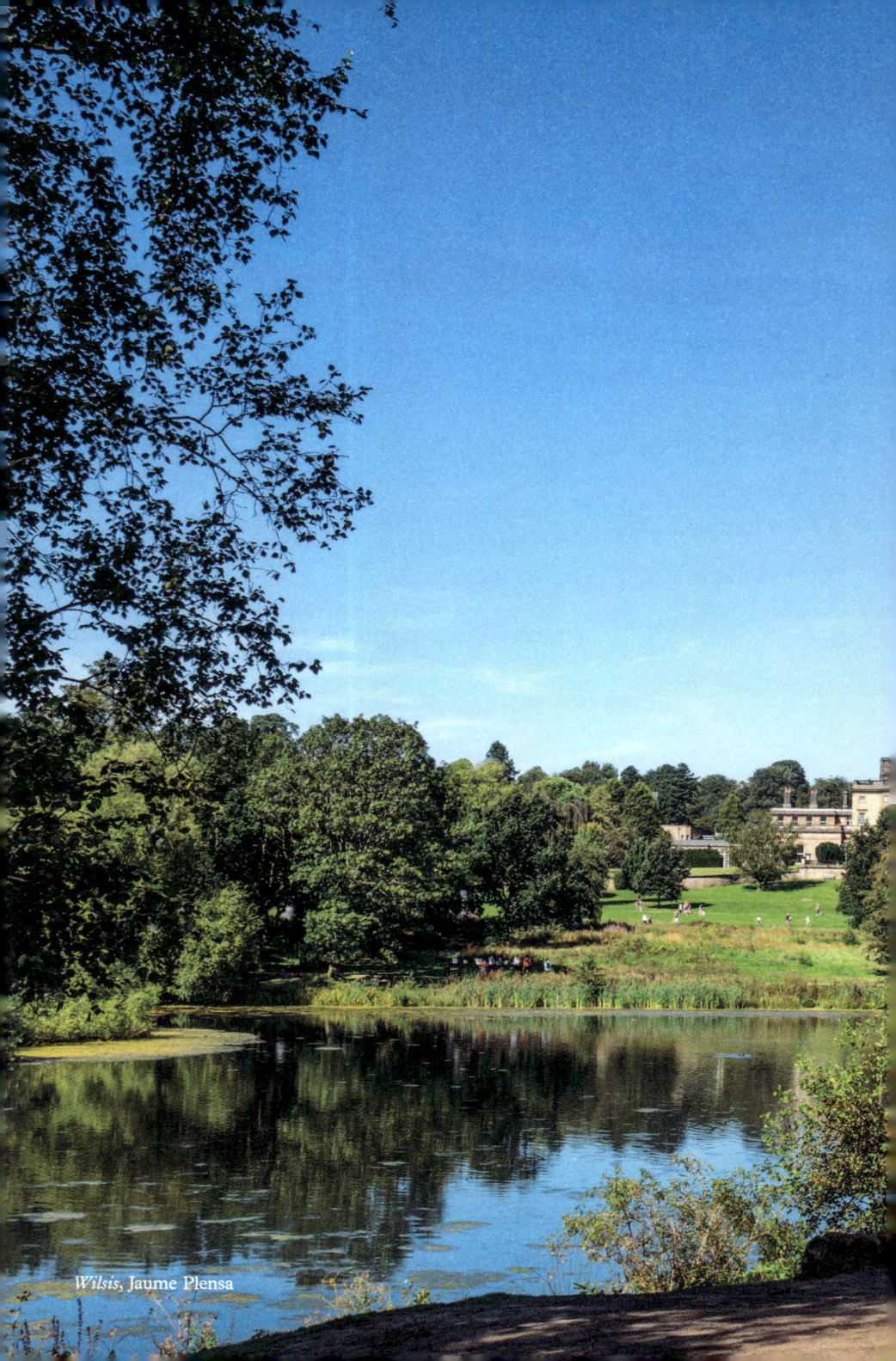

Wilsis, Jaume Plensa

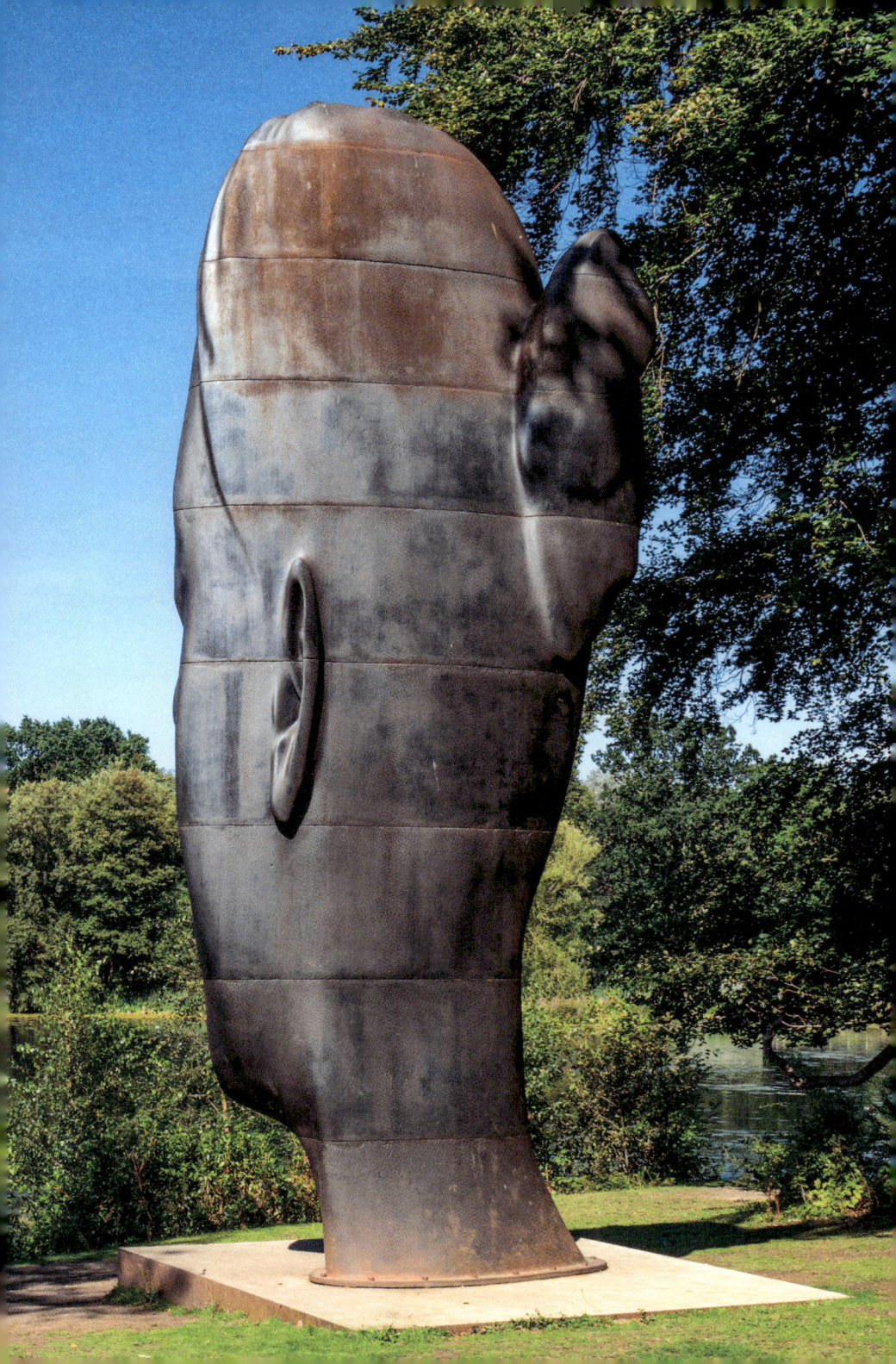

IRWELL SCULPTURE TRAIL

UK's largest open-air art route

All the destinations in this book make for a superb day out, but this snaking northern sculpture trail, the largest in the UK, affords the opportunity for several. Extending an ambitious 33 miles between the former Lancashire mill town of Bacup and the iconic Salford Quays, this picturesque route, featuring more than 70 artworks, has been helpfully split into nine manageable segments – each one perfectly proportioned for a single day's exploring. Biking buffs will go wild for Stacksteads Cluster's exhilarating trails, which occupy two former quarries and connect a trio of Robin Dobson sculptures celebrating the area's industrial heritage. Meanwhile, the family-friendly Close Park boasts larger-than-life effigies of a shiny trainer-wearing cheetah, a dinosaur and a cupcake boy by sculptor Mark Jalland, along with a children's play area. Maximise your cultural intake with a visit to one of the indoor art destinations that cross the trail, be it Bury Art Museum (home to Turners and Constables) or Salford's gleaming Lowry (p.172).

Bacup, OL13 9DN
to Salford Quays, M50 3UB
irwellsculpturetrail.co.uk

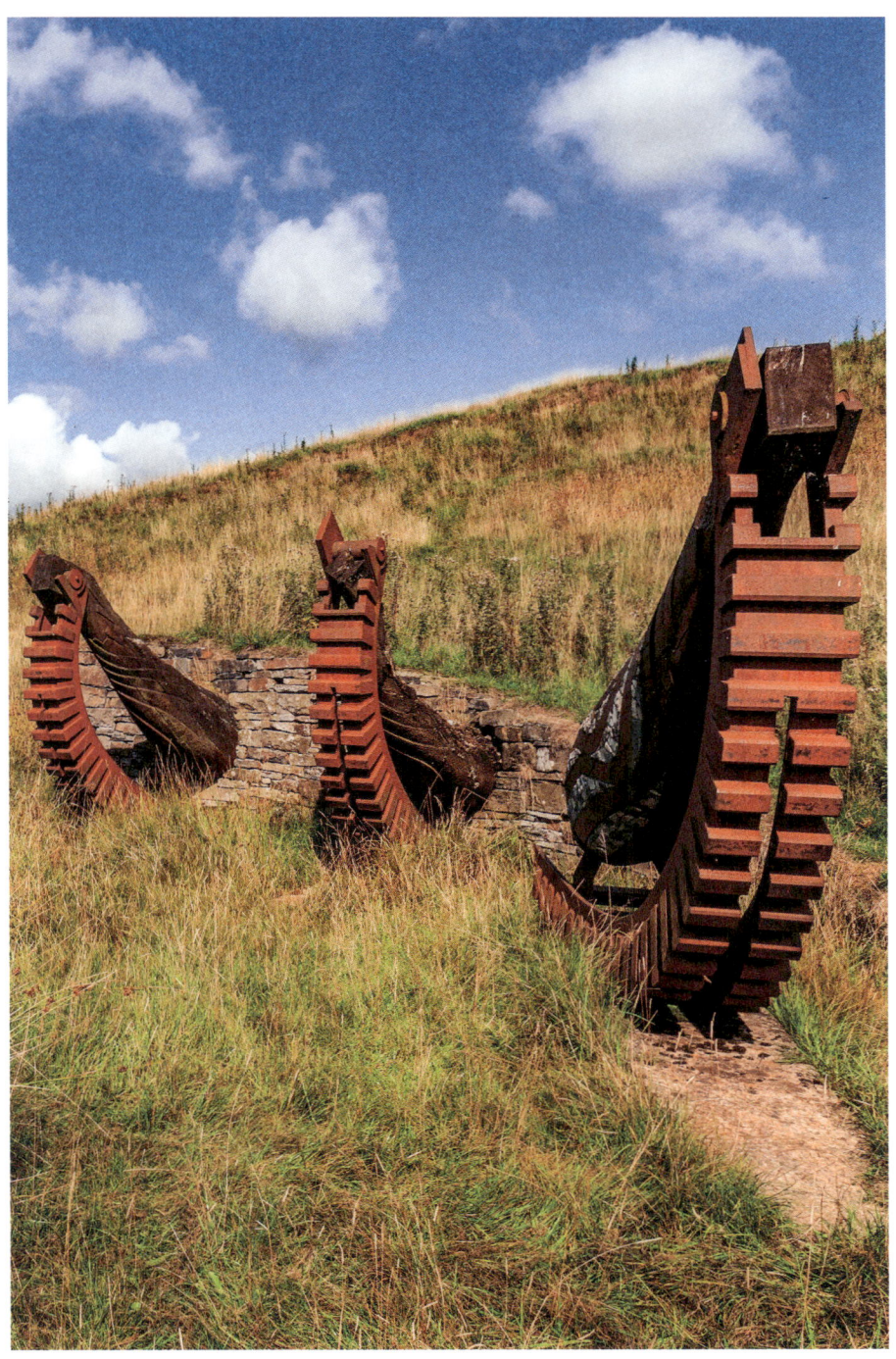

Remnant Kings, Ian Randall

CHATSWORTH HOUSE

Grand estate with princely hoard

Just as Rome wasn't built in a day, Chatsworth's glittering art collection has taken almost half a millennium – and 17 generations – to amass. One of Britain's prominent 'Treasure Houses', this opulent Peak District pile is home to a vast and eclectic hoard spanning 4,000 years of history, from a Rembrandt acquired by the 3rd Duke of Devonshire to a Michael Craig-Martin digital work commissioned by the son of the 12th. Its impressive sculpture gallery was immortalised by the 2005 film adaptation of *Pride & Prejudice* (you'll find the original Mr Darcy bust prop in the gift shop). Beyond the Frans Hals and Van Dycks, Chatsworth is a renowned destination for contemporary sculpture – most notably its annual summer exhibition, which has seen everything from Marc Quinn's monumental marble baby to Barry Flanagan's dancing bronze hares occupying the sprawling house and garden.

Bakewell, DE45 1PP
chatsworth.org

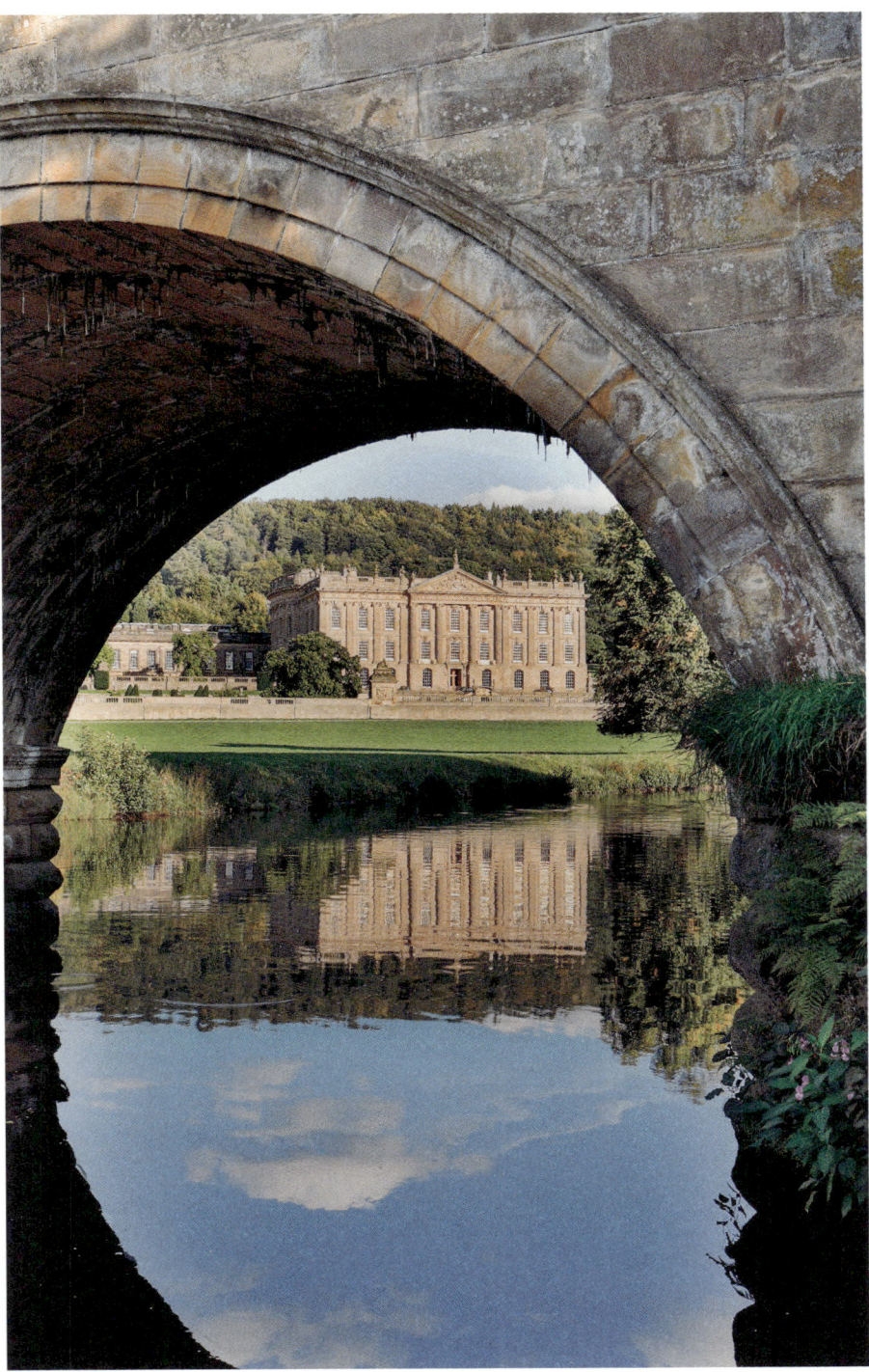

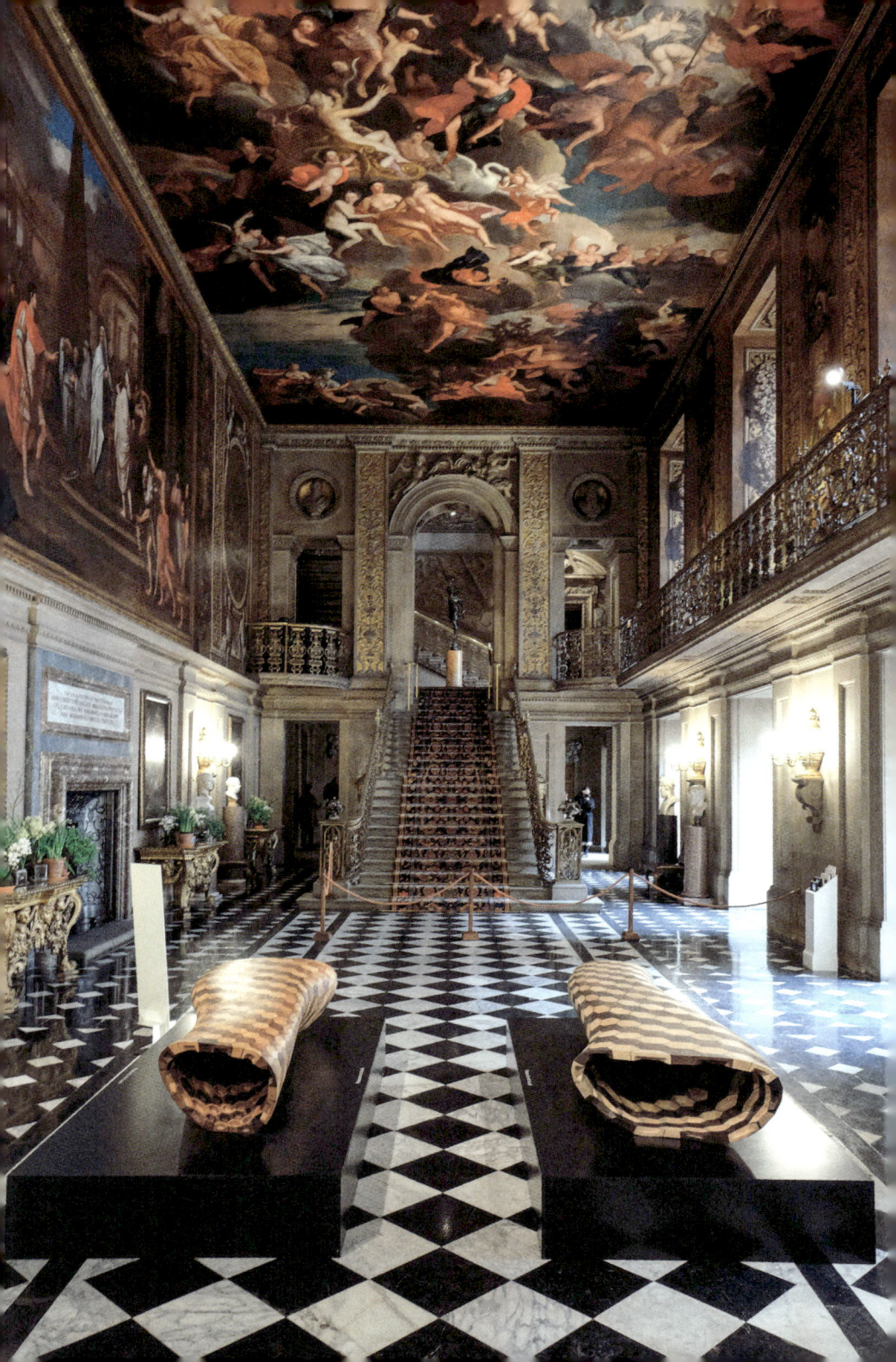

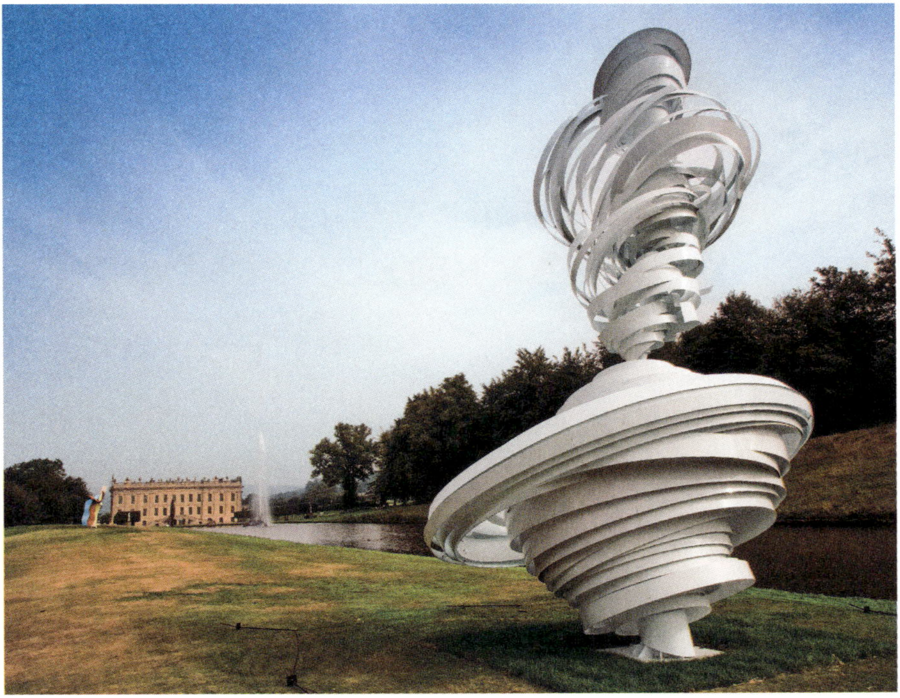

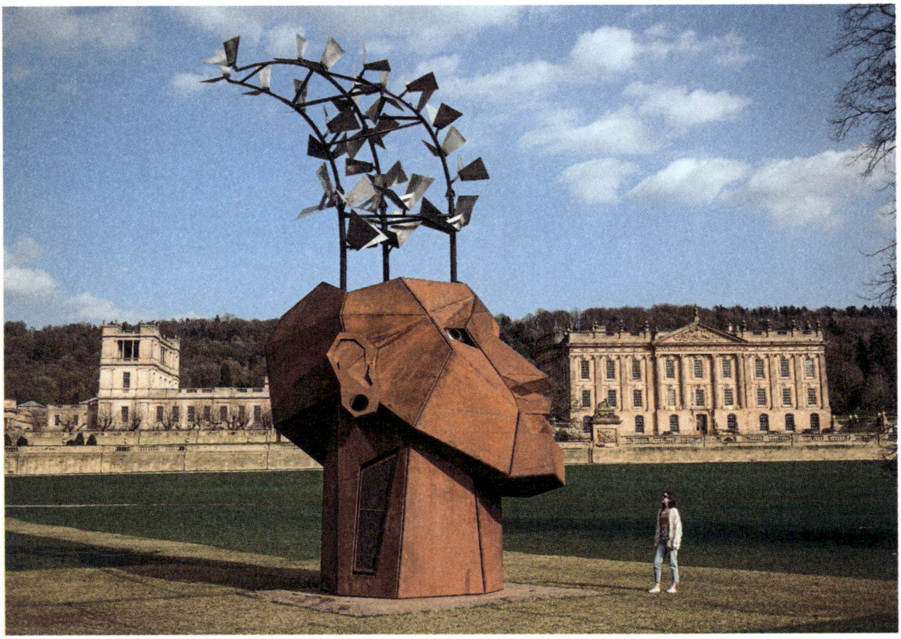

Above: *Cyclone Twist*, Alice Aycock
Below: *The Flybrary*, Christina Sporrong

THE HEPWORTH WAKEFIELD

Ambitious gallery in sculptor's hometown

Rising impressively from the River Calder like a gargantuan Hepworth masterpiece, this Chipperfield-designed gallery pays felicitous tribute to the Wakefield native, who was born in the city in 1903. Unveiled as Wakefield Art Gallery's successor in 2011, this striking building takes the form of ten interconnected trapezoidal concrete volumes, each housing its own capacious gallery on the light-flooded first floor, and a delightful shop and cafe at ground level. Sculptures such as *Mother and Child* and *Winged Figure* are Hepworth highlights, but the gallery is far from a one-woman show, with significant works by Eva Rothschild, L.S. Lowry, Martin Parr and Anthea Hamilton all part of its 5,000-artwork arsenal. Temporary exhibitions have spanned everything from Sheila Hicks' colourful textiles to Anthony McCall's *Solid Light Works*, as well as numerous Hepworth retrospectives and surveys focusing on different phases of her career. Don't miss the tranquil garden, where a handful of Hepworth sculptures (among other artists' works) can be relished in the open air – just as she intended.

Gallery Walk, Wakefield, WF1 5AW
hepworthwakefield.org

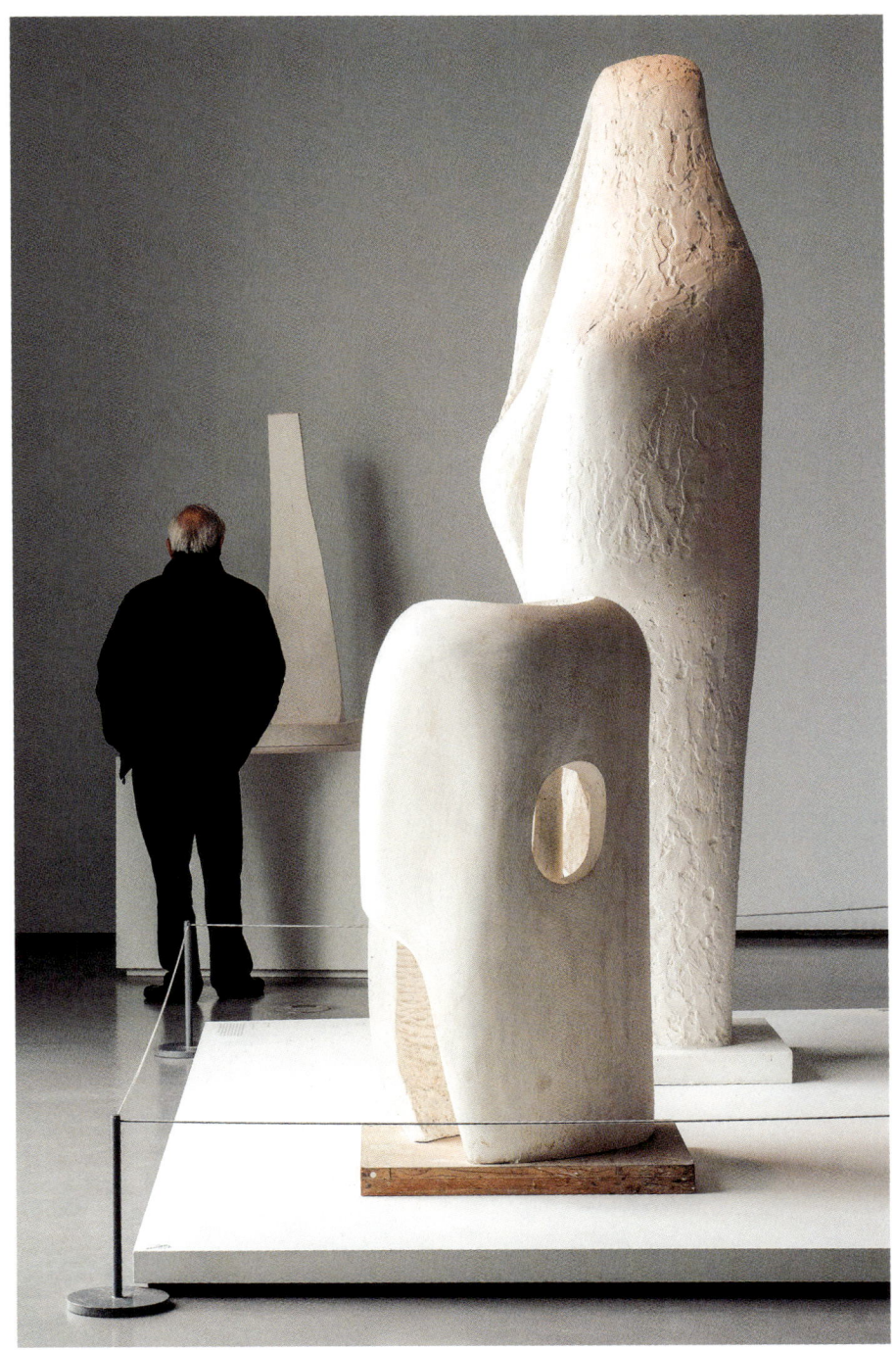

The Hepworth Plasters, Barbara Hepworth

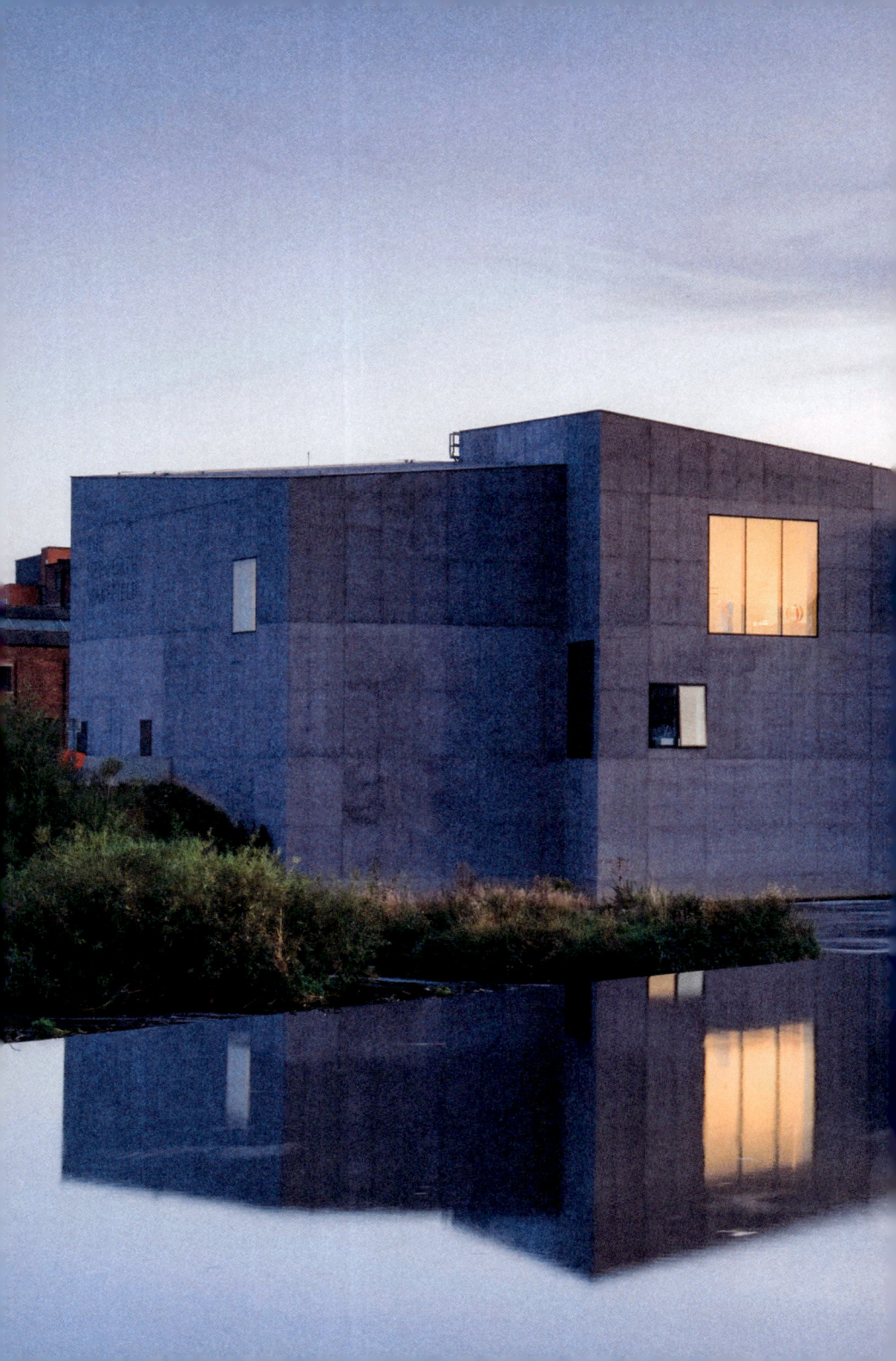

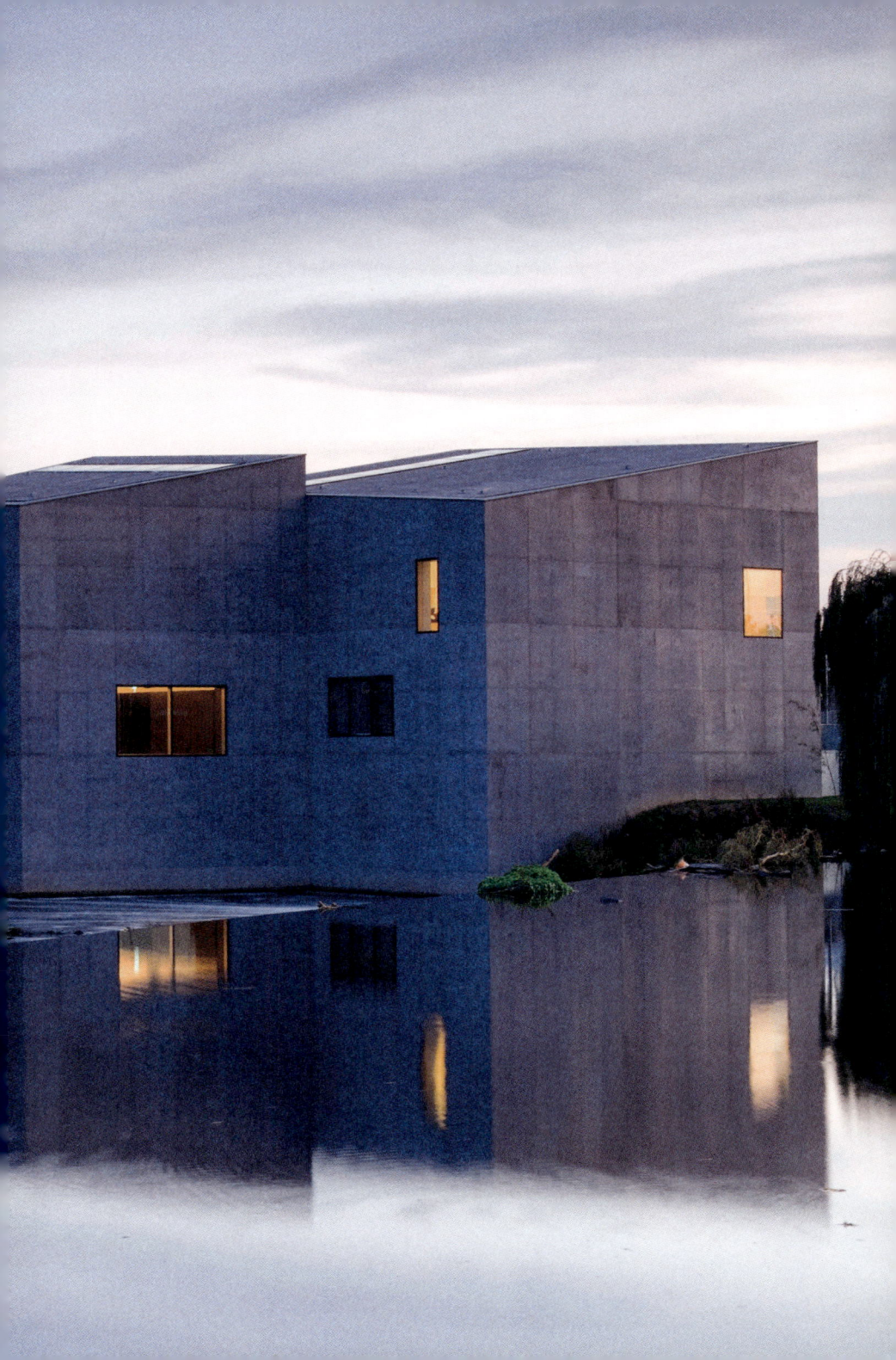

THE MACKINTOSH HOUSE

Art Nouveau architect's reconstructed home

The 'Glasgow style' isn't so-called for nothing: the city is stuffed with examples of this distinctive Art Nouveau design, developed by Charles Rennie Mackintosh and his circle around the turn of the 20th century. *House for an Art Lover*, built posthumously to his exacting designs, and *The Hill House*, the mansion commissioned by publisher Walter Blackie, are must-sees for fans of his work. But perhaps the most atmospheric of Mackintosh's Glasgow houses is the one he lived in himself – or, at least, the recreation of it. Painstakingly assembled from the salvaged fixtures and fittings of the since-demolished original, the reconstructed home offers a unique glimpse into Mackintosh's work and life across four exquisitely preserved, faithfully furnished rooms. Standing a mere 100 metres from its original 78 Southpark Avenue address, the terraced house emerges incongruously from the corner of the University of Glasgow's Brutalist Hunterian Art Gallery – itself home to a captivating display of Mackintosh designs.

82 Hillhead Street, Glasgow, G12 8QQ
gla.ac.uk/hunterian/visit/our-venues/mackintosh-house

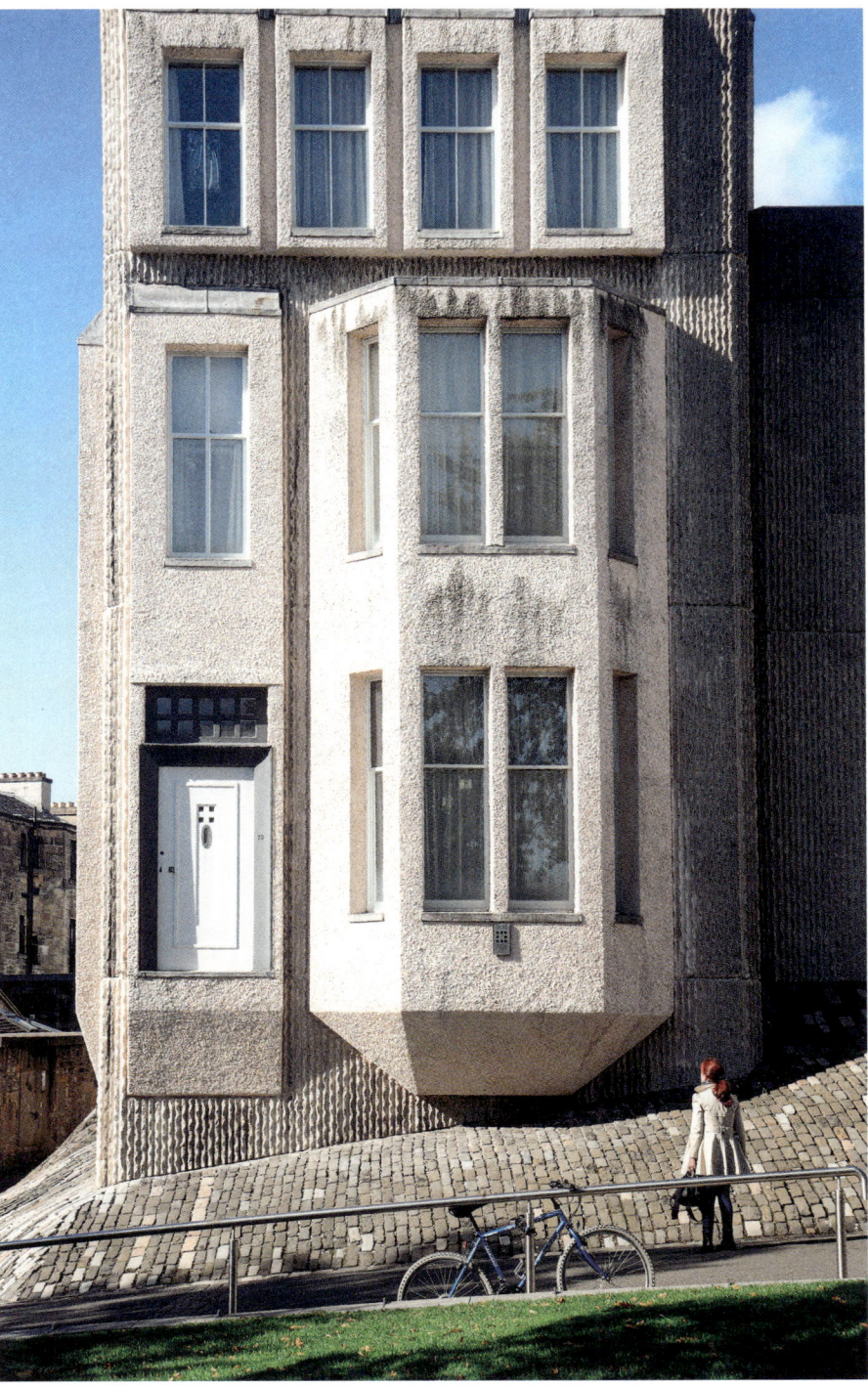

THE BURRELL COLLECTION

Eclectic treasures in parkland setting

A staggering 9,000 works of art comprise this glittering Glasgow trove. As impressive for its eclecticism and magnitude as the fact it was amassed entirely by local shipping magnate William Burrell and his wife Constance, the collection was bequeathed to the city in 1944 in an extraordinary act of philanthropy. Burrowed deep in Glasgow's verdant Pollok Country Park, the award-winning gallery was custom-built to Burrell's exacting instructions, which stipulated that visitors be allowed to appreciate its diverse riches in a bucolic setting. Everyone from Manet's beer-drinking women to Rodin's pensive bronze *The Thinker* and Degas' crimson-skirted dancers appear within its largely glass-clad walls, interspersed with important collections of Egyptian, Chinese and Islamic paintings and objects spanning six millennia. An art destination for all ages, the gallery boasts regular artist-led sessions for families, along with a busy programme of enlightening collection tours and workshops for all.

Pollok Country Park, 2060 Pollokshaws Road,
Glasgow, G43 1AT
burrellcollection.com

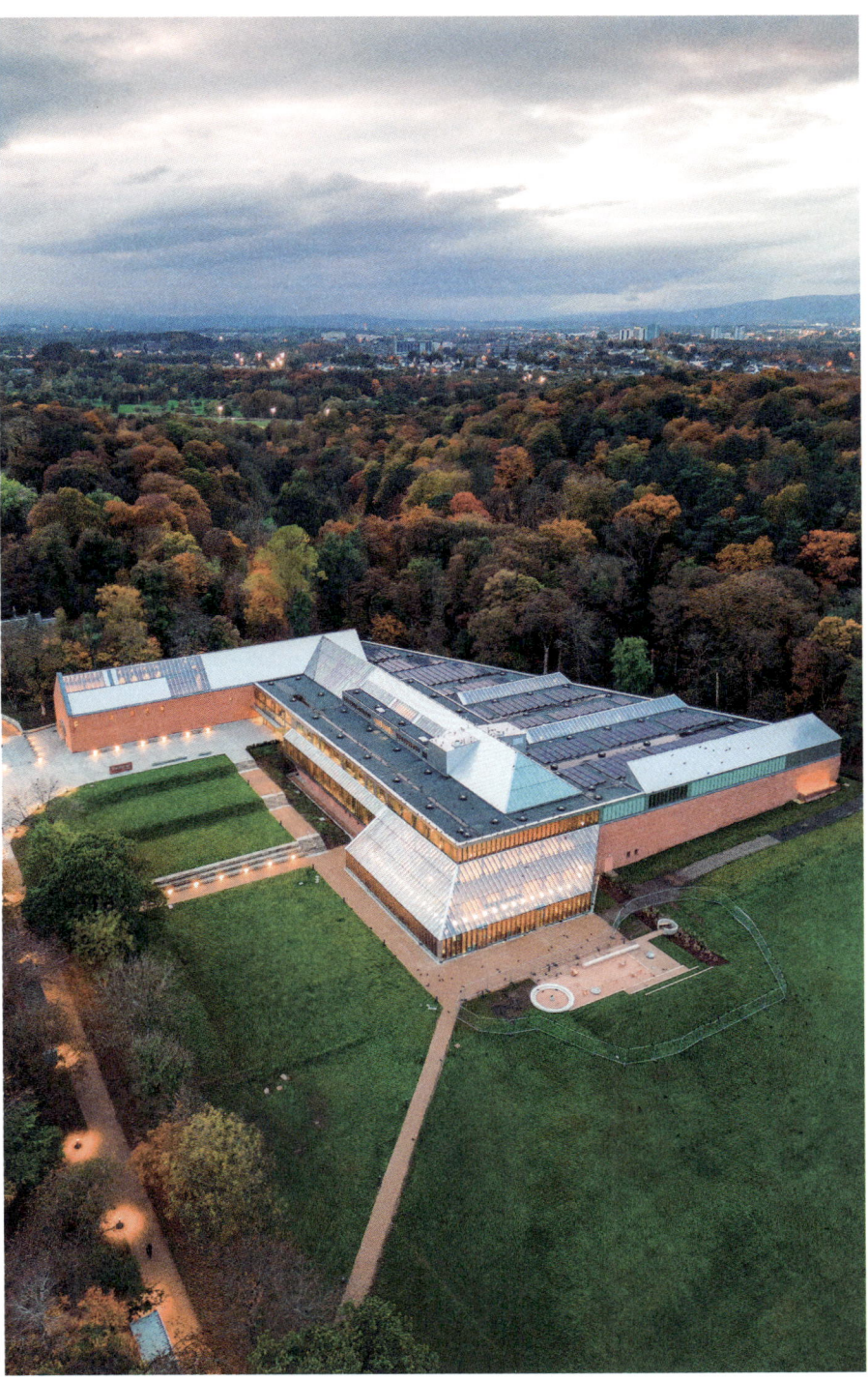

FRUITMARKET

Central Edinburgh gallery with experimental exhibits

Perched above Edinburgh Waverley Station for the past 50 years, this gallery's salad days might be over, but the former fruit-and-veg market still feels tantalisingly fresh. Astutely described by exhibiting artist Gabriel Orozco as 'a kind of laboratory', this spontaneous platform feels like a place where almost anything could happen – be it pioneering performance art or the total transformation of the interior, courtesy of an apocalyptic Martin Boyce installation or a hypnotic Jim Lambie floor. The expertly curated bookshop justifies a visit by itself – as does the on-site cafe with its comforting hot sandwiches and inventive cakes (think Persian pistachio and rosewater sponge). Once you've had your fill – of both art and cake – proceed next door in pursuit of the 104 historic Scotsman Steps, each crafted from a different type of marble by the artist Martin Creed, who was commissioned by the gallery in 2011.

45 Market Street, Edinburgh, EH1 1DF
fruitmarket.co.uk

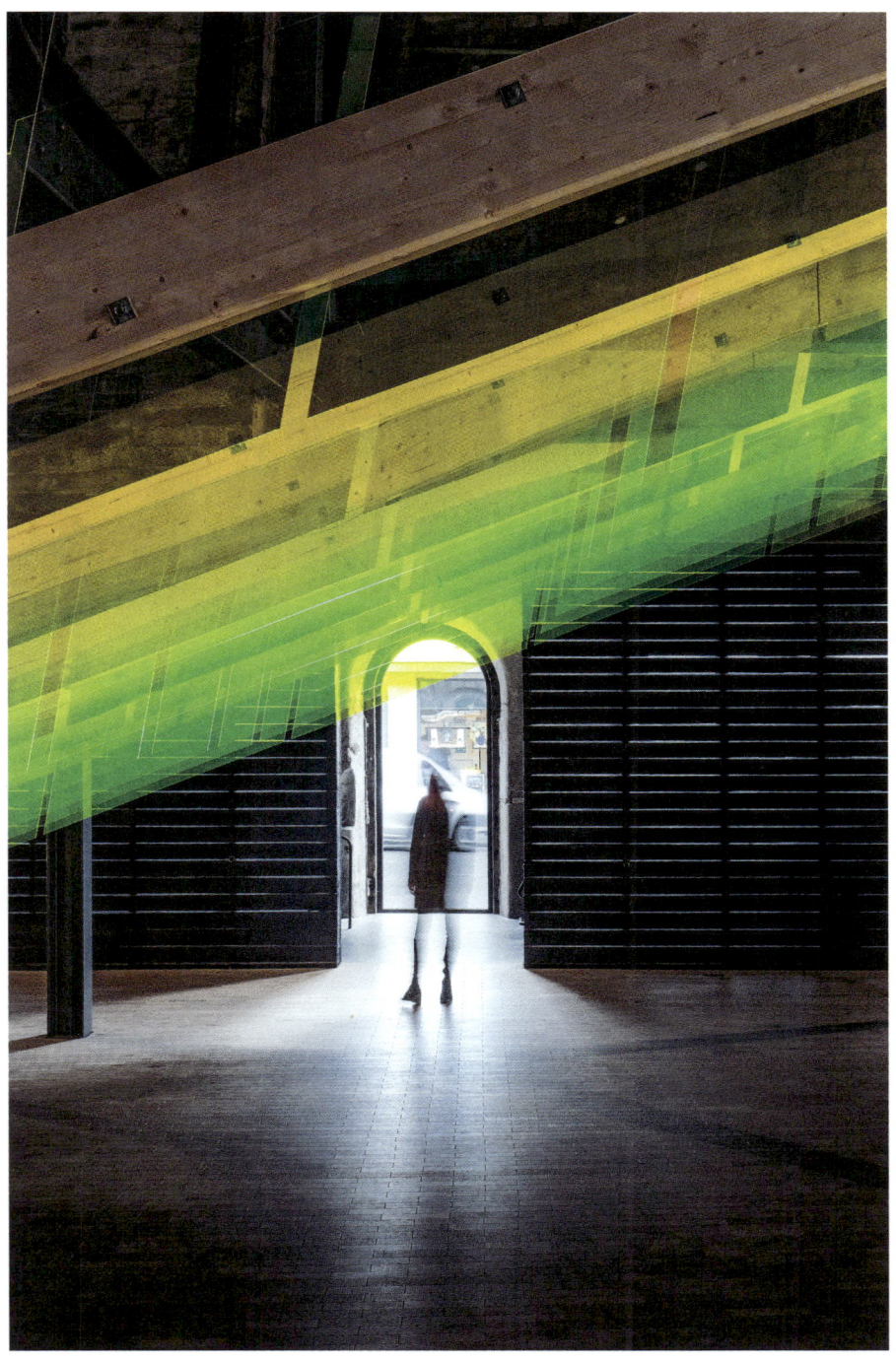

Pardes, Jyll Bradley

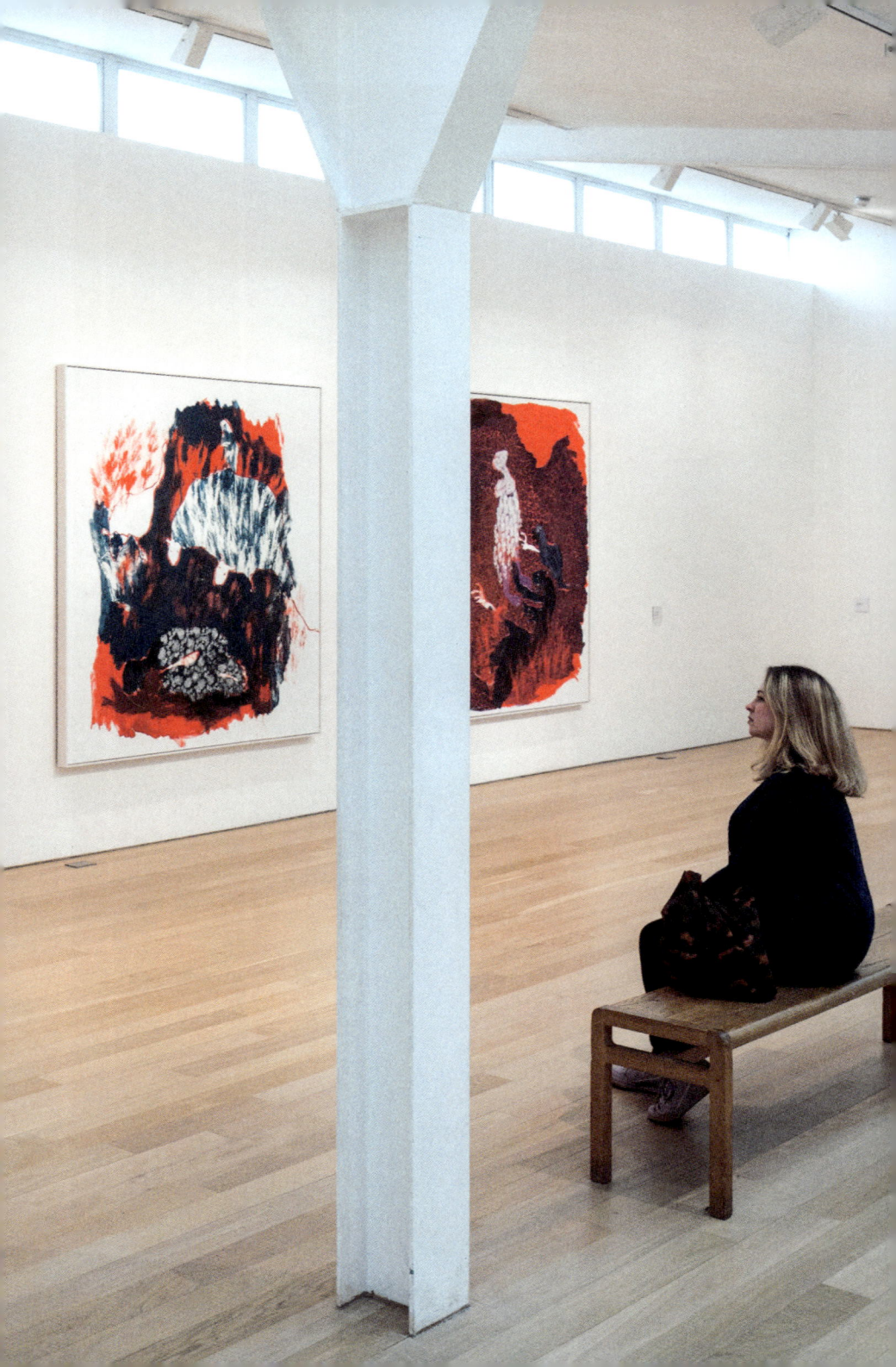

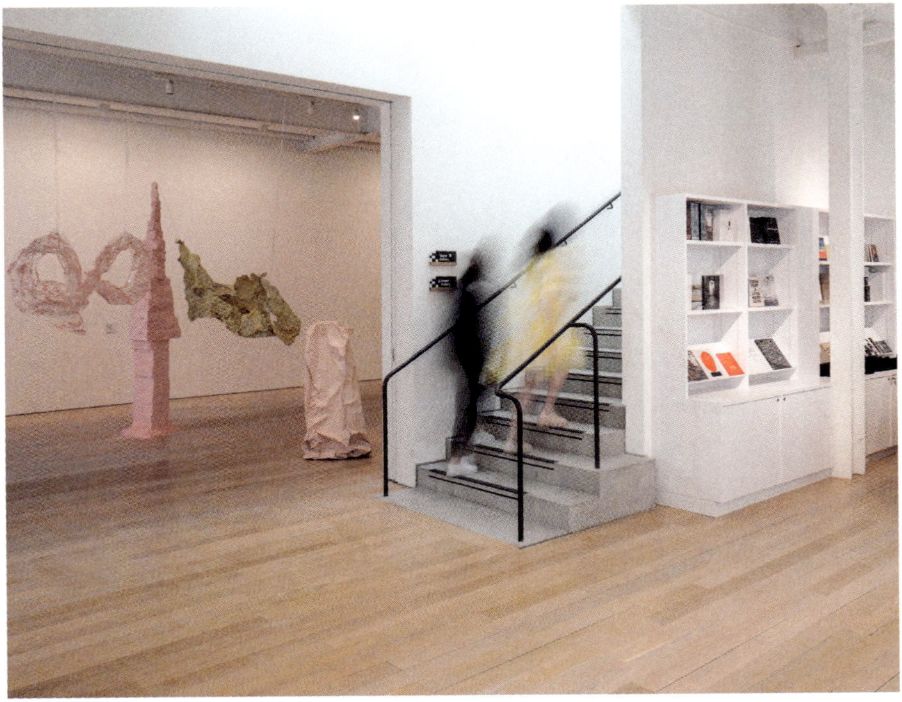

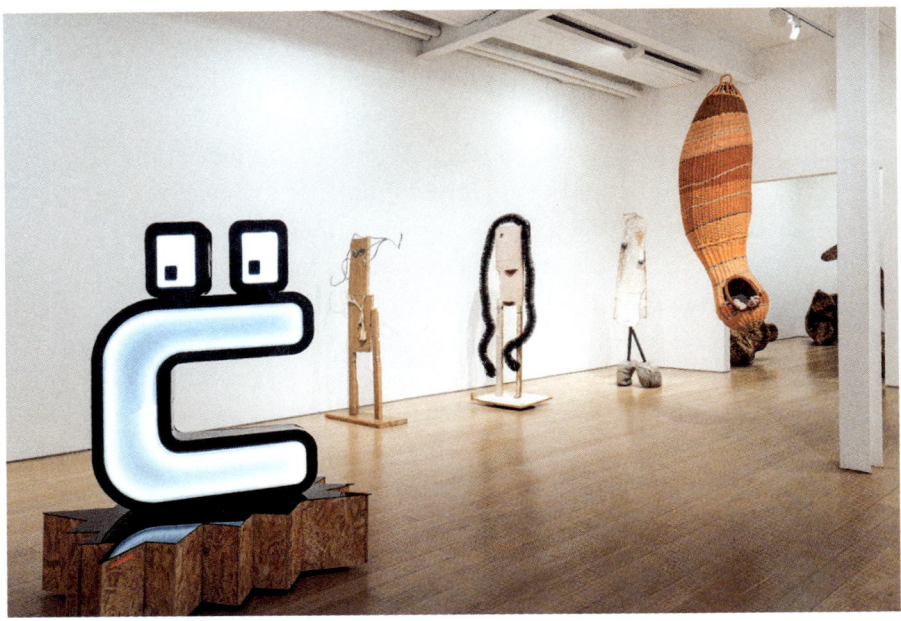

Opposite: *Zvakazarurwa*, Portia Zvavahera
Above: *Sculptures (2001–2021) details for a retrospective*, Karla Black
Below: *Poor Things*, various artists

JUPITER ARTLAND

Unearthly garden of sculptural delights

With its otherworldly landscape and unconventional artworks, this suitably named sculpture park promises a delightfully surreal experience. Opened in 2009 by art collectors Nicky and Robert Wilson in the grounds of West Lothian's Bonnington House, the weird and wonderful gallery-without-walls affords visitors some unusually engrossing encounters, from climbing Charles Jencks' undulating landform artwork to taking a dip in Joana Vasconcelos's technicolour swimming pool. Arranged across 120 acres of breathtaking woodland and meadow just outside Edinburgh, the park's thought-provoking sculptures include Cornelia Parker's colossal shotgun, Anish Kapoor's caged void, Rachel Maclean's abandoned toy shop and Laura Ford's sinister quintet of crying girls, as well as a revolving line-up of temporary commissions. While the scenery is stunning, Jupiter's indoor offering is as much of a treat, with Lindsey Mendick's visceral ceramics and Andrew Sim's dreamy paintings both lighting up the galleries in recent years.

The Steadings, Bonnington House, Wilkieston,
Edinburgh, EH27 8BY
jupiterartland.org

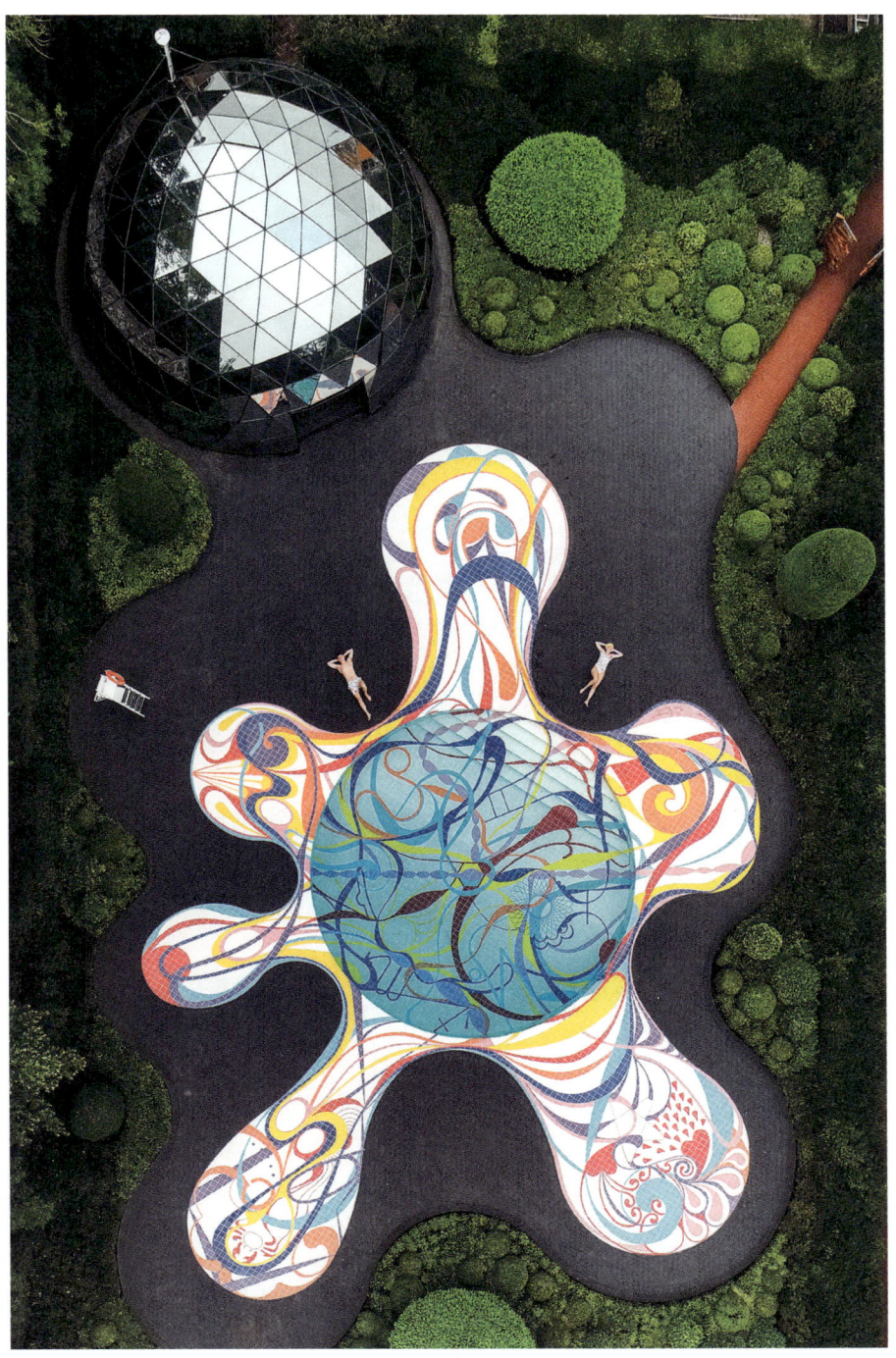

Gateway, Joana Vasconcelos

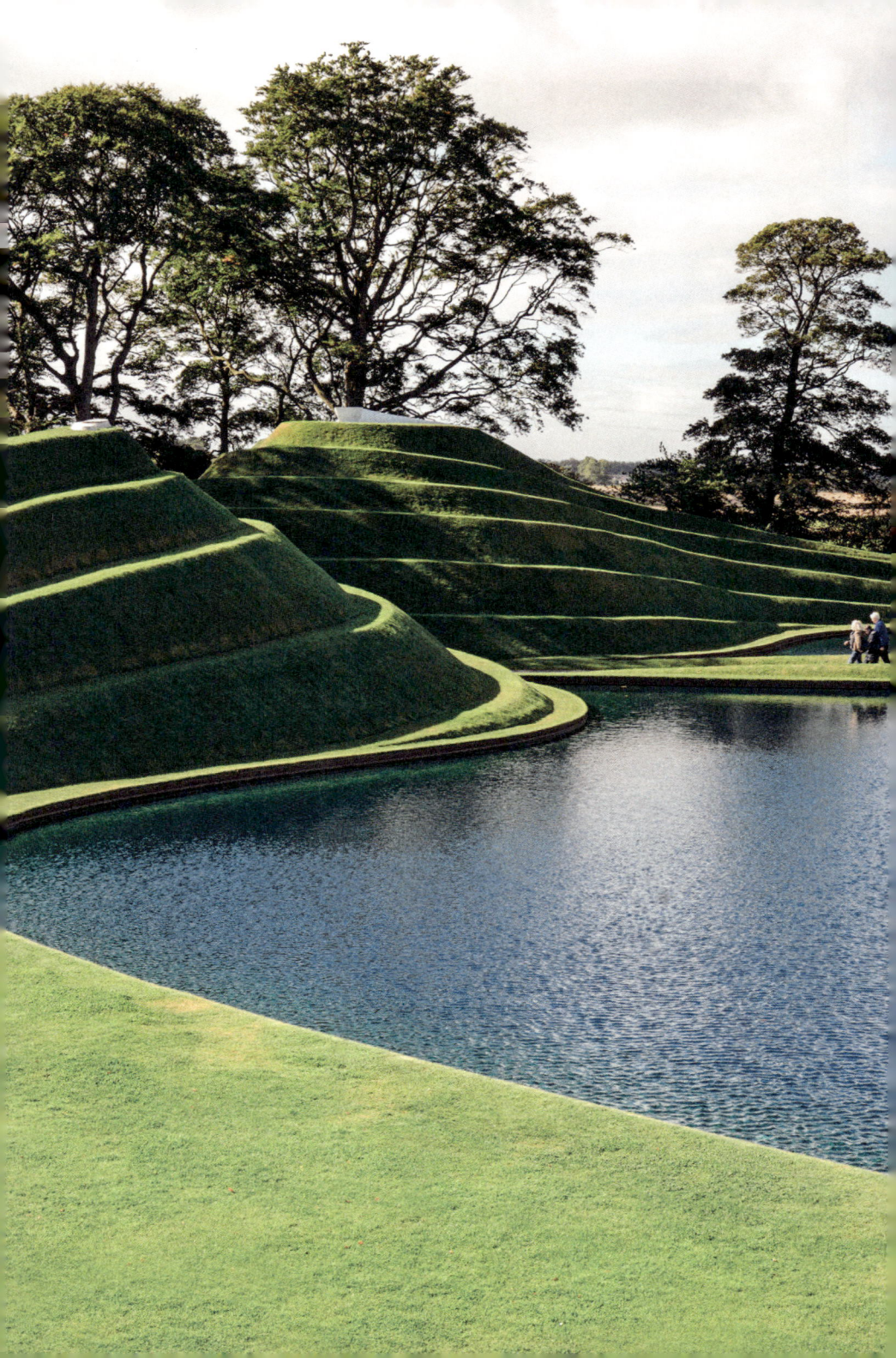

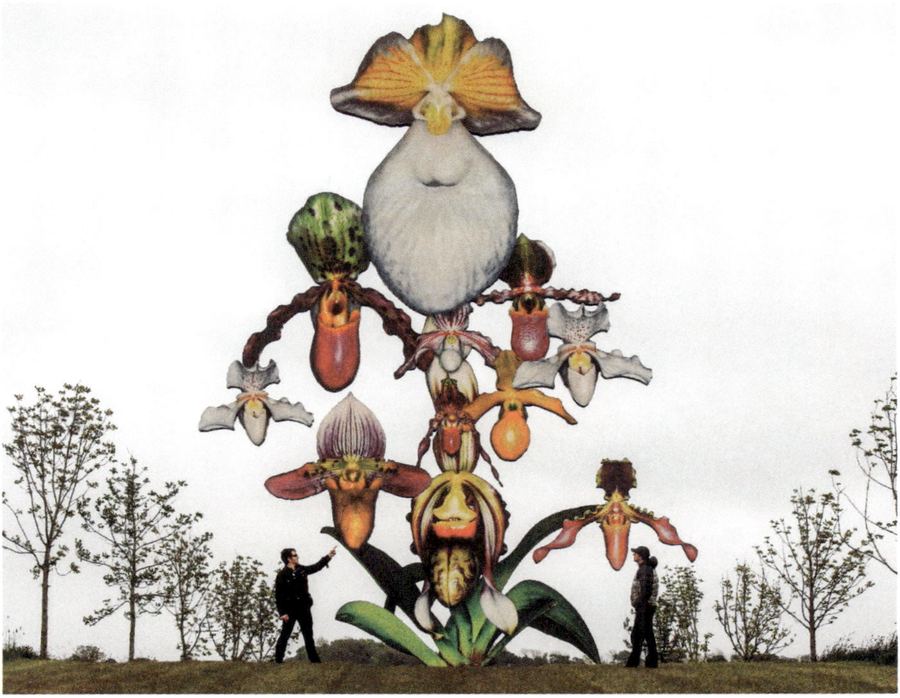

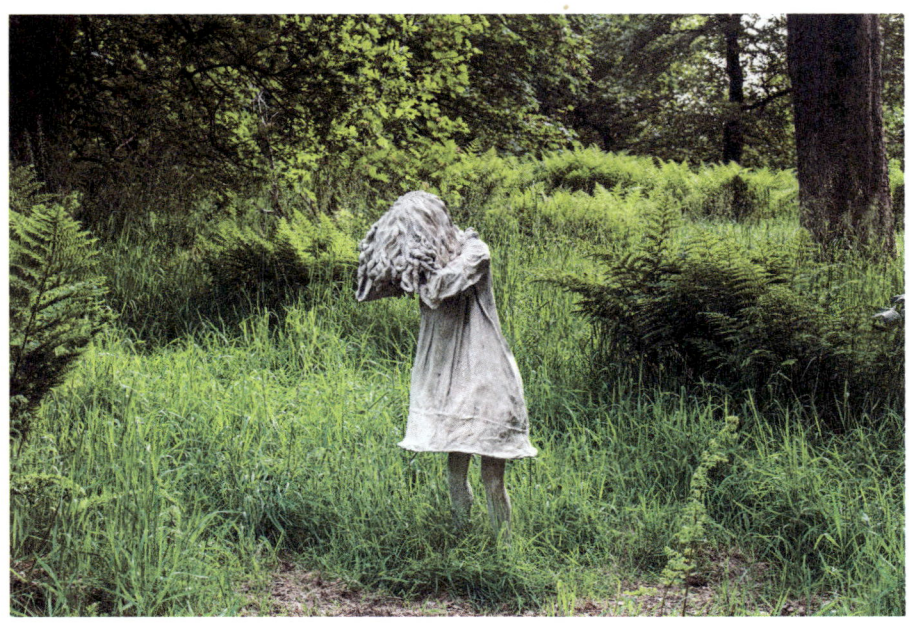

Opposite: *Cells of Life*, Charles Jencks
Above: *Love Bomb*, Marc Quinn
Below: *Weeping Girls*, Laura Ford

NATIONAL GALLERIES OF SCOTLAND

Big three north of the border

You could spend a week attempting to assimilate the contents of Scotland's three national galleries and barely begin to scratch the surface. Spread across four prominent buildings stretching from the West End to Holyrood, Edinburgh's holy trinity offers a cornucopia of delights for every mood, from post-war painting in a neoclassical mansion to portraits of famous Scots in a neo-Gothic palace, along with countless dramatic depictions of Scotland's diverse landscape. Time-strapped visitors should head straight for the Portrait's Great Hall, whose star-studded astronomical ceiling mural is well worth the neck cramp, or to the National Gallery in search of enigmatic national treasure *The Skating Minister*. Eduardo Paolozzi buff? Make a beeline for the Modern, where a meticulous recreation of the Scottish sculptor's studio and the eponymous Paolozzi Kitchen – home to his looming Vulcan sculpture and a delectable menu of Scottish twists on Italian classics – await.

National: The Mound, Edinburgh, EH2 2EL
Portrait: 1 Queen Street, Edinburgh, EH2 1JD
Modern: 73 & 75 Belford Road, Edinburgh, EH4 3DR
nationalgalleries.org

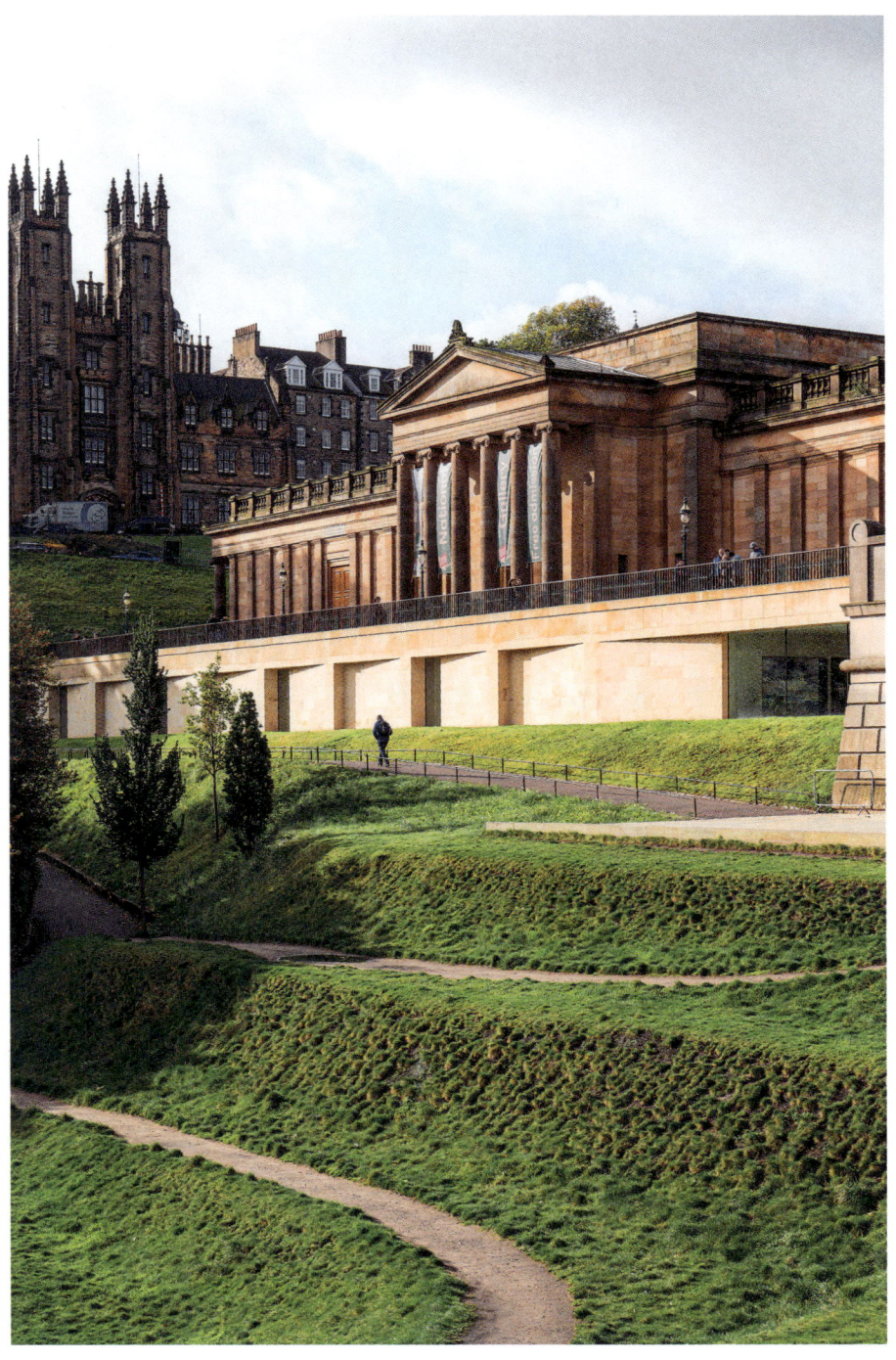

Scottish National Gallery

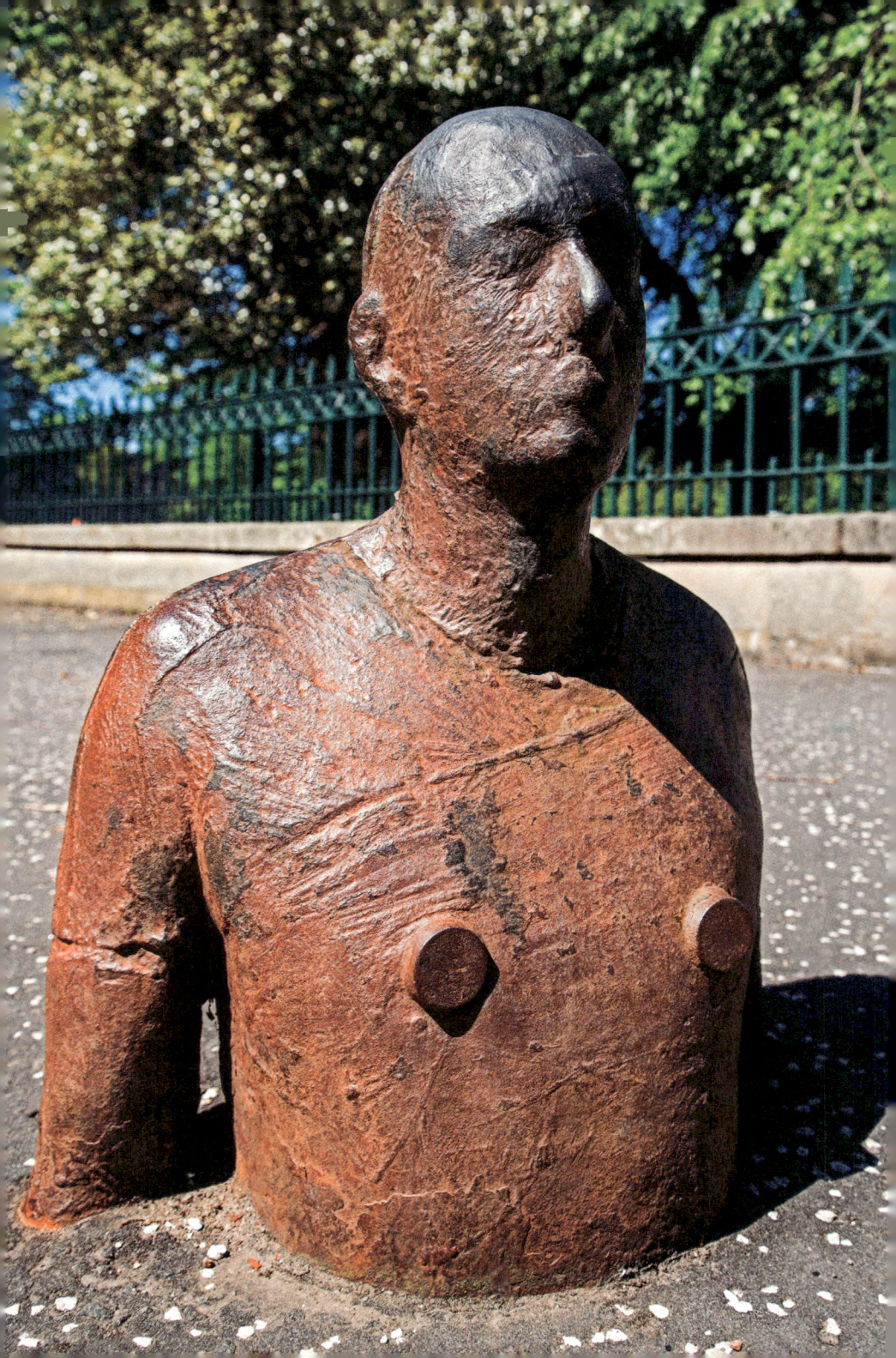

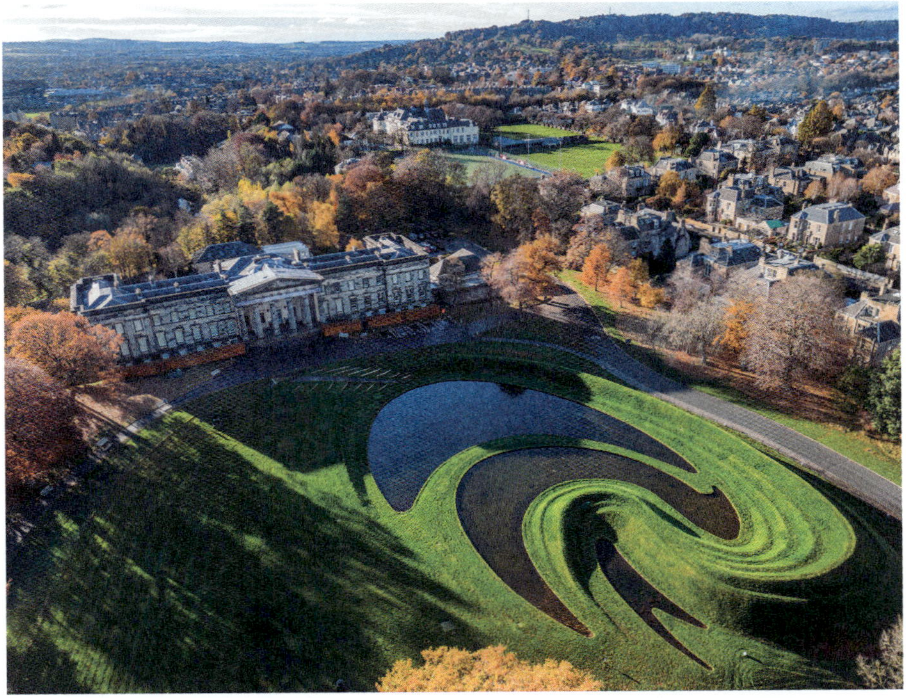

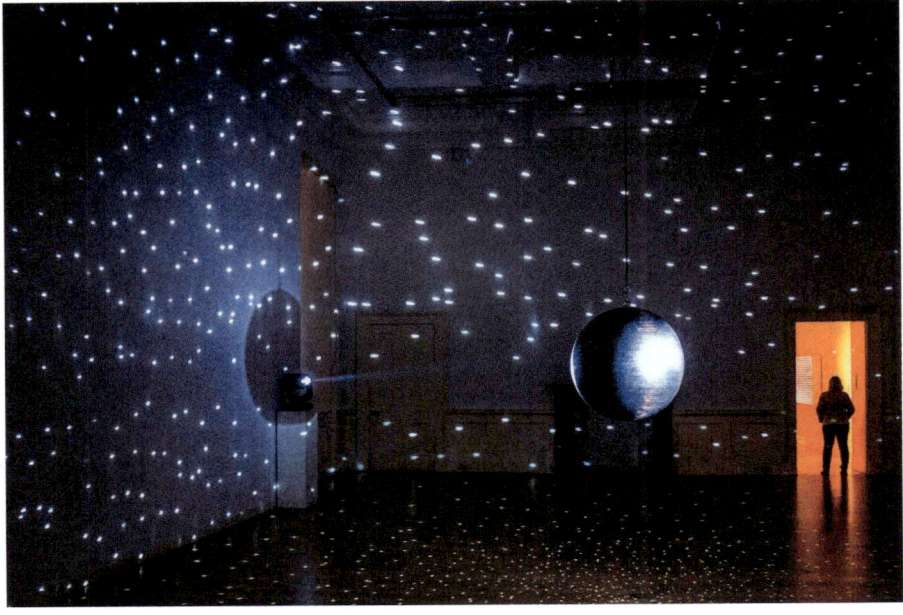

Opposite: *6 TIMES*, Antony Gormley
Above: *Landform*, Charles Jencks, Scottish National Gallery of Modern Art (Modern One)
Below: *Totality*, Katie Paterson, Scottish National Gallery of Modern Art (Modern One)

British Art Destinations
First edition, first printing

First published in 2025 by Hoxton Mini Press, London
Copyright © Hoxton Mini Press 2025. All rights reserved.

Text by Emmy Watts
Editing by Kate Overy
Production design by Dom Grant
Production control by David Brimble
Proofreading by Florence Ward
Editorial support by Richard Enright and Flora MacKenzie
Cover design by Tom Etherington

ISBN: 978-1-914314-92-6

Printed and bound by Balto Print, Lithuania

Manufacturer:
Hoxton Mini Press, 104 Northside Studios,
16-29 Andrews Road, London E8 4QF, UK
www.hoxtonminipress.com

Represented by
Authorised Rep Compliance Ltd.
Ground Floor, 71 Lower Baggot Street
Dublin D02 P593, Ireland
www.arccompliance.com

Hoxton Mini Press is an environmentally conscious publisher, committed to offsetting our
carbon footprint. This book is 100 per cent carbon compensated, with offset purchased from
Stand For Trees.

Every time you order from our website, we plant a tree:
www.hoxtonminipress.com

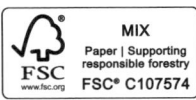

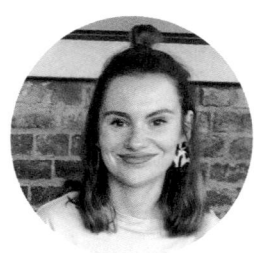

EMMY WATTS

Emmy Watts is a writer, blogger and art enthusi-
ast. She's authored 15 books for Hoxton Mini Press,
including *The Art of Play: Designing the World's Greatest Playscapes* and *Opinionated Guides* to everything
from London's most creative playgrounds to its best
vegan eateries. She's lived in London almost her entire
adult life, but can very easily be tempted elsewhere by
a great gallery.

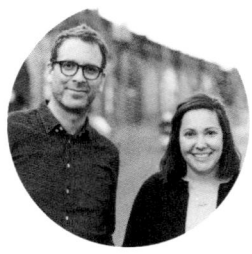

HOXTON MINI PRESS

Hoxton Mini Press is a small independent publisher
based in east London. We are committed to making
beautiful but affordable books that don't screw up
the planet. We offset all our printing, and we hope
that the trees we do use will continue their life as
books that you'll pass on to your grandchildren.